Frommer's™

FIRST EDITION

# CHICAGO
# Free &
# dirt cheap

## by Laura Tiebert

WILEY

John Wiley & Sons Canada, Ltd.

Published by:

**John Wiley & Sons Canada, Ltd.**
6045 Freemont Blvd.
Mississauga, ON L5R 4J3

ISBN 978-0-470-73650-0

Editor: Gene Shannon
Production Editor: Elizabeth McCurdy
Project Coordinator: Lynsey Stanford
Editorial Assistant: Katie Wolsley
Cartographer: Lohnes & Wright
Vice President, Publishing Services: Karen Bryan
Production by Wiley Indianapolis Composition Services

For reseller information, including discounts and premium sales, please call our sales department: Tel. 416-646-7992. For press review copies, author interviews, or other publicity information, please contact our publicity department: Tel. 416-646-4582; Fax: 416-236-4448.

Wiley also publishes its books in a variety of electronic formats. Some con-tent that appears in print may not be available in electronic formats.

Manufactured in the United States

1 2 3 4 5 RRD 14 13 12 11 10

# CONTENTS

# LIST OF MAPS

## About the Author

**Laura Tiebert** is a bargain-hunting travel writer who's always happy to score a dirt-cheap deal, and who believes that the best things in life are indeed free. She lives with her husband and two sons in Wilmette, Illinois.

## Acknowledgments

This book is better for the insightful editing of Gene Shannon, and was inspired by many friends and friends of friends who sent me e-mails describing their favorite free Chicago experiences, from dancing under the stars at Summerdance in Millennium Park, to scoring vintage clothing at Unique Thrift. Thank you!

## An Invitation to the Reader

In researching this book, we discovered many wonderful places—hotels, restaurants, shops, and more. We're sure you'll find others. Please tell us about them, so we can share the information with your fellow travelers in upcoming editions. If you were disappointed with a recommendation, we'd love to know that, too. Please write to:

*Frommer's Chicago Free & Dirt Cheap,* 1st Edition
John Wiley & Sons Canada, Ltd. • 6045 Freemont Blvd. •
Mississauga, ON L5R 4J3

## An Additional Note

Please be advised that travel information is subject to change at any time—and this is especially true of prices. We therefore suggest that you write or call ahead for confirmation when making your travel plans. The authors, editors, and publisher cannot be held responsible for the experiences of readers while traveling. Your safety is important to us, however, so we encourage you to stay alert and be aware of your surroundings. Keep a close eye on cameras, purses, and wallets, all favorite targets of thieves and pickpockets.

## Other Great Guides for Your Trip:

*Frommer's Chicago*

*Frommer's Chicago Day by Day*

*Frommer's Portable Chicago*

*Frommer's Chicago with Kids*

## Free & Dirt Cheap Icons & Abbreviations

We also use **four feature icons** that point you to the great deals, in-the-know advice, and unique experiences that separate urban adventurers from tourists. Throughout the book, look for:

**FREE**  Events, attractions, or experiences that cost no more than your time and a swipe of your Metrocard.

FINE PRINT  The unspoken conditions or necessary prepartations to experience certain free and dirt cheap events.

★  The best free and dirt cheap events, dining, shopping, living, and exploring in the city.

  Special events worth marking in your calendar.

## Frommers.com

Now that you have this guidebook to help you plan a great trip, visit our website at **www.frommers.com** for additional travel information on more than 4,000 destinations. We update features regularly to give you instant access to the most current trip-planning information available. At Frommers. com, you'll find scoops on the best airfares, lodging rates, and car rental bargains. You can even book your travel online through our reliable travel booking partners. Other popular features include:

- Online updates of our most popular guidebooks
- Vacation sweepstakes and contest giveaways
- Newsletters highlighting the hottest travel trends
- Podcasts, interactive maps, and up-to-the-minute events listings
- Opinionated blog entries by Arthur Frommer himself
- Online travel message boards with featured travel discussions

*No one puts out a welcome sign (or a show!) like Chicago, and the famous Chicago Theatre. See p. 158.*

# THE BEST THINGS IN LIFE ARE FREE

**T**he best things in life really are free (or at least dirt cheap). A perfect day under blue skies at North Avenue Beach. The sounds of the symphony enveloping you in the Pritzker Pavillion at Millennium Park. Gazing upon the architectural wonder of a Frank Lloyd Wright building. You can't put a price on those experiences.

Fortunately, you don't need money to be embraced by the City of Big Shoulders. What you need is an adventurous spirit—Chicago is a town that's down-to-earth, that prides itself on being no-frills, and whose best-known icons are free. Yes, I said, *free*. The lakefront, with its chain of 13 emerald parks? Free. Millennium Park, featuring the glorious Cloud Gate (aka "the bean"), Pritzker Pavillion, the Lurie Gardens? Free. Lincoln Park Zoo? Free. Best architecture in the United States? Free for the viewing. The world-famous Chicago hot dog, loaded up with chopped onions, hot peppers, sliced tomatoes, and mustard, on a poppyseed bun? Okay, not free, but at $1.75, definitely dirt cheap.

Although Chicago is the third-largest city in the U.S., it is only the sixth most expensive. Your dollar gets you farther here than it will in New York, Los Angeles, Miami, Honolulu, or San Francisco. The founders of Chicago themselves showed their free and dirt cheap spirit when they declared the lakeshore "Forever open, clear, and free." That legacy lives on in every aspect of Chicago today.

This is a guide that blurs the boundaries, straddles the lines: It's for the visitor who wants a rock-bottom, dirt-cheap (but fun!) trip to Chicago; for the potential resident who is wondering how the heck the people who live here can manage to eat, sleep, *and* enjoy themselves; and for the resident, new and longtime, who is always looking for a good bargain, a happy hour, a class or lecture, or a city program he or she hasn't discovered yet to make life in this amazing city a little bit better.

Yes, $16 martini lounges and eye-poppingly expensive restaurants are plentiful in the city, but that's not where we, the locals, hang out or dine. Going out to play on a tight budget here means doing what most of the denizens do every day: eating at the city's many affordable restaurants, enjoying the wonderful parks and neighborhoods, and taking advantage of its wide variety of free or inexpensive attractions, events, and performances. And if you do as the locals do, you're far more likely to experience the hidden secrets of Chicago that only a frugal adventurer, such as yourself, will discover.

We've got the best collection of museums on one campus in the nation, and I'll show you how to score free or cheap tickets to all of them. Laughter is free—and you'll be belly laughing knowing that you only paid $5 to watch some of the best up-and-coming comedians do improv battle onstage. Lest I forget, the blues is Chicago's own music. The blues and dirt cheap go hand-in-hand, and you'll be able to check out a broad sampling of the music scene for very few bucks.

What I discovered in researching this book was that I felt ridiculous for ever having spent more than $20 on any outing in the city. Forget the expensive souvenirs and collect experiences instead. Chicago, with its incredible array of possibilities, beckons.

Some of the greatest Chicago experiences—like the "Cloud Gate" sculpture in Millennium Park (see p. 100)—will let you see a whole new side of yourself.

# BEST OF FREE
# & DIRT CHEAP
# CHICAGO

**T**hree things I already know about you: 1) You are the savviest of savvy travelers because you know that travel is not about how much money you spend, but about how many experiences you bank; 2) You are willing to go off the beaten track in search of a cheap or free adventure; and 3) You never, ever pay full price. It's practically a religion with you.

Okay, these are just guesses, albeit educated ones (you bought this book, didn't you?). Here's another educated guess: You're going to love Chicago. Many of the natives see eye-to-eye with you. We know a good bargain when we see one, and we flock to enjoy those attractions and events en masse. In Chicago, you can experience what amounts to a real urban miracle: open-air concerts that are free and fabulous; the best architecture in the world, free for the gazing; a new interactive park that's become the city's "front lawn"; and a lakefront that was declared "forever open, clear, and free" by our city's founders.

Visiting Chicago on a dime and a prayer? Taking a family vacation on a shoestring budget? Moving here to get your life started, or to start over? Welcome aboard. You have found yourself in a city that not only embraces, but celebrates, the free and dirt cheap philosophy. What follows are the best of the best dirt cheap and free experiences in Chicago.

## 1 Best Free Only-in-Chicago Experiences

- **Best Way to Feel like a Real Chicagoan:** Strolling, biking, running, or simply sitting and gazing at the scene on the **lakefront.** Unless you have actually walked down the Magnificent Mile, one of the best shopping districts in the world, through the pedestrian tunnel, and onto Oak Street Beach—a veritable Club Med atmosphere in the summer—you haven't experienced one of the most unique aspects of living in Chicago. Kick off your shoes, step into flip-flops and shorts, and head to the beach for a game of pick-up volleyball. I guarantee you'll be enamored of summer in the city faster than you can say, "That's a lake? But you can't see across it!" See p. 100.

- **Best Open-Air Dancing:** Chicago natives learn to salsa, mambo, or swing dance under the stars at **Chicago Summer-Dance.** Now in its 13th year, the hugely popular, annual 11-week dance festival runs from June to September and takes place in the **Spirit of Music Garden** (601 S. Michigan Ave.) in Grant Park. Free, 1-hour dance lessons from professional instructors are followed by 2 hours of live music and dancing on a 4,600-square-foot open-air dance floor. Top-notch bands play everything from swing, salsa, and afrobeat to reggae, funk, and klezmer. In an informal survey of friends, SummerDance ranked as the number-one free activity in the city. Why not join in the fun? SummerDance events occur every Thursday, Friday, and Saturday evening, 6 to 9:30pm, and Sunday afternoon, 4 to 7pm, weather permitting.

Admission is free and open to the public. See p. 188.

- **Most Bang for Your Buck:** Twice weekly, from late May to early September, there's a free **fireworks display** at Navy Pier, Wednesdays at 9:30pm and Saturdays at 10:15pm. Fireworks also take place for special events the rest of the year; for exact times and dates, check out www.navypier.com. When the weather is fine, grab a beverage at one of the Navy Pier outdoor beer gardens and enjoy the view. Even better, combine my previous recommendation with this one, and check out Chicago **SummerDance at Navy Pier** for live music, dancing, and the best view of the fireworks—hands-down one of the best free-and-cheap date nights in the city. In 2009, there were three different Summer-Dance evenings at the Navy Pier beer garden. Lessons are from 6 to 7pm, dancing from 7:30 to 10pm, and fireworks at 9:30pm. See p. 102.

- **Best Neighborhood Festival:** Garden walks are a summer tradition in Chicago; what began as a chance to tour backyard gardens has grown to become a number of huge street festivals with food, drink, games, and more. The **Sheffield Garden Walk (www.sheffield festivals.org)**, which takes place in mid-July in Lincoln Park, is one of the largest and best organized. The **Dearborn Garden Walk (www.dearborn gardenwalk.com)** allows rare glimpses into the good life on the Gold Coast, also on a weekend in mid-July. Pick up a map and take a self-guided, free tour of the gardens, and see how the other half lives. See p. 104.

- **Best Pageantry: Venetian Night** During the last weekend in July, approximately 35 boats decked out in lights and props sail along the shoreline of Lake Michigan, between the Shedd Aquarium at Roosevelt Road and the Chicago Yacht Club at Monroe Street. It's a bit like a floating parade, and it gets a little crazy. People of all ages stake out spots along the lakefront as early as 9am to ensure a good view of the event. Venetian Night is the longest running event that the City of Chicago produces, and attracts about 675,000 spectators—so public transportation, walking, or biking to Venetian Night is suggested. See p. 105.

- **Best Stroll: Lincoln Park Zoo** (2200 N. Cannon; ☎ **312/742-2000**) is a free, beautiful green oasis in the heart of the city, and it's open 365 days a year.

This is the ideal place to take the kids, or just take a stroll. Not to be missed during your stroll: The Kovler Lion House, an architecturally beautiful interior, with an up-close view of the big cats (don't worry, there are vertical wires separating you and that jaguar!). See p. 102.

● **Best Place to Escape Chicago's Winters: Garfield Conservatory** (300 N. Central Park; ℂ **312/746-5100**) offers the only city-run indoor playground for kids. Add in the array of amazing blooms on display, and you have an unbeatable combination (the Spring Flower Show in April is especially inspiring after a long Chicago winter). The conservatory was designed by the great landscape architect Jens Jensen in 1907, and is one of the largest gardens under glass in the world. Admission is free, but make sure to play it safe when traveling here, as the conservatory is located in a blighted neighborhood. If you drive (the conservatory is located just 10 min. west of downtown Chicago), there's free parking adjacent to the conservatory, just to the south, and it's manned by security. Or, take the CTA Green Line to the Conservatory–Central Park Drive

station. The conservatory is open every day, and always free. Hours are 9am to 5pm, and on Wednesdays, it's open 9am to 8pm. See p. 106.

● **Best Totally Free Architectural Tour:** Sure, you can pay $15 to tour Frank Lloyd Wright's Home and Studio in Oak Park, but you can walk the surrounding neighborhood for free. Oak Park is home to the world's largest collection of Wright-designed buildings, so set out and explore the Historic District surrounding the Home and Studio at your own pace, and marvel at the exteriors of a wide selection of Wright-designed, Prairie-style, and Victorian homes (you know, the ones that drove Frank Lloyd Wright crazy with their traditional styling). See p. 106.

● **Best Open-Air Concert Series:** Chicago is the last city in America to still present a free, open-air, professional series of orchestral concerts each summer. The **Grant Park Music Festival** takes place at the glorious Jay Pritzker Pavilion in Millennium Park. You won't believe how fantastic the sound system is until you hear it with your own ears. Started during the Depression to lift Chicagoans' spirits, the Festival features the Grant Park Orchestra and Chorus. The Festival is still lifting spirits today: Lawn and general seating is free—no tickets necessary. Get there an hour before the concert starts to claim a good spot on the lawn. See p. 103.

- **Best Free Ride:** Navy Pier offers daily **free trolley service** between Navy Pier and State Street along Grand Avenue and Illinois Street. Hop on and hop off along the way, and laugh along as the drivers regale riders with entertaining Chicago stories. Start at the Grand Avenue subway station (at State St.). Runs Memorial Day to Labor Day, Sunday through Thursday 10am to 11pm, Friday and Saturday 10am to 1am. See p. 285.

- **Best Historic Adventure:** If you spook easily, this place is best avoided (particularly at dusk on Oct. 31, for example), but at any other time of year, **Graceland Cemetery** is full of amazing Chicago history lessons—all free. I, for one, am a huge fan of visiting cemeteries when I travel, and I don't think I'm alone in this sort-of strange obsession. Make sure to stop by the administrative office for a map of notable graves and a brochure. Chicago notables Potter Palmer, Marshall Field, George Pullman, Cyrus McCormick, and more have graves here. Don't miss the final resting place of Daniel Burnham, who got an island all to himself, on the edge of a beautiful pond. See p. 111.

## 2 Best Dirt Cheap Only-in-Chicago Experiences

- **Best Cheap Cruise:** A bona fide cruise on the Chicago River and Lake Michigan will set you back nearly $50. But, hitch a ride on the Chicago Water Taxi and you'll pay only $2 to cruise the Chicago River from the Loop to Michigan Avenue. Better yet? On the weekend, the water taxi will transport you to Chinatown, where you can delve into a super inexpensive and delicious meal, then hop back on the taxi for a scenic—and cheap—ride home. Board between 2 North Riverside Plaza (Madison St. stop), 325 North LaSalle St. (LaSalle/Clark), and 400 N. Michigan Ave. (6:30am–6:30pm weekdays; 9:45am–6:00pm Sat, 10:45am–4:45pm Sun). ℂ **312/ 337-1446;** www.chicagowater taxi.com. See p. 132.

● **Best Food Fest:** Admission is free to the **Taste of Chicago,** and so is the music at the Petrillo Music Shell. If you want to actually taste something at the Taste, tickets are sold in strips of 12 for $8—not cheap, but not insanely expensive, either. You can eat a fair amount for your $8, as "taste portions" (smaller portions of restaurant menu items) are two to four tickets each. Large portions (giant turkey leg, rib sandwich) go for 9 to 12 tickets, side portions for 6 to 8 tickets, and soft drinks, 4 tickets. I have to admit that this is not my favorite Chicago event (the heat and the crowds combined with a million food smells tend to be more overwhelming than appetizing), but I'm clearly in the minority. Some 3.7 million people can't be wrong, can they? See p. 23.

● **Best Food for Thought:** The **Uptown Poetry Slam with Marc Smith** is the granddaddy of all poetry slams—it's been running for more than 2 decades at the historic Green Mill jazz club (4802 N. Broadway; ⓒ **773/878-5552**). The event takes place every Sunday and includes an open mic at 7pm, scheduled performers at 8pm, and a slam competition at 9pm. Admission is $6. See p. 194.

● **Best Cheap Laughs:** Chicago is one of the hottest cities in the world for improv comedy, and the popular cage match series at **iO Chicago** (3541 N. Clark; ⓒ **773/880-0199**) pits up-and-coming improvisational groups against each other at midnight on Saturdays. Sketches range from racy to obnoxious to witty to sarcastic . . . and all are worth your $5 ticket. See p. 189.

● **Best Theater for the Roll of a Die:** The longest-running show in Chicago is also one of the best dirt cheap deals. The **Neo-futurists** (5153 N. Ashland; ⓒ **773/878-4577**) are currently celebrating the 20th anniversary of "Too Much Light Makes the Baby Go Blind," an attempt to perform 30 plays in 60 minutes. Tickets are $9 plus the roll of a single six-sided die (meaning, you'll pay between $10–$15), and it's cash only. Each show is written by a performer, honed by the ensemble, and randomly mixed with 29 other plays with the help of you, the audience. The show is performed Friday and Saturday nights at 11:30pm (doors open at 11pm); Sunday nights at 7pm (doors open at 6:30pm), every weekend except the last 2 weeks in December. To make sure you get in (the theater seats 150), get there at 10:45pm on Fridays, 10:30pm on Saturdays, and 6:30pm on Sundays. See p. 184.

## 3 Best Dirt Cheap Dining

- **Best Happy Hour Steal:** Savvy Loop workers know that the best place to head for an inexpensive, gourmet happy-hour buffet is **Trattoria No. 10** (10 N. Dearborn St.; 𝒞 312/984-1718), a warm and cozy Italian spot that's also popular for pre-theater dining for North Loop Theater District patrons. But the real value here isn't on the dinner menu, it's the all-you-can-eat buffet spread out on the bar for $12 (plus a $6 drink minimum), where you can sample beef tenderloin, shrimp and various pasta specialties. Skip lunch and fill up here! Served weekdays from 5-8 p.m. See p. 58.

- **Best Dim Sum:** The spacious, fairly elegant **Phoenix** (2131 S. Archer Ave., btw. Wentworth Ave. and Cermak Rd.; 𝒞 312/328-0848) has plenty of big tables for family and friends to enjoy the Cantonese and Szechuan cuisine, and it attracts lots of Chinatown locals, especially for Dim Sum brunch. Come early to avoid the wait. Late night, stop by the more casual **Saint's Alp Teahouse** downstairs (𝒞 312/842-1886), an outpost of the Hong Kong chain, which is open until midnight daily. See p. 62.

- **Best Inexpensive Outdoor Dining: Pegasus** (130 S. Halsted St., btw. Monroe and Adams sts.; 𝒞 312/226-3377), with its rooftop patio serving drinks, appetizers, and desserts, offers wonderful views of the Loop's skyline. The restaurant is a good bet for gyros, Greek salads, shish kabobs, and the classic moussaka. Good for large groups. See p. 63.

- **Best Burrito:** Burrito? Come on, we can do better than that! In a city that excels at Mexican cuisine, picking the best Mexican restaurant is a tough call. Pilsen is home to the city's highest concentration of Mexican restaurants, and two good choices include **Nuevo Leon** (1515 W. 18th St., at Laflin St.; 𝒞 312/421-1557), a popular choice for the standard offerings. Across the street, **Plaza Azul** (1514 W. 18th St., at Laflin St.; 𝒞 312/421-2552) serves authentic Mexican seafood dishes, salads, and soups. See p. 63.

● **Best Lunch in the Loop:** Loud, crowded, and casual, **Heaven on Seven** (111 N. Wabash Ave.; ✆ **312/263-6443**) is a no-frills spot that buzzes with energy. Chef/owner Jimmy Bannos's Cajun and Creole specialties come with a cup of soup and include such Louisiana staples as red beans and rice, a catfish po' boy sandwich, and jambalaya. If you don't have a taste for Tabasco, the extensive coffee-shop-style menu covers all the traditional essentials: grilled-cheese sandwiches, omelets, tuna—the works. Indulge in chocolate peanut butter pie or homemade rice pudding for dessert. See p. 57.

● **Best Pierogi:** Chicago is home to a huge Polish population. If you're hankering for some hearty, stick-to-your-ribs Polish food, the best-known restaurant is **Red Apple** (Czerwone Jabluszko) (3121 N. Milwaukee Ave.; ✆ **773/588-5781**). Dining here is strictly buffet, and the lineup includes Polish specialties such as pierogi (meat- or cheese-stuffed dumplings) and blintzes, as well as a huge selection of roast meats, salads, and bread. Best of all is the price: $8.50 on weekdays and $9.50 on weekends for all you can eat. See p. 96.

● **Best Tavern Lunch:** Chicago is a town filled with neighborhood taverns. Chicago is a town filled with neighborhood taverns. **The Billy Goat Tavern** (430 N. Michigan Ave; ✆ **312/222-1525**), while a little on the grungy side, is a famed hangout for media workers and writers, and the service style inspired a classic *Saturday Night Live* skit with John Belushi. Most famous for its "cheezeborgers" ($3), all the prices are diner-cheap, with nothing on the menu over $6, and many items under $4. See p. 65.

● **Best Beef Sandwich: Mr. Beef** (666 N. Orleans St.; ✆ **312/337-8500**) is basically a fast-food stand, without much atmosphere or room for seating. Despite these drawbacks, Mr. Beef is a much-loved Chicago institution. Its claim to fame is the classic Italian beef sandwich ($5), the Chicago version of a Philly cheese steak. The Mr. Beef variety is made of sliced beef dipped in jus, piled high on a chewy bun, and topped with sweet or hot peppers. Heavy, filling, and *very* Chicago. See p. 69.

- **Best Creative Sandwich: Bourgeois Pig** (738 W. Fullerton Pkwy; ✆ 773/883-5282) is located near DePaul University in Lincoln Park, and caters to an intellectual crowd. "The Sun Also Rises," "Hamlet," and "The Old Man and the Sea" are among the menu's 25 gourmet sandwiches. Baked goods, including ginger molasses cookies, are homemade. The Pig always ranks high in surveys for best cup of coffee in Chicago, so don't miss one of the four varieties brewed daily, or one of a mind-bending array of espresso drinks. Juices, shakes, and root beer made here are also great bets. The huge sandwiches will only set you back about $8. See p. 80.

- **Best Do-It-Yourself Meal:** Get creative at this build-your-own-stir-fry restaurant. If you've never been to **Flat Top Grill** (319 W. North Ave.; ✆ 312/787-7676; check www.flattop grill.com for more locations) before, you might want to follow the suggested recipes on the giant blackboards. But of course, if you decide to strike out on your own with a unique combo that turns out to be less than edible (horseradish tofu sauce over stir-fried pineapple, anyone?), you can always start over for free, since the price of $9.99 for lunch and $13 for dinner includes multiple visits to the food line. See p. 82.

- **Best Stand-Out Hot Dog Stand:** Chicago is home to many standout hot-dog stands and shops, but one, **Hot Doug's** (3324 N. California Ave.; ✆ 773/279-9550), takes encased meats to a new level, featuring several gourmet sausages on a bun every day except Sunday (plan on standing in line no matter which day you show up—it's always worth it). Hot Doug's also serves a great classic Chicago dog just like many other stands in town. See p. 71.

## 4 Best Low-Cost Lodging

- **Best Cheap Lodging Deal, Hands Down: Hostelling International Chicago** wins this crown easily. Named the best hostel in the world in 2007, the J. Ira & Nikki Harris Family Hostel (Hostelling International), located at 24 E. Congress Pkwy (✆ 312/360-0300), is a standout in a city with a dearth of dirt cheap, super clean, and safe lodging options. You can't lose on the location in the South Loop, a great jumping-off point for adventures in the Loop, Millennium Park, and beyond. You'll find volunteer staffers who provide everything from insider tips on the best shopping, bus routes, and museum fees to their own well-organized walking tours. Each room is large by hostel standards and includes a locker (make sure to bring your own lock). There's an 11pm quiet rule, but no curfew. There's a beautiful kitchen, so you can prepare your own meals, and free breakfast. Because the hostel is located within walking distance to the Blue Line (O'Hare), it's easy to get to and from the airport from here. See p. 38.

● **Best Dirt Cheap Loop Hotel:** Clean, neat rooms for reasonable prices, and a location near the Loop and Museum Campus, draw you to the **Travelodge Chicago Downtown** (65 E. Harrison, at S. Wabash Ave.; ℂ **888/515-6375**). You'll only be half a block from Grant Park and the summer music festivals, and only 4 blocks from the Field Museum. The hotel was built in 1925 as the Harrison Hotel, and for many years was one of the premier hotels in the city. Okay, it's not so

premier anymore, but it's definitely dirt cheap. See p. 39.

● **Best Dirt Cheap Magnificent Mile Hotel:** The **Red Roof Inn Chicago Downtown** (162 E. Ontario St., ½ block east of Michigan Ave.; ℂ **800/733-7663**) is your best bet for the lowest-priced lodgings in the heart of the Magnificent Mile, and it's located within blocks of high-priced hotels like the Ritz Carlton and Peninsula. For the same stellar location, you'll pay a quarter of the price here. Guest rooms are stark and small, so make sure to ask for a room facing Ontario Street, where you'll get western exposure and some natural light. See p. 47.

● **Best Cheap Neighborhood Hotel:** Located on the North Side, a few doors down from the El stop on Belmont Avenue, the charming **City Suites** Hotel (933 W. Belmont Ave., at Sheffield Ave.; ℂ **800/248-9108**) has a 1930s Art Deco feel, and double rooms for under $100 (you might even do better than that rate, particularly on weekdays and off-season). The amenities are super for a hotel at this price point. There are plush robes and complimentary continental breakfast, and refrigerators and microwaves are available upon request. Be aware, though, that most rooms can be fairly noisy, due to the El tracks and the location on busy Belmont Avenue (bring earplugs!). See p. 49.

- **Best Cheap Hotel When Baseball Is on the Agenda:** Sister hotel to the City Suites, the **Majestic Hotel** (528 Brompton St., at Lake Shore Dr.; 𝒞 800/727-5108) offers an excellent location, particularly if Wrigley Field is a major attraction for you. Located on a charming tree-lined street, convenient to the many shops and restaurants of Lincoln Park, the hotel offers large suites with sun porches. Many of the rooms are dark due to apartment buildings on all sides. See p. 50.

- **Best Hotel with Free Parking:** This former motor lodge isn't going to win any design prizes, but the **Best Western River North Hotel** (125 W. Ohio St., at LaSalle St.; 𝒞 800/528-1234) has got some of the most affordable rates to be found in this busy neighborhood, within easy walking distance of Chicago's art-gallery district and numerous restaurants. Rooms are spacious if rather generic (with comfortable bedding and down pillows). A big selling point for families is the indoor pool, with an adjoining outdoor roof deck.

The almost unheard-of free parking in the hotel's parking lot can add up to significant savings for anyone who drives. See p. 46.

- **Best Cheap Family Hotel, River North:** The family-friendly **Hampton Inn & Suites Chicago Downtown** (33 W. Illinois St., at Dearborn St.; 𝒞 800/HAMPTON [426-7866]) manages to appeal to both adults and kids—the Prairie-style lobby and breakfast lounge give the place a tranquil feel, while the indoor pool and free hot breakfast are a plus for families. Built in 1998, the hotel still feels brand-new; the rooms have an urban look, with dark wood furniture and plush duvets. There's even a complimentary continental breakfast with two hot items per day; you won't need much lunch if you fill up here each morning. See p. 44.

- **Best Family Hotel off the Beaten Track:** If you're looking for a neighborhood inn away from the tourist hordes, **Best Western Hawthorne Terrace** (3434 N. Broadway Ave., at Hawthorne Place; 𝒞 888/401-8781) fits the bill. Located in Lakeview—within walking distance of Wrigley Field, Lake Michigan, and the Lincoln Park walking and

# Chicago's Top Five Best-Kept Free Secrets

**1** Sadly, free money is not on offer at **The Chicago Fed Money Museum** (230 S. LaSalle St., at Quincy St.; *©* **312/322-2400**). Disappointing, I know, but this little museum provides more than just the standard history-of-banking displays: The center has a giant cube that holds a million dollars and an exhibit that lets you try to detect counterfeit bills. There's even a section where visitors can pretend to be Ben Bernanke (for a moment), with a display that shows how changes in interest rates affect the economy. See p. 110.

**2** The annual **Christkindlmarket** takes place from Thanksgiving weekend until Christmas Eve. Daley Plaza (btw. Washington, Clark, and Dearborn sts.) is transformed into a German Christmas market. Admission is free; for $7 you can splurge and buy a souvenir mug filled with Gluhwein, the hot German mulled wine, imported from Nuremberg; you can refill it for $5. (If you're not a wine drinker, $7 buys you a mug of German beer.) Check out the free musical entertainment, and browse the market's authentic German ornaments, nativity scenes, cuckoo clocks, as well as marzipan, schnitzel, and stollen. While you're there, check out the city's official Christmas tree (also at Daley Plaza), and stroll across State Street to check out Macy's holiday windows. See p. 27.

**3** The **Chicago Architecture Foundation**'s permanent exhibition, *Chicago: You Are Here,* in the ArcelorMittal CitySpace Gallery—with

bike paths—the hotel is set back from busy Broadway Avenue. The relatively large rooms are bright and cheery, with spotless bathrooms. The ground-level exercise room is especially welcoming, with large windows to let light in and a glass-enclosed hot tub. The hotel's extremely varied clientele—from business travelers in search of a homey environment, to diehard baseball fans, to lesbian and gay travelers in town for the annual Gay Pride Parade—is part of its charm. See p. 50.

its bold, innovative approach to telling the story of the construction of Chicago—features a scale model of downtown Chicago. The ArcelorMittal CitySpace Gallery provides the perfect orientation to Chicago's built landscape and is open to the public every day from 9:30am to 5pm. The organization presents exhibitions, lectures, and youth and adult education programs, many of which are open to the public free of charge. See p. 158.

④ It's hard to fathom, but yes, I am recommending a visit to the **Fermi National Accelerator Laboratory** (otherwise known as Fermilab), located in the western suburb of Batavia. The government-run facility hosts free "Ask a Scientist" discussions on the first Sunday of most months, open to anyone ages 10 and up at their site (Wilson and Kirk roads, Batavia; ℭ **630/840-8258**). Past topics have included future accelerators and magnets. Go and soak up the intellectual power at this national laboratory specializing in high-energy particle physics. See p. 208.

⑤ The **Chicago Public Library at the Harold Washington Library Center** itself is no secret, but this is: If you (or someone you know) have a Chicago Public Library card, you can check out museum passports good for free admission to a dozen area cultural venues. Nine branches of the public library will even loan you fishing poles! See p. 110.

## FREE & DIRT CHEAP CALENDAR OF EVENTS

Chicago is a festival city, with ethnic parades, food, music, art and flower fairs, and street celebrations packing the calendar. Best of all, most of these events are free. Of course, if you want to buy a beer at a neighborhood festival, or a car at the Auto Show (joking, of course), the events can become somewhat pricier. But viewing the parades, the autos, the flowers, and whatever else is on display is always free.

Particularly in the summer, it can be tough to choose among activities. In winter you'll have fewer choices, but some of the perennial favorites take place then. Even though these are annual events, the dates move around a lot, so call or log on to make sure you're in the right free place at the right free time.

To discover the latest and greatest special events in the city, ask the Chicago Office of Tourism (℃ 877/CHICAGO [244-2246]; www.choose chicago.com) or the Illinois Bureau of Tourism (℃ 800/2CONNECT [226-6632]; www.enjoyillinois.com) to mail you a copy of the Chicago Visitor's Guide, an excellent quarterly publication that surveys special events, including parades and street festivals, concerts and theatrical productions, and museum exhibitions. You can also download the guide in PDF form from www.choosechicago.com (look under

"visitors" and then search for "city guides"). Also ask to be sent the latest materials produced by the Mayor's Office of Special Events (℃ 312/744-3315, or the Special Events Hot Line 312/744-3370, TTY 312/744-2964; www.cityofchicago.org/specialevents), which keeps current with citywide and neighborhood festivals. You'll find food, music and flower fairs, garden walks, and more.

Remember that new events might be added every year, and that occasionally special events are discontinued or rescheduled. So, to avoid disappointment, be sure to telephone in advance or check the website of the sponsoring organization, the Chicago Office of Tourism, or the Mayor's Office of Special Events to verify dates, times, and locations.

## JANUARY

**Winter Delights**    Throughout January and February, the city's Office of Tourism (℃ **877/CHICAGO** [244-2246]; www.choose chicago.com) offers special travel deals to lure visitors during tourism's low season. Incentives include bargain-priced hotel packages, affordable prix-fixe dinners at downtown restaurants (a typical three-course meal will go for $20), and special music and theater performances. Families with cabin fever should seek great deals on hotels with pools—it's a great weekend away from the snow and cold. Early January through February.

**Chicago Boat, RV & Outdoor Show**    McCormick Place, 23rd Street and Lake Shore Drive (℃ **312/946-6200;** www.chicagoboatshow.com). This extravaganza has been a Chicago tradition for nearly 70 years. All the latest boats and recreational vehicles are on display, plus there's trout fishing, a climbing wall, boating-safety seminars, and big-time entertainment. Late January.

## FEBRUARY

**FREE** **Chinese New Year Parade**    Wentworth and Cermak streets (℃ **312/326-5320;** www.chicagochinatown.org). The twisting dragon is sure to please as it winds down the street at this annual celebration. Call to verify the date, which varies from year to year, depending on the lunar calendar (usually btw. Jan 21 and Feb 19).

**Chicago Auto Show** McCormick Place, 23rd Street and Lake Shore Drive (📞 **630/495-2282;** www.chicagoautoshow.com). More than a thousand cars and trucks, domestic and foreign, are on display at this show, a tradition since 1901. Get behind the wheel of the latest models at this event, which draws nearly a million car owners or wannabe owners a year. Look for packages at hotels that include tickets. Mid-February.

**International Cluster of Dog Shows** McCormick Place South, 23rd Street and South Lake Shore Drive (📞 **773/237-5100;** www.ikcdogshow.com). See canines great and small strut their stuff. They're all adorable, but only one can win Best in Show. More than 10,000 AKC (American Kennel Club) purebred dogs of all breeds heat up the competition. It's quite a scene, particularly in the poodle area, where you can see dogs getting their hair blow-dried until they look like canine rock stars. Third week in February.

## MARCH

FREE **Spring Flower Shows** Spring is sprung a little earlier in the conservatories than it is outside in the real world, and thank goodness. See the lilies, daffodils, tulips, pansies, and other flowering perennials at **Lincoln Park Conservatory** (📞 **312/742-7737**) and **Garfield Park Conservatory** (📞 **312/746-5100**). Throughout March and April.

FREE **St. Patrick's Day Parade** Even the Chicago River puts on the green for St. Patrick's Day—it's actually dyed Kelly green for the occasion. The parade runs along Dearborn Street from Wacker Drive to Van Buren; the best place to view it is around Wacker and Dearborn. Saturday closest to March 17.

## APRIL

**Major League Baseball** Bundle up and join the die-hard fans at the ballpark (and die-hard fans know to wear long underwear, so follow their lead). Optimism reigns supreme in the early season and fans hope again that this will be their season. And even if it's not, hot dogs and peanuts will take some of the edge off. Check the team websites for various discounts: you should be able to find outfield upper deck seats for about $10. For the Cubs, call ⓒ **773/404-CUBS** (2827) or visit www.cubs.mlb.com; for the White Sox, call ⓒ **312/674-1000** or visit www.whitesox.mlb.com. Early April.

## MAY

FREE **Buckingham Fountain Color Light Show** Held in Grant Park, at Congress Parkway and Lake Shore Drive, the water and the ever-changing colored lights put on their show in the landmark fountain nightly until 11pm. May 1 through October 1.

FREE **Celtic Fest Chicago** The city's newest music festival celebrates the music and dance of Celtic traditions from around the world. Early May, Millennium Park (ⓒ **312/744-3315;** www.explorechicago.org).

**The Ferris Wheel & Carousel at Navy Pier** For $5, get a bird's-eye view of Chicago from the Ferris wheel (those who are slightly less fond of heights can stay closer to earth on the carousel), when it starts spinning again after a long winter's sleep. From Memorial Day through Labor Day, Navy Pier also hosts twice-weekly fireworks shows Wednesday nights at 9:30pm and Saturday nights at 10:15pm. May through October, 600 E. Grand Ave. (ⓒ **312/595-PIER** [7437]; www.navypier.com).

## JUNE

**Ravinia Festival** Summer wouldn't be summer without Ravinia, a Chicago tradition. Basically, it's an outdoor concert venue with a covered pavilion and plenty of lawn seating. Offerings range from classical to pop. Enjoy a picnic on the lawn while reveling in the music of the Chicago Symphony Orchestra. Pack a picnic, jump on the Metra commuter railroad, and join the crowds sitting under the stars on the lawn. Lawn seats are the cheap way in at $12. FINE PRINT Ravinia is so popular that many of the first-rate visiting orchestras, chamber ensembles, pop artists, and dance companies sell out in advance. June through September, at Ravinia Park, in suburban Highland Park, north of Chicago (ⓒ **847/266-5100** for ticket reservations; www.ravinia.com).

FREE **Chicago Blues Festival** The lineup looks better every year at this festival. Admission is free, but get there in the afternoon to stake out a spot on the lawn for the evening shows. You'll discover young up-and-coming blues stars (including some who are the off-spring of blues greats, such as Shamekia Copeland, daughter of Johnny Copeland). A shuttle bus will take you from the park to blues clubs. Call for information. First week in June, Petrillo Music Shell, at Jackson Drive and Columbus Drive in Grant Park (© **312/ 744-3315**).

FREE **57th Street Art Fair**  This is the oldest juried art fair in the Midwest—in 2007, it celebrated its 60th anniversary. Kids will especially enjoy the arts and crafts projects and the fun rides. First weekend in June, at 57th and Kimbark streets in Hyde Park (© **773/ 493-3247;** www.57thstreetartfair.org).

FREE **Chicago Gospel Festival**  This is the largest outdoor, free-admission event of its kind. Blues may be the city's more famous musical export, but Chicago is also the birthplace of gospel music: Thomas Dorsey, the "father of gospel music," and the greatest gos-pel singer ever, Mahalia Jackson, were South siders. This 3-day festival offers music on three stages with more than 40 perfor-mances. Early June, Petrillo Music Shell, at Jackson Drive and Columbus Drive in Grant Park (© **312/744-3315**).

FREE **Printers Row Book Fair**  One of the largest free outdoor book fairs in the country, this weekend-long event features readings by children's-book authors, book signings, and panel discussions on everything from writing your first novel to finding an agent. Also on offer are more than 150 booksellers displaying new, used, and antiquarian books for sale; a poetry tent; and special activities for children. Early June, on Dearborn Street from Congress to Polk (© **312/222-3986**).

FREE **Old Town Art Fair**  More than 200 painters, sculptors, and jewelry designers exhibit here from the Midwest and around the country. The fair also features an art auction, a garden walk, and food and drink. Second weekend in June, historic Old Town neigh-borhood, at Lincoln Park West and Wisconsin Street (© **312/337-1938;** www.oldtowntriangle.com).

FREE **Wells Street Art Festival**  Held on the same weekend as the Old Town Art Fair, this arts fest is lots of fun, with 200 arts and crafts vendors, food, music, and carnival rides. Second weekend in June, Wells Street from North Avenue to Division Street (© **312/ 951-6106;** www.oldtownchicago.org).

`FREE` **Andersonville Midsommarfest**   You can relive the Scandi-navian heritage of Andersonville, once Chicago's principal Swedish community. The treats at the Swedish Bakery, north of the Swedish-American Museum, are not to be missed. Second weekend in June, along Clark Street from Foster to Balmoral avenues (© **773/728-2995**).

`FREE` **Puerto Rican Fest**   One of Chicago's animated Latino street celebrations, this festival includes 5 days of live music, theater, games, food, and beverages. It peaks with a parade that wends its way from Wacker Drive and Dearborn Street to the West Side Puerto Rican enclave of Humboldt Park. Mid-June, at Humboldt Park, Division Street and Sacramento Boulevard (© **773/292-1414;** www.prparadechicago.com).

**Jammin' at the Zoo**   One featured musical act (which could be rock, zydeco, or reggae music), rocks the zoo on the lovely lawn south of the zoo's Park Place Café, certainly one of the more unusual outdoor venues in the city. The first of three summer concerts (ticket prices vary) is held in late June, Lincoln Park Zoo, 2200 N. Cannon Dr., at Fullerton Parkway (© **312/742-2000;** www.lpzoo.com). Admission to the zoo itself is free.

`FREE` **Grant Park Music Festival**   The free outdoor musical con-certs in the park begin the last week in June and continue through August. Also worthwhile are the movies in the park, shown out-doors on a large screen. Pritzker Music Pavilion, in Millennium Park (© **312/742-7638;** www.grantparkmusicfestival.com).

`FREE` **Taste of Chicago**   The largest free outdoor food fest in the nation (according to the City of Chicago), "The Taste," as it's known to locals, can be hot, sweaty, and claustrophobic. If your kids are small or don't do well in crowds, avoid it. Going on a weekday morning will help you miss the heaviest crowds. Three-and-a-half million people eat their way through cheesecake, ribs, pizza, and more, all carted to food stands set up throughout the park by scores of Chicago restaurants. On the evening of July 3, things get pretty hairy when Chicago launches its Independence Day fireworks, and crowds are at their sweaty peak. Admission is free; you pay for the sampling, of course. Late June and the first week of July, Grant Park (℃ **312/744-3315**).

**FREE** Chicago Country Music Festival It's less claustrophobic than Taste of Chicago, and it's free. You'll see big-name entertainers of the country-and-western genre. Late June (during the first weekend of Taste of Chicago), Petrillo Music Shell, at Jackson Drive and Columbus Drive in Grant Park (℃ **312/744-3315**).

**FREE** Chicago Pride Parade This parade is flamboyant and colorful, the culmination of a month of activities by Chicago's gay and lesbian community. The floats, marching units, and colorful characters will keep you entertained, so pick a spot on Broadway for the best view. Last Sunday in June, on Halsted Street, from Belmont Avenue to Broadway, south to Diversey Parkway, and east to Lincoln Park (℃ **773/348-8243;** www.chicagopridecalendar.org).

**FREE** Farmers' Markets They open at two dozen sites all over the city at the end of the month and continue weekly through October. Downtown sites are Daley Plaza (every other Thurs) and Federal Plaza (every Tues). For other locations and times, call ℃ **312/744-3315.**

## JULY

**FREE** Independence Day Celebration Celebrated in Chicago on July 3 (this way, people can also attend their community's own celebrations on the 4th), concerts and fireworks are the highlights of the festivities in Grant Park. The sight of fireworks exploding over and reflecting off of Lake Michigan is well worth braving the crowd. Take public transportation, or walk; ℃ **312/744-3315.**

Irish-American Heritage Festival If you're into Irish dancing, made famous by *Riverdance,* make sure to check out this festival, featuring Irish music, dance, food, readings, and children's entertainment. Second weekend in July, Irish-American Heritage Center, 4626 N. Knox Ave., at Montrose Avenue (℃ **773/282-7035**).

Sheffield Garden Walk One of Chicago's largest street parties, the Sheffield Garden Walk sounds a bit more refined than it actually is—but here's your chance to snoop into the lush backyards of Lincoln Park homeowners. There are also live bands, children's activities, and food and drink vendors on tap. Suggested donation is $6, $10 after 3 p.m. Mid-July, starting at Sheffield and Webster avenues (© **773/929-WALK** [9255]; www.sheffieldfestivals.org).

**FREE** **Chicago Yacht Club's Race to Mackinac Island**   If you love boating, you're sure to get a kick out of watching the start of this 3-day competition. At Monroe Street Harbor, boats set sail on Saturday for the grandest of the inland water races. Mid-July (© **312/861-7777;** www.chicagoyachtclub.org).

**FREE** **Chicago SummerDance**   From July to early September, the city's Department of Cultural Affairs transforms a patch of Grant Park into a lighted outdoor dance venue on Thursday, Friday, and Saturday from 6 to 9:30pm, and Sunday from 4 to 7pm. The 4,600-square-foot dance floor provides ample room for throwing down moves while live bands play music—from ballroom, jazz, klezmer, and country-and-western to samba, zydeco, blues, and soul. One-hour lessons are offered from 6 to 7pm. Free admission, east side of South Michigan Avenue between Balbo and Harrison streets (© **312/742-4007**).

**Taste of Lincoln Avenue**   This is one of the largest and most popular of Chicago's many neighborhood street fairs; it features 50 bands performing music on five stages. Neighborhood restaurants staff the food stands, and there's also a kids' carnival. Third weekend in July, Lincoln Park, between Fullerton Avenue and Wellington Street (© **773/868-3010;** www.wrightwoodneighbors.org).

**FREE** **Venetian Night**   Whimsical decorations on a carnival of illuminated boats make this a colorful event. Fireworks and synchronized music by the Grant Park Symphony Orchestra complete the scene. Watch from the shoreline, or, if you can swing it, get on board a friend's boat. Last Saturday in July, from Monroe Harbor to the Adler Planetarium (© **312/744-3315**).

**FREE** **Newberry Library Book Fair & Bughouse Square Debates**   If you have an interest in history or a love of books, this fair is for you. At the fair, held over 4 days, Newberry Library sells tens of thousands of used books, most for under $2. The highlight is soapbox orators re-creating the Bughouse Square Debates in Washington Square Park, just across the street. Pulitzer Prize–winning author Studs Terkel emcees the spirited chaos among left-wing agitators.

Late July, 69 W. Walton St. and Washington Square Park (© **312/ 255-3501;** www.newberry.org).

## August

**FREE** Chicago Air & Water Show   This hugely popular show is held on the lake at North Avenue Beach and overhead, where you'll see Stealth bombers, F-16s, and special appearances by the U.S. Air Force Thunderbirds and Navy Seals. Because the crowds are intense at North Avenue Beach, try grabbing a portable radio and hanging at Oak Street Beach, along the Gold Coast. Admission is free. Mid-August, North Avenue Beach (© **312/744-3315**).

**FREE** Viva! Chicago Latin Music Festival   Salsa, mambo, and the latest Latin rock groups hit the stage for this free festival. Last weekend in August, Petrillo Music Shell, at Jackson Drive and Columbus Drive in Grant Park (© **312/744-3370**).

## September

**FREE** Chicago Jazz Festival   This festival features Chicago-style jazz, with several national headliners always on hand. The event is free; kids are welcome. First weekend in September, Petrillo Music Shell, Jackson Drive and Columbus Drive in Grant Park (© **312/ 744-3315**).

**FREE** Mexican Independence Day Parade   Chicago is home to the nation's second-largest Mexican-American population, and that makes for a great parade. Another parade is held on the next day on 26th Street in the Little Village neighborhood (© **773/521-5387**). Mid-September, along Dearborn Street between Wacker Drive and Van Buren Street (© **312/744-3315**).

World Music Festival Chicago   This relatively new and enormously popular festival is a major undertaking by the city's Department of Cultural Affairs. Call ahead for tickets, because many events sell out. The festival is held at venues around town—notably, the Chicago Cultural Center, Museum of Contemporary Art, Old Town School of Folk Music, and Hot House. You'll see top performers from Zimbabwe to Hungary to Sri Lanka performing traditional, contemporary, and fusion music. Shows are a mix of free and ticketed ($10 or less) events. Call for information and to receive updates on scheduled performances. Late September, various locations around the city (② **312/742-1938;** www.cityofchicago.org/worldmusic).

## OCTOBER

**FREE** **Chicago Marathon**    Whether or not you're a runner, cheering on the harriers is an uplifting experience. Sponsored by LaSalle Bank, Chicago's marathon is a major event on the international long-distance running circuit, with some of the world's top runners competing. It begins and ends in Grant Park, but can be viewed from any number of vantage points along the race route. The website offers a free downloadable "spectator guide." Second Sunday in October (② **888/243-3344** or 312/904-9800; www.chicago marathon.com).

**FREE** **Spooky Zoo Spectacular**    Dress your tots in their Halloween finest for the free treats that are dispensed at various animal habitats. Bozo the Clown—himself a Chicago native—kicks things off with a parade through the zoo grounds. Late October, Lincoln Park Zoo, 2200 N. Cannon Dr. at Fullerton Parkway (② **312/742-2000;** www.lpzoo.com).

## NOVEMBER

**FREE** **Magnificent Mile Lights Festival**    Beginning at dusk, a colorful parade of Disney characters makes its way south along Michigan Avenue, from Oak Street to the Chicago River, with holiday lights being illuminated block by block as the procession passes. Carolers, elves, and minstrels appear with Santa along the avenue throughout the day and into the evening, and many of the retailers serve hot chocolate and other treats. Saturday before Thanksgiving (② **312/642-3570;** www.gnmaa.com).

**FREE** **State Street Thanksgiving Parade**    An annual event that takes place on Thanksgiving morning beginning at 8:30am. The parade marches up State Street, from Congress to Randolph (② **312/781-5681**).

**FREE** **Christmas Tree Lighting**    The switch is flipped on the day after Thanksgiving, around dusk. Daley Center Plaza, in the Loop (② **312/744-3315**).

`FREE` **Zoo Lights Festival**   Colorful illuminated displays brighten long nights during the holidays. Another special tradition is the annual Caroling to the Animals, a daylong songfest on a Saturday early in the month. Late November through the first week in January, Lincoln Park Zoo, 2200 N. Cannon Dr. (© **312/742-2000**).

## DECEMBER

`FREE` **Christkindlmarket**   This German-style Christmas market features free music, inexpensive food, and excellent holiday shopping (including a stellar selection of decorations and ornaments) in the shadow of the city's Christmas tree. German beer and mulled wine make sure everyone is full of good cheer. Daley Plaza, 55 W Randolph St, © **312/494-2175;** www.christkindlmarket.com.

Great deals can be found at many excellent Chicago hotels (like the Talbott Hotel, see p. 48) if you know where to look.

# CHEAP SLEEPS

In a city that thrives on the business traveler and a large convention trade, hotel rooms often go for a premium—not good news for those of us on the free and dirt cheap travel plan. However, several amazing accommodations deals can be found in the heart of Chicago.

The best of these, hands down, is the J. Ira and Nikki Harris Hostel (part of the Hostelling International organization), one of the world's best hostels as voted by members of www.hostelworld.com. Located in the South Loop, with rooms for about $30, along with easy access to transportation and many of Chicago's best attractions, you won't find a better deal in the city.

Another *huge* secret weapon for the traveler seeking to steal a room in a Chicago hotel is a little Chicago-only secret called **www.hot rooms.com**. With options ranging from moderate to deluxe, you'll get the low-down, cheapest rates at the best hotels in town. A search in the height of the summer tourist season actually turned up rooms in four different hotels ranging from $99 for queen rooms at the Howard Johnson Inn in River North or Congress Plaza in the South Loop, to $109 for the Comfort Inn & Suites Downtown, again in River North. Imagine what off-season and weekday rates might be! Other services that are nationwide, and that might help you score a cheap room include **www.hotwire.com** and **www.priceline.com**.

So, even in the busy and pricey Michigan Avenue area, with a little work and strategic thinking (both of which are right up your alley) it's possible to score a room for around $100. And if you're willing to go a bit farther west, into River North, or north, to Lakeview, options for motel lodgings and small hotels mean more cheap deals. Of course, when you forego a major hotel, you'll be making minor sacrifices, some very minor (no freshly baked cookies at turn-down), to less minor (locations that are, well, more than a bit off-the-beaten track). As you'd expect, if you avoid the heavily touristed area of Michigan Avenue and the Loop, and instead hang your hat in a real Chicago neighborhood like Lakeview, you might find yourself taking a bus or the El into the central areas of the city, but you'll save a bundle.

## RESERVATION SERVICES

For discounted rooms at more than 30 downtown hotels, try the aforementioned **Hot Rooms** (✆ **800/468-3500** or 773/468-7666; www.hotrooms.com). I've used this service and was very pleased to get a night in a top-rated downtown hotel for about half the regular price. The service is free, but if you cancel a reservation (and you must adhere to each individual hotel's cancellation policy), you're assessed a fee of $25. If you're in the heat of checking out hotel rooms, follow Hot Rooms on Twitter for up-to-the-minute updates on specials.

The Chicago Visitor Guide, published by the **Chicago Convention and Tourism Bureau,** will give you a comprehensive look at hotels; to find the latest deals on lodging, including hotel discounts as well as complete weekend packages, you can call ✆ **800/2CONNECT** (226-6632), or check out **www.choosechicago.com**.

## Ride That Wave

Everyone recognizes that the best way to stay free in Chicago is to crash on a friend's couch, or failing that, the couch of a friend of a friend. Or a friend of a friend of a friend. Or your boss' nephew's friend, who happens to be a nice guy. You get the idea. Failing that, there's **www.couchsurfing.org**. This nonprofit organization promotes couch surfing as a way to connect people internationally. There is a "vouching" system in which potential hosts can find out if others can vouch for the person who wants to stay on their couch. At press time, the site claimed 1.5 million successful surf or host experiences, and some 144,000 couches were available in the U.S. Further inspiration: Testimonials on the site demonstrate that some people are managing to couchsurf for an entire year, going through Europe, for example.

## APARTMENT RESERVATIONS

A centralized reservations service called **At Home Inn Chicago,** P.O. Box 14088, Chicago, IL 60614 (© **800/375-7084** or 312/640-1050; www.athomeinnchicago.com), lists more than 70 accommodations in Chicago. If you're of an adventurous bent, and of course you are, you'll find options ranging from high-rise and loft apartments to guest rooms carved from a former private club on the 40th floor of a Loop office building. Most lie within 3 miles of downtown (many are located in the Gold Coast, Old Town, and Lincoln Park). This can be an especially good budget option if you're planning a longer stay in the city, because of the special weekly rates. Studios and one-bedroom apartments in central neighborhoods can be rented for $100 and under (for example, a studio on the north end of Michigan Ave. was available for $99). Rates can be even lower by the week. If you call, the reservations service will work on rates with you.

## LANDING THE BEST ROOM

Somebody has to get the best room in the house: It might as well be you. You can start by joining the hotel's frequent-guest program, which may make you eligible for upgrades. A hotel-branded credit card usually gives its owner "silver" or "gold" status in frequent-guest programs for free. Always ask about a corner room. They're often larger and quieter, with more windows and light, and they often cost the same as standard rooms. When you make your reservation, ask if the hotel is renovating; if it is, request a room away from the construction. Ask about nonsmoking rooms, rooms with views, rooms with twin, queen-, or king-size beds. If you're a light sleeper, request a quiet room away from vending machines, elevators, restaurants, bars, and discos. Ask for a room that has been most recently renovated or redecorated. If you aren't happy with your room when you arrive, ask for another one. In a word: Ask. Most lodgings will be willing to accommodate you.

We give the listed "rack rates," for the hotels in this chapter, so be aware that these are the hotel's published prices, and they are on the high side. You may well score rooms for much less. The rates given in this chapter are per night and do not include taxes, which are quite steep at 15.4%, or any discounts. Prices are always subject to availability and vary according to day of the week and seasonally. (The lower rates tend to be offered Jan–Mar and on nonholiday weekends.)

We also include several hostels in this chapter (see section below), depending on just how cheap you are willing to sleep; if you require your own room, then you'll pay more than for a room shared with other travelers-on-the-cheap. (Remember, too, that many hostels offer private rooms.)

Best of all is the option of bunking with a friend, or friend-of-a-friend who actually lives in the city. Not only do you get a taste of real life in our fair city, but it's *free* (of course it's always nice to bring a host/hostess gift and treat that person to a nice dinner in exchange for your free digs—both of which won't add up to more than 1 night in a downtown hotel).

## HOSTEL? THEY WERE VERY NICE TO ME . . .

By far the cheapest stay in Chicago, hostels provide a no-frills opportunity to bunk down in a room with a bunch of other travelers, make new friends from around the world, and save loads of cash. Back in the day, you'd have to bring your own bedding, and there was a daytime "lockout" period. No longer. Hostels are open 24/7, and linens are usually included in the price.

If you haven't stayed at a hostel, expect to choose from a shared room (either same-sex or mixed; Hostelling International hostels have only single-sex dorm rooms) with shared bathrooms, usually for less than $50; prices vary by season. Some hostels offer private rooms for one, two, or three people, or en suite bathrooms, with prices rising accordingly. The top end for private rooms is still usually well under $100.

Hostelling International hostels offer free breakfast and free Wi-Fi, and you can count on the hostel to be clean, safe, and well-managed (the international nonprofit organization's mission is to "promote international understanding of the world and its people through hostelling.") You don't have to be a member of HI to stay, but you do get a slight discount if you are a member. There is only one HI hostel in Chicago proper, the J. Ira and Nikki Harris Hostel, but it's fabulous and large, with capacity for 500 guests (see review below). For information on how to join Hostelling International USA (which also gives you membership in all international HI hostels), visit www.hiusa.org. Membership is free if you're 17 or under, $28 annually for people 18 to 54. As a member, you can make prepaid reservations at HI hostels, and are eligible for a lot of discounts, from long-distance calling to bus tours to organized tours.

Most hostels of any type offer a communal kitchen/dining area, a lounge area, and lockers or other locked storage (be sure to bring a lock, since locks are not provided). Some of the better hostels provide free or low-cost organized activities, ranging from local tours, movies, and pub crawls, to day or overnight trips. Staff members are trained to help you plan individual excursions based on your interests. Private hostels can be just as expensive as, and sometimes more laid-back than, HI places. You may stay in a co-ed dorm room, find a bar on premises, and find a bulletin board offering rides or temp jobs. You may also find a noisier, more partying crowd, which may be a plus or a minus, depending what you're looking for.

You'll find a comprehensive listing of hostels, both HI and private (as well as budget hotels and guesthouses) at www.hostels.com, which claims to list "every hostel, everywhere." The website gives properties a "satisfaction rating" based on user reviews, which you can read. Granted, like most Internet reviews, they can be artificially inflated (or deflated), but you can at least get an idea of what to expect and, if you like it, make reservations through that website, or go directly to the hostel's site.

In addition to the HI hostel we list in this chapter, some of the other top-rated hostels in the Chicago area at press time include:

● **Arlington House International Hostel,** 616 W. Arlington Place (© **773-929-9380;** www.arlingtonhouse.com), ranks high for its Lincoln Park location. Features 24-hour security, Wi-Fi access, and a barbecue area. Prices range from $25 to $36 in high season. Internet access and linens are included in the price. Subway/El: Red Line to Fullerton.

● **AAE Chicago Parthenon Hostel,** 314 W. Halsted (© **304/268-8981;** www.chicago.aaeworldhotels.com), has the advantage of being a short walk from the Amtrak and Greyhound stations. Located in the heart of Greektown, you'll be near an abundance of inexpensive restaurants and nightlife. Breakfast is included in the price, which ranges from $24 to $55 in high season. Valet parking is available for a very reasonable $10 per night. Subway/El: Blue Line to Halsted.

● **Chicago International Hostel,** 6318 N. Winthrop Ave. (© **773/262-1011**), is located on the far north side of the city, near Loyola University's campus and the Rogers Park neighborhood. Linens are included in the price, which ranges from $23 to $40 in high season. The downside is a 30-minute subway ride to the Loop. Free parking is available behind the hostel. Subway: Red Line to Granville.

Beyond hostels, hotels, and motels, you need to get creative, and you can find some really cheap ways to stay. Cheapest of all is staying with a friend, or friend of a friend, or if you feel comfortable, couch surfing (see "Ride That Wave," earlier in this chapter). You might also consider staying at an inexpensive chain hotel outside of the city. Those hotels are particularly abundant near O'Hare International Airport. And while none of Chicago's YMCAs offer accommodations, a north suburban YMCA does (see p. 224), and that too can make for a bargain stay.

## 1 Central Chicago Accommodations

**Hilton Chicago**   When it opened in 1927, this massive brick-and-stone edifice billed itself as the largest hotel in the world. Today the Hilton still runs like a small city, with numerous restaurants and shops and a steady stream of conventioneers. Its colorful history includes visits by Queen Elizabeth, Emperor Hirohito, and every president since FDR—and riots outside its front door during the 1968 Democratic Convention. The classical-rococo public spaces—including the Versailles-inspired Grand Ballroom and Grand Stair Lobby—are magnificent, but

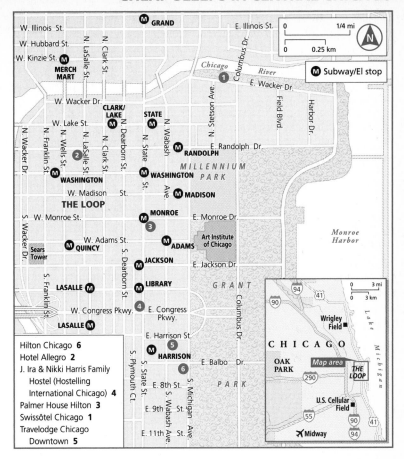

Hilton Chicago **6**
Hotel Allegro **2**
J. Ira & Nikki Harris Family
  Hostel (Hostelling
  International Chicago) **4**
Palmer House Hilton **3**
Swissôtel Chicago **1**
Travelodge Chicago
  Downtown **5**

the rest of the hotel falls into the chain-hotel mold: comfortable and well-run but fairly impersonal. You can score rooms for a great price here, but be prepared for them to be on the small side. Luckily, even the smallest room feels homey, thanks to the warm cherry furniture. Many of the standard rooms have two bathrooms (great if you're traveling in a group of friends). Rooms facing Michigan Avenue offer sweeping views of Grant Park and the lake. The Hilton is a great choice for budget travelers thanks to its bargain prices on the less-desirable small rooms, and its proximity to major museums and Grant Park.

720 S. Michigan Ave. (at Balbo Dr.), Chicago, IL 60605. (C) **800/HILTONS** (445-8667) or 312/922-4400. Fax 312/922-5240. www.hilton.com. 1,544 units. $129–$399 double. AE, DC, DISC, MC, V. Subway/El: Red Line to Harrison. **Amenities:** 4 restaurants (cafe,

American, steakhouse, Irish pub w/live music); 2 lounges; babysitting; concierge; health club w/indoor track, hot tubs, sauna, and steam room; indoor pool; 24-hr. room service. *In room:* A/C, TV w/pay movies, hair dryer, minibar, Wi-Fi.

**Palmer House Hilton**   The longest continually operating hotel in North America (since 1871), the Palmer House was named for legendary State Street merchant prince Potter Palmer. The building's grand Italianate lobby retains a Gilded Age aura (it's worth a look even if you're not staying here), but don't come here expecting to be swept back in time. The massive complex depends heavily on large business groups, so the hotel often feels like an extension of the McCormick Place Convention Center. With so many rooms to fill, you stand a good chance of scoring a deal when they're looking to fill the hotel. At press time, rooms were on offer for $139 for full-pay-ment-in-advance rooms (meaning, you pay up front and don't have the option of getting your money back in case of cancellation). Rooms that were previously decorated in drab, motel-worthy colors have been upgraded in the past few years with new, cheerier bedding and carpets. (If you get a chance, go to the lower level and peek at the newly restored grand ballroom: it's a knockout of balconies, Italianate moldings, and crystal chandeliers). Standard double rooms are quite spacious, with plenty of room to spread out. Bathrooms are small but serviceable (some rooms come with two bathrooms, a plus if you're traveling in a small group). FINE PRINT No matter where your room is located, don't expect grand views of surrounding skyscrapers; most rooms look out into offices across the street.

17 E. Monroe St. (at State St.), Chicago, IL 60603. ✆ **800/HILTONS** (445-8667) or 312/726-7500. Fax 312/917-1797. www.hiltonchicagosales.com. 1,639 units. $129–$350 double. AE, DC, DISC, MC, V. Subway/El: Red Line to Monroe. **Amenities:** 3 restaurants; 2 lounges; babysitting referrals; children's programs; concierge; executive-level rooms; health club w/indoor pool, Jacuzzi, and sauna for $10/day or $20/entire stay; room service until 2am. *In room:* A/C, TV w/pay movies, hair dryer, high-speed Internet access, minibar.

★ **Swissôtel Chicago**   This sleek, modern hotel is all business and may therefore feel a bit icy to some visitors, but its wonderful location on the river, just east of the Michigan Avenue bridge, and the amazing discounts offered on weekends (superior king rooms, for example, can sometimes go for less than $100 on weekend nights) makes it

## Cheap Hotel Chains

If all else fails and all the recommendations in this chapter are booked, and you have not managed to find a friend of a friend with a free couch, you can try an area chain hotel. Some of these have specific hotels listed in this chapter; others will mean you have to go a bit farther from the city and take transportation in daily. Staying outside of the city is not ideal, but it is cheap, and one area that is full of cheap hotel options is the area surrounding O'Hare airport. There, you will find a Super 8, a Motel 6, and a Comfort Inn, with rates that range from $69 to $125 per night. To check on any Chicago location and room rate, here are the toll-free numbers for America's most popular cheap hotel chains: **Best Western** (© 800/528-1234); **Comfort Inn** (© 800/228-5150); **Doubletree Hotels** (© 800/222-TREE [222-8733]); **Econo Lodges** (© 800/55-ECONO [553-2666]); **Holiday Inn** (© 800/HOLI-DAY [465-4329]); **Howard Johnson** (© 800/654-2000); **La Quinta Motor Inns** (© 800/531-5900); **Motel 6** (© 800/466-8356); **Ramada** (© 800/2-RAMADA [276-6232]); **Rodeway Inns** (© 800/228-2000); **Super 8** (© 800/800-8000); and **Travelodge** (© 800/255-3050).

especially attractive to budget travelers in search of tranquility. The hotel's triangular design gives every room a panoramic vista of Lake Michigan, Grant Park, and/or the Chicago River. The spacious rooms have separate sitting areas and warm contemporary furnishings. It's always worth asking to upgrade to an Executive Level room, which are sometimes empty on weekends. On that level, you'll receive complimentary breakfast and hors d'oeuvres and have access to a lounge with Internet connections, a library, and a personal concierge. Active travelers will want to break a sweat in the lofty environs of the Penthouse Health Club and Spa, perched on the 42nd floor.

323 E. Wacker Dr., Chicago, IL 60601. © **888/737-9477** or 312/565-0565. Fax 312/565-0540. www.swissotelchicago.com. 632 units. $129–$409 double. AE, DC, DISC, MC, V. Subway/El: Red, Brown, Orange, or Green line to Randolph. **Amenities:** 2 restaurants (steakhouse, American); lounge; babysitting; concierge; executive-level rooms; penthouse fitness center w/indoor pool, spa, Jacuzzi, and sauna; 24-hr. room service. *In room:* A/C, TV w/pay movies, hair dryer, Internet, minibar.

## CHEAP SLEEPS

★ **J. Ira & Nikki Harris Family Hostel (Hostelling International Chicago)**
Clean, safe, inexpensive, and centrally located, this hostel should
rank high on any budget traveler's list. For around $30 a night, you
can stay at this, the second-largest hostel in the U.S., in a comfy room
in Chicago's South Loop, a fantastic jumping-off point for all your
adventures. It is hands-down the best dirt cheap lodging in the city,
and was named the best hostel in the world in 2007 (the hostel was
completely remodeled in 2000). Each room is large by hostel standards and includes a locker (make sure to bring your own lock).
There's an 11pm quiet rule, but no curfew. Everyone has access to a
full kitchen, so you can prepare your own meals. Volunteers staff an
information desk and can answer questions about bus routes, fees,
museums, walking tours, and more. Free breakfast and free Wi-Fi,
too! Walking distance to the Blue Line, so it's easy to get to and from
O'Hare International Airport.

24 E. Congress Pkwy. (at Wabash Ave.), Chicago, IL 60605. ✆ **312/360-0300.** Fax
312/360-0313. www.hichicago.com. 500 beds. $29–$35 per bed (additional $3 per
person per night if you don't have a Hostelling International membership). Maximum 14-day stay. Children 18 and under must be accompanied by an adult. MC, V.
Subway/El: Blue Line to LaSalle, Red Line to Harrison, Brown Line to Library, Purple
Line to Library, Green Line to Adams, Orange Line to either Adams or Library. No
pets. **Amenities:** Self-service kitchen with dining room; lobby with free Wi-Fi; meeting rooms; library; TV room; 24-hour security; 24-hour luggage storage; lockers in-
room; linens, towels, and pillows provided.

## WORTH A SPLURGE

**Hotel Allegro**   A boutique hotel with a fun, lighthearted vibe, the
Kimpton Group's splashy Allegro is a good value. Although its published rates are similar to those of its sister properties, the Hotel
Monaco and Hotel Burnham (both too pricey to be included in this
guide), the Allegro is far larger and therefore more likely to offer special rates to fill space, especially on weekends and in the winter. In
January, you might score a romantic weekend package with champagne, roses, strawberries, and breakfast included for $159 during the
City of Chicago's Winter Delights promotion. Guests of the Allegro
enter a lobby with plush, boldly colored furnishings. That whimsical
first impression segues into the cheery, pink-walled guest rooms.

## Sites Where Savings Add Up

Not to be confused with alligators or aggravators, aggregators are online services that will search multiple sites for travel deals. One that I prefer is www.kayak.com. You'll find featured deals on everything from cruises to ski vacations, and when it comes to hotels, you can sort by price, distance to the city center, and user reviews. Other aggregators to check out include www.sidestep.com, www.cheapflights.com, www.travelaxe.com (which searches only hotels), Yahoo's www.farechase.com, www.mobissimo.com, www.qixo.com and SuperSearch, a subsidiary of online discount agency www.travelzoo.com. Most aggregators have a broader online network than the "big three" (www.travelocity.com, www.expedia.com, and www.orbitz.com), so they offer a wider variety of options, and therefore, a wider variety of prices.

Most rooms are small (without much space beyond the bed, an armoire, and one chair), but manage to feel cozy rather than cramped. Suites have foldout couches and separate bathrooms that come with robes and two-person Jacuzzi tubs. The hotel's restaurant, 312 Chicago, attracts nonguests in search of excellent Italian cuisine.

1 W. Randolph St. (at LaSalle St.), Chicago, IL 60601. © **800/643-1500** or 312/236-0123. Fax 312/236-0917. www.allegrochicago.com. 483 units. $139–$299 double. Kids 17 and under stay free in parent's room. Rollaways are available free depending on room; cribs free. AE, DC, DISC, MC, V. Subway/El: All lines to Washington. Pets allowed. **Amenities:** Restaurant (northern Italian); lounge; concierge; exercise room (and access to nearby health club w/indoor pool for $10/day); limited room service. *In room:* A/C, TV w/pay movies, hair dryer, free high-speed Internet access, minibar.

**Travelodge Chicago Downtown**    Travelodge promises and delivers neat, clean rooms at reasonable prices. The hotel's location near the Loop and Museum Campus is excellent: You are half a block from Grant Park and all the summer festivals, and only 4 blocks from the Field Museum. This 12-story hotel is one of few budget lodgings you'll find in the heart of the Loop. The hotel was built in 1925 as the Harrison Hotel, and for many years was one of the premier hotels in the city. Ever since Travelodge acquired the property, they've been promoting it as "a touch of old Chicago" and working to restore the property. To date, all guest rooms and the lobby have been renovated. Some rooms offer refrigerators and microwaves, and groups might seek out the rooms that feature two beds and two bathrooms. There's no pool, but two in-hotel restaurants cater to budget travelers: Chicago Carry-Out offers full breakfasts and sandwiches, and Charming Wok serves inexpensive Chinese fare from 11am to 11pm.

65 E. Harrison St. (at S. Wabash Ave.), Chicago, IL 60605. ℂ **888/515-6375** or 312/427-8000. Fax 312/427-8261. www.travelodge.com. 250 units. $103–$165 double. Kids 17 and under stay free in parent's room. Rollaways $10/night; cribs free. AE, DC, DISC, MC, V. Subway/El: Red Line to State/Harrison. **Amenities:** 2 restaurants. *In room:* A/C, TV w/pay movies, fax, hair dryer, minibar.

## 2  Near North & River North Accommodations

**Allerton Crowne Plaza**    A historic hotel that received a fairly bland makeover, the Allerton's main appeal is its central location and relatively reasonable rates. Built in 1924 as a "club hotel," providing permanent residences for single men and women, the Allerton is now one of the flagship hotels of the Crowne Plaza chain. The Italian Renaissance–inspired exterior has been painstakingly restored to its original dark-red brickwork, stone carvings, and limestone base. Too bad the distinctive exterior style wasn't replicated inside. The rooms have a generic chain-hotel feel, and because the hotel was originally built for single men and women, the rooms are fairly small (the "Petite Classic" rooms are—surprise, surprise—tiny). Still, all the rooms and public areas have a warm and homey feel. Snag one overlooking Michigan Avenue to get the best views (or at least stop by the hotel's Renaissance Ballroom for a peek at the Mag Mile).

701 N. Michigan Ave. (at Huron St.), Chicago, IL 60611. ℂ **800/621-8311** outside Illinois, or 312/440-1500. Fax 312/440-1819. www.ichotelsgroup.com. 443 units. $109–$299 double. AE, DC, DISC, MC, V. Subway/El: Red Line to Chicago. **Amenities:** Restaurant (American); lounge; concierge; fitness center (w/excellent city views); 24-hr. room service. *In room:* A/C, TV w/pay movies, hair dryer, high-speed Internet access, minibar.

**Courtyard by Marriott Chicago Downtown**    Marriott's budget chain offers good value in the heart of River North. You're a short walk from Michigan Avenue, the Loop, and the many galleries and nightclubs of

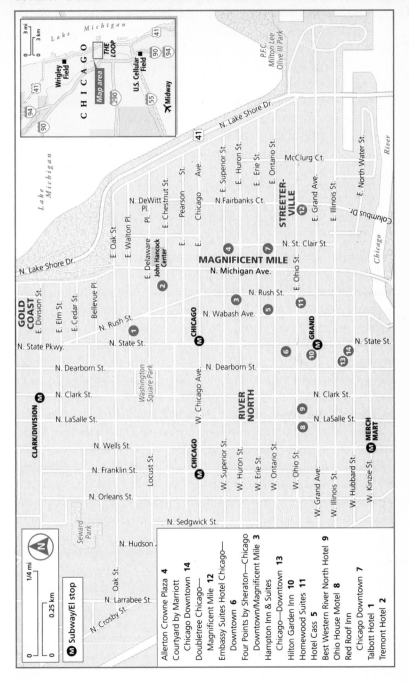

Allerton Crowne Plaza **4**
Courtyard by Marriott
  Chicago Downtown **14**
Doubletree Chicago—
  Magnificent Mile **12**
Embassy Suites Hotel Chicago—
  Downtown **6**
Four Points by Sheraton—Chicago
  Downtown/Magnificent Mile **3**
Hampton Inn & Suites
  Chicago—Downtown **13**
Hilton Garden Inn **10**
Homewood Suites **11**
Hotel Cass **5**
Best Western River North Hotel **9**
Ohio House Motel **8**
Red Roof Inn
  Chicago Downtown **7**
Talbott Hotel **1**
Tremont Hotel **2**

River North. The trolley to Navy Pier stops a block from the hotel (on State St.). Plus, you'll get access to an indoor pool, a particularly nice fitness center with a view over the Chicago River, plus a whirlpool, sauna, and sun deck. Guest rooms feature granite vanities, high-speed Internet access, and sofas, some with pullout beds. Rooms especially good for groups and families include connecting rooms (both double-bedded and king-size), and suites that offer a bedroom plus a sitting room with a sofa bed.

30 E. Hubbard St. (at State St.), Chicago, IL 60611. ✆ **800/321-2211** or 312/329-2500. Fax 312/329-0293. www.marriott.com. 337 units. $119–$209 double; $159–$400 suite. Kids 18 and under stay free in parent's room. Rollaway beds and cribs free. AE, DC, DISC, MC, V. Subway/El: Red Line to Grand/State. **Amenities:** Restaurant; lounge; concierge; exercise room; indoor pool; room service. *In room:* A/C, TV w/pay movies, hair dryer, high-speed Internet access.

**Doubletree Chicago—Magnificent Mile** The soaring modern atrium lobby is impressive, as is the location east of the Magnificent Mile and close to the Ohio Street Beach and Navy Pier. Although the public spaces have the impersonal feel of a conference center, the rooms are cheerily decorated, and the large windows allow sweeping city views from the upper floors. (I recommend the rooms on the north side of the building, which look toward the Hancock Building.) But it's the amenities that help this hotel stand out, making it one of the best values in the city.

Fitness devotees will delight in the fact that the hotel adjoins the Lakeshore Athletic Club, where guests may enjoy the extensive facilities free of charge (including an indoor pool, fitness classes, and sauna); you don't even have to go outside to get there. The hotel also has its own spacious outdoor pool and sun deck; in the summer you can sit back and enjoy a drink at the outdoor bar. (Be forewarned, however, that the hotel fills up during summer vacation; book as far in advance as possible for July–Aug). The Doubletree is a good bet for the budget-conscious family, as kids 17 and under stay free in their parent's room. Leave the pay-per-view movies one night and head to the massive AMC theaters next door, where all 21 screens offer stadium seating.

300 E. Ohio St. (at Fairbanks Court), Chicago, IL 60611. ✆ **312/787-6100.** Fax 312/787-6259. www.doubletreemagmile.com. 500 units. $109–$270 double. Rollaways $20; cribs free. AE, DC, DISC, MC, V. Subway/El: Red Line to Grand. **Amenities:** 3 restaurants (American, cafe); bar; babysitting; concierge; executive-level rooms; complimentary access to nearby health club w/whirlpool and sauna, outdoor and indoor

pools; 24-hr. room service. *In room:* A/C, TV w/pay movies and video games, hair dryer, high-speed Internet access.

**Embassy Suites Hotel Chicago—Downtown**    You might fancy yourself in Florida when you first set foot in this hotel, where a gushing waterfall and palm- and fern-lined landscaped ponds lie at the bottom of the huge central atrium. But you're not in the Tropics: You're in one of Chicago's more budget-friendly hotels, even though it bills itself as a business hotel and does a healthy convention business. Accommodations are spacious enough for a group: All guest rooms are suites, which have two rooms, consisting of a living room with a sleeper sofa, a round table, and four chairs; and a bedroom with either a king-size bed or two double beds. At one end of the atrium, the hotel serves a complimentary cooked-to-order breakfast and, at the other end, supplies complimentary cocktails and snacks in the evening. And yes, there's a pool. Families might prefer the location of Embassy Suites' other Chicago hotel, a lovely tower located at 511 N. Columbus Dr. (© 312/836-5900), just a few blocks from Navy Pier.

600 N. State St. (at W. Ohio St.), Chicago, IL 60610. © **800/EMBASSY** (362-2779) or 312/943-3800. Fax 312/943-7629. www.embassysuiteschicago.com. 366 units. $139–$279 king suite; $169–$319 double suite. Kids 17 and under stay free in parent's room. Few rollaways available, ask upon check-in (sofa beds in every suite); cribs free. AE, DC, DISC, MC, V. Subway/El: Red Line to Grand/State. **Amenities:** Restaurant (Italian); coffee bar; babysitting; concierge; exercise room w/whirlpool; indoor pool; limited room service. *In room:* A/C, TV w/pay movies and video games, hair dryer, high-speed Internet access, kitchenette.

★ **Four Points by Sheraton—Chicago Downtown/Magnificent Mile** This hotel's location puts you in the heart of the action—just 1 block west of the central part of Michigan Avenue, with its shopping and great restaurants. You'll also be a block from the stop for the No. 151 bus, which will whisk you south to Millennium Park and the Art Institute, or the No. 146, the express bus that goes to Museum Campus. Rooms feature whirlpool tubs, free Internet service, and flatscreen TVs. The pool and whirlpool area is bright and airy. At press time, self-parking was only $28, a bargain compared to many Magnificent Mile hotels.

630 N. Rush St. (just west of Michigan Ave.), Chicago, IL 60611. © **312/981-6600.** www.starwoodhotels.com. 226 units. From $125 double; $215 junior suite; $245 king suite. Kids 14 and under stay free in parent's room. Rollaway beds $25; cribs free. AE, DC, DISC, MC, V. Subway/El: Red Line to Grand/State. **Amenities:** Snack bar; fitness room; indoor pool and whirlpool; room service. *In room:* A/C, TV w/pay movies, fridge, free Internet access, microwave.

**Hampton Inn & Suites Chicago—Downtown**  The Hampton, with its combination of rooms, two-room suites, and studios, is a smart choice for families and small groups. Kids will appreciate the indoor pool and in-room movies after a busy day of sightseeing. Built in 1998, the hotel still feels brand-new; the Prairie-style lobby and breakfast lounge give the place a tranquil feel. The rooms have an urban look, with dark wood furniture and plush duvets. Request a room overlooking Illinois or Dearborn streets if you crave natural light; most rooms don't offer much of a view. The standard rooms include a desk, armchair, and ottoman; a studio has a microwave, sink, and minifridge along one wall; and the apartment-style suites feature galley kitchens with fridges, microwaves, dishwashers, and cooking utensils, and a separate bedroom. Nice touches include a nightlight in the bathroom and clock radios with guides to local radio stations. You won't have to cook breakfast in your kitchenette—the hotel offers a complimentary breakfast buffet, with two hot items per day.

33 W. Illinois St. (at Dearborn St.), Chicago, IL 60610. ℂ **800/HAMPTON** (426-7866) or 312/832-0330. Fax 312/832-0333. www.hamptoninn.com. 230 units. $109–$199 double; $199–$309 suite. Kids under 18 stay free in parent's room. Rollaways $10/night; cribs free. AE, DC, DISC, MC, V. Subway/El: Red Line to Grand/State. **Amenities:** Restaurant (Italian); exercise room w/sauna; indoor pool w/Jacuzzi and sun deck; room service. *In room:* A/C, TV w/pay movies and video games, hair dryer, high-speed Internet access.

**Hilton Garden Inn**  Although it might seem out of place in these urban climes, this Hilton Garden Inn, located on prime real estate between North Michigan Avenue and the River North neighborhood, is every inch a big-city player. The hotel caters to business types, so budget travelers just might score a great deal on the weekends, when the usual clientele clears out. The building is adjacent to ESPN Zone and the Shops at North Bridge mall. The hotel doesn't have much personality—the lobby is strictly business and feels cold. What the place does have going for it—besides location—are ample rooms, located between the 13th and the 23rd floors. Views higher up, especially on the east side and from corner suites facing north and south, afford dramatic vistas of the cityscape and skyline.

10 E. Grand Ave. (at State St.), Chicago, IL 60611. ℂ **800/HILTONS** (445-8667) or 312/595-0000. Fax 312/595-0955. www.hilton.com. 357 units. $99–$309 double. Kids 18 and under stay free in parent's room. Rollaways $20/night; cribs free. AE, DC, DISC, MC, V. Subway/El: Red Line to Grand/State. **Amenities:** Restaurant; lounge;

babysitting; concierge; fitness center w/Jacuzzi and sauna; indoor pool; limited room service. *In room:* A/C, TV w/pay movies, fridge, hair dryer.

**Homewood Suites** An excellent choice for budget travelers, this hotel offers a handy location and fresh, clean rooms with some nice extras. Because all of the rooms are suites with full kitchens, you can prepare your own meals, and there's plenty of room in the suite for everyone to spread out. Housed just off the Mag Mile in a sleek tower above retail shops, offices, and a health club—and adjacent to ESPN Zone—the hotel's design aesthetic is best described as "Italian Renaissance meets Crate & Barrel." Distressed-leather sofas, Mediterranean stone tile, wrought-iron chandeliers, and beaded lampshades adorn its sixth-floor lobby. Rooms—one- and two-bedroom suites and a handful of double-double suites, which can connect to king suites— feature velvet sofas that are all sleepers, and the beds have big, thick mattresses. Each comes with a dining-room table that doubles as a workspace and decent-size bathrooms. The hotel provides a complimentary buffet breakfast and beverages and hors d'oeuvres every evening; there is also a free grocery-shopping service and free access to an excellent health club next door.

40 E. Grand Ave. (at Wabash St.), Chicago, IL 60611. © **800/CALL-HOME** (225-5466) or 312/644-2222. Fax 312/644-7777. www.homewoodsuiteschicago.com. 233 units. $99–$359 for a 2-room suite. Kids under 18 stay free in parent's room. Rollaways and cribs free. AE, DC, DISC, MC, V. Subway/El: Red Line to Grand/State. **Amenities:** Babystting; concierge; fitness room w/small pool and views of the city. *In room:* A/C, TV w/pay movies, hair dryer, high-speed Internet access, kitchen.

**Hotel Cass** A hidden gem, the Hotel Cass is tucked just 2 blocks off the Magnificent Mile, within easy walking distance of shopping, restaurants, and far-mmore-expensive luxury hotels. Space may be at a premium here—the check-in area and lobby-lounge are fairly compact—but everything is bright and stylish. The rooms are quite small (in some, there's barely room for the flatscreen TVs, which are mounted on the mechanical arms that reach over the bed)O, and some only have views of the building next door. But the beds are soft and comfortable, with masses of pillows (helpfully labeled "soft" and "firm"), and bathrooms tuck stylish amenities like rectangular sinks into a compact space. A bonus for budget-conscious travelers: the complimentary buffet breakfast, which includes eggs, bacon, and decadently delicious cinnamon rolls.

640 N. Wabash Ave. (btw. Erie and Ontario sts), Chicago, IL 60611. ℂ **800/799-4030**, 312/787-4030. www.casshotel.com. 175 units. $99–$189 double. AE, DC, DISC, MC, V. Subway/El: Red Line to Grand. **Amenities:** Business center; access to nearby health club for $10/day; same-day laundry service. *In room:* A/C, TV w/pay movies, high-speed and Wi-Fi Internet access, coffeemaker, hair dryer, iron, safe.

## CHEAP SLEEPS

**Best Western River North Hotel**   This former motor lodge and cold-storage structure conceals a very attractive, sharply designed interior that scarcely resembles any Best Western in which you're likely to have spent the night before. One of the few hotels located right in the midst of River North—one of the busiest nightlife and restaurant zones in the city—it lies within easy walking distance of interesting boutiques and Chicago's art-gallery district. Rooms are spacious, and the bathrooms are spotless (though no-frills). One-room suites have a sitting area, while other suites have a separate bedroom; all suites come with a sleeper sofa (the Family Suite has two separate bedrooms and two bathrooms). A big selling point is the indoor pool, with an adjoining outdoor roof deck (a smallish fitness room looks out onto the pool). The Best Western's reasonable rates will appeal to travelers on a budget—and the almost-unheard-of free parking can add up to significant savings for anyone who drives here for a visit. FINE PRINT There's a 2-night minimum for weekend stays May through October.

125 W. Ohio St. (at LaSalle St.), Chicago, IL 60610. ℂ **800/528-1234** or 312/467-0800. Fax 312/467-1665. www.rivernorthhotel.com. 150 units. $89–$199 double; $225-$295 suite. Kids under 18 stay free in parent's room. Rollaways $10/night; cribs free. AE, DC, DISC, MC, V. Free parking for guests (1 car per room) with in-out privileges. Subway/El: Red Line to Grand/State. **Amenities:** Restaurant (pizzeria); lounge; exercise room; indoor pool with sun deck; room service. *In room:* A/C, TV w/pay movies and video games, hair dryer, Wi-Fi.

★ **Ohio House Motel**   Endearingly retro, this hotel rates high for being cheap, clean, and superbly located (Portillo's Hot Dog is just across the street—you can't beat it for cheap, super delicious eats). Free parking and free Wi-Fi make this a no-brainer. Seriously, the free parking alone is worth at least $30 a day. Rates start at $89 and shouldn't go much higher than $119 during most times of the year. The quaint coffee shop is known for its fabulous breakfast. Don't miss the "Deuces Wild," with two eggs, two strips of bacon, two sausage patties, and two pancakes for $4.95. Rooms are simple and small, but

## Is It Fun to Stay at the YMCA?

None of Chicago's YMCAs offers short-term housing, but if you're willing to stay in north suburban Niles, you may be able to score a room for as little as $45 per night, and you don't even need to be a member of the YMCA to stay here. What could be more fun than a deal like that? You'll get a TV with basic cable, private bath, housekeeping services, guest laundry, optional microwave and refrigerator rental, and free Wi-Fi in the common areas. Plus, there's a 24-hour lounge and vending area, and desk staff is available around the clock. Better yet? Free parking in the YMCA lot. Accessible to the Edens Expressway, which will take you to downtown Chicago, the Leaning Tower YMCA is located at 6300 W. Touhy Avenue, Niles, IL 60714. If you're taking public transit from downtown, take the Red Line El to Howard. Exit the El and transfer to the Pace Bus No. 290 headed west to Niles. The bus stops directly in front of the YMCA. That trip will take you about an hour. For reservations, call ℂ 847/410-5100; or see www.leaningtower ymca.org.

what do you expect for a killer price in a killer location? I think you'll find little to complain about and a lot to like at this oasis of cheap.

600 N. LaSalle St. (at Ohio St.), Chicago, IL 60654. ℂ 866/601-6446 or 312/943-6000. Fax 312/943-6063. http://ohiohousemotel.com. 195 units. $89–$119 double. Kids 17 and under stay free in parent's room. No rollaways; cribs free. AE, DC, DISC, MC, V. Free parking. Subway/El: Red Line to Grand/State. *In room:* A/C, TV w/pay movies, hair dryer, Wi-Fi.

★ **Red Roof Inn Chicago Downtown**    This hotel is your best bet for consistently low-priced lodgings in downtown Chicago. The location is its main selling point: right off the Magnificent Mile (and within blocks of the Ritz-Carlton and Peninsula, where rooms will cost you at least four times as much). The guest rooms are stark and small (much like the off-the-highway Red Roof Inns), but the hotel makes continual efforts to update linens and room decor. Ask for a room facing Ontario Street, where you'll get western exposure and some natural light. Groups of three or four should go for the king suite, which has a sofa bed, microwave, and refrigerator.

162 E. Ontario St. (½ block east of Michigan Ave.), Chicago, IL 60611. ✆ **800/733-7663** or 312/787-3580. Fax 312/787-1299. www.redroof-chicago-downtown.com. 195 units. $89–$140 double; $105–$159 king suite. Kids 17 and under stay free in parent's room. No rollaways; cribs free. AE, DC, DISC, MC, V. Subway/El: Red Line to Grand/State. **Amenities:** Free morning coffee in lobby. *In room:* A/C, TV w/pay movies, hair dryer, Internet.

## WORTH A SPLURGE

★ **Talbott Hotel**    The family-owned Talbott is a small, European-style gem that's one of the city's best small, independent hotels, and with rooms starting at $139, a fine choice for budget travelers. Constructed in the 1920s as an apartment building, the Talbott was converted to a hotel in 1989. That's great news if you're traveling with friends or as a family, because the hotel has many suites with two bedrooms and two bathrooms, plus kitchen facilities. The location just off the Magnificent Mile is superb. The hotel's wood-paneled lobby, decorated with leather sofas and velvety armchairs, two working fireplaces, tapestries, and numerous French horns used for fox hunts, is intimate and inviting. The homey, non–chain hotel atmosphere, large suites, availability of kitchens, and prime location make this one of my favorites. Rooms are decorated in neutral tones, with furniture chosen for its residential feel, such as carved wooden desks, plus European linens and plasma TVs. They vary in size, so ask when making reservations. You might score a hotel with more extensive facilities, for the same price, but the cozy atmosphere and personal level of service here appeal to visitors looking for the feeling of a small inn rather than a sprawling, corporate hotel.

20 E. Delaware Place (btw. Rush and State sts.), Chicago, IL 60611. ✆ **800/TALBOTT** (825-2688) or 312/944-4970. Fax 312/944-7241. www.talbotthotel.com. 149 units. $139–$449 standard kings; $260–$671 suites. Kids under 18 stay free in parent's room. Rollaways $20/night; cribs free. AE, DC, DISC, MC, V. Subway/El: Red Line to Chicago/State. **Amenities:** Restaurant (Italian); lounge; concierge; complimentary access to nearby health club; 24-hr. room service. *In room:* A/C, TV, hair dryer, minibar, Wi-Fi.

**Tremont Hotel**    Slightly more upscale than the Talbott but with the same small, European-style feel, the Tremont is ideal for couples, as most guest rooms tend to be on the small (or shall we say, "intimate") side. In fact, all rooms except the suites have only one bed and accommodate two people. Rooms in the Tremont House—a separate building next door—have kitchenettes, a wonderful money-saving option, especially for making quick breakfasts and sandwich lunches. Suites are designed so one room includes a king-size bed with its own television, minibar, and bathroom. The adjoining living room includes a sofa bed, a television, minibar, and bathroom. The cozy lobby with a fireplace sets the mood from the start. The furnishings are tasteful without being somber, and rooms are cheery, with yellow walls and large windows. The steak-and-chops restaurant off the lobby, the memorabilia-filled Mike Ditka's Restaurant, is co-owned by the legendary former Chicago Bears football coach. It's pricey, so your best bet is to sit at the bar for a drink and an appetizer. (Don't be surprised if you find yourself sitting next to Da Coach himself—he's a frequent patron.)

100 E. Chestnut St. (1 block west of Michigan Ave.), Chicago, IL 60611. © **800/621-8133** or 312/751-1900. Fax 312/751-8650. www.tremontchicago.com. 130 units. $79–$279 double. Kids under 18 stay free in parent's room. Cribs free. AE, DC, DISC, MC, V. Subway/El: Red Line to Chicago/State. **Amenities:** Restaurant; babysitting; concierge; small exercise room (and access to nearby health club). *In room:* A/C, TV/VCR, CD player, hair dryer, Internet, minibar.

# 3 Lincoln Park & North Side Accommodations

City Suites Hotel   A few doors down from the El stop on Belmont Avenue, this charming small hotel has a 1930s Art Deco aesthetic, and feels more like an urban bed-and-breakfast than a big hotel. Most rooms are suites, with separate sitting rooms and bedrooms, all furnished with first-rate pieces and decorated in a homey and comfortable style. Families should ask about the king suite, with a king-size bed and sitting area with sofa bed; they can also accommodate a crib. The amenities are excellent for a hotel in this price range, including plush robes and complimentary continental breakfast. Fridges and microwaves are available upon request in suites. A bonus—or drawback, depending on your point of view—is the hotel's neighborhood setting. Most rooms can be fairly noisy; those facing north overlook Belmont Avenue, where nightlife continues into the early-morning hours, and those facing west look right out over rumbling El tracks. On your way in and out of the hotel, you'll mingle with plenty of locals, from young professional families to gay couples to punks in full regalia. Blues bars, nightclubs, and restaurants abound hereabouts, making the City Suites a find for the bargain-minded and adventuresome. Room service is available from Ann Sather, a Swedish diner and neighborhood institution (p. 78).

933 W. Belmont Ave. (at Sheffield Ave.), Chicago, IL 60657. ⓒ **800/248-9108** or 773/404-3400. Fax 773/404-3405. www.cityinns.com. 45 units. $139–$249 double; $199–$409 suite. Rates include continental breakfast. Kids 12 and under stay free in parent's room. No rollaways (sofa beds in suites); cribs free. AE, DC, DISC, MC, V. Subway/El: Red Line to Belmont. **Amenities:** Concierge; free access to Bally's health club 5 blocks away; limited room service. *In room:* A/C, TV, hair dryer, Wi-Fi.

**Majestic Hotel**   Owned by the same group as the City Suites Hotel, the Majestic blends seamlessly into its residential neighborhood. Located on a charming tree-lined street (but convenient to the many restaurants and shops of Lincoln Park), the hotel welcomes kids with open arms. Guests receive a complimentary continental breakfast and afternoon cookies in the lobby. Some of the larger suites—the most appealing are those with sun porches—offer butler's pantries with a fridge, microwave, and wet bar. Groups and families should ask about the two-room king suite, which includes a bedroom with king-size bed, a living room with a sofa bed, and a kitchenette with refrigerator and microwave. Other than the larger suites, many of the rooms are fairly dark because you're surrounded by apartment buildings. Avoid the claustrophobic single rooms with alley views. The hotel is ideally suited for enjoying the North Side and only a short walk from both Wrigley Field and the lake.

528 W. Brompton St. (at Lake Shore Dr.), Chicago, IL 60657. ⓒ **800/727-5108** or 773/404-3499. Fax 773/404-3495. www.cityinns.com. 52 units. $99–$179 double; $129–$219 suite. Rates include continental breakfast. Kids under 12 stay free in parent's room; age 12 and over, $10 per person. No rollaways (sofa beds in suites); cribs free. AE, DC, DISC, MC, V. Subway/El: Red Line to Addison; walk several blocks east to Lake Shore Dr. and then 1 block south. **Amenities:** Free passes to nearby Bally's health club; limited room service. *In room:* A/C, TV w/pay movies, hair dryer, minibar, Wi-Fi.

## CHEAP SLEEPS

**Best Western Hawthorne Terrace**   A fantastic bargain for travelers who don't mind staying a bit north of the beaten track, this hotel offers plenty of space for a great price. Located in Lakeview—within walking distance of Wrigley Field, Lake Michigan, and the Lincoln Park walking and bike paths—the hotel is set back from busy Broadway Avenue, thanks to a charmingly landscaped terrace (a good spot to enjoy your complimentary continental breakfast when the weather's nice). Inside, the relatively large rooms won't win extra style points,

# CHEAP SLEEPS IN LINCOLN PARK & NORTH SIDE

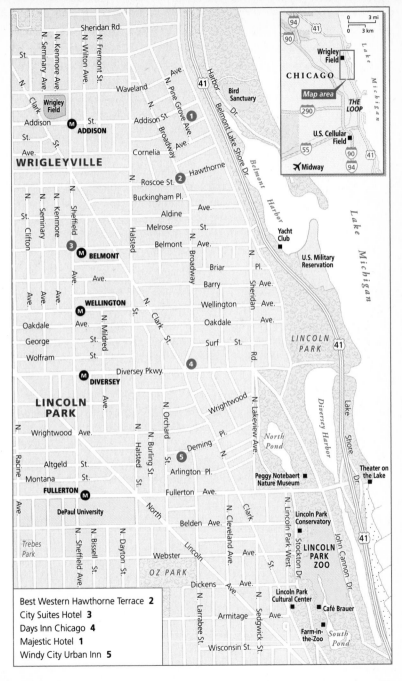

Best Western Hawthorne Terrace  2
City Suites Hotel  3
Days Inn Chicago  4
Majestic Hotel  1
Windy City Urban Inn  5

but most are bright and cheery, with spotless bathrooms (another plus: many rooms have two windows, a bonus if you crave natural light). Junior suites provide a room with two double beds, and an adjoining living room with a pullout couch; families of four will fit comfortably in one of these suites, which can also accommodate a crib. The ground-level exercise room is especially welcoming, with large windows to let light in and a glass-enclosed hot tub. Best of all? Parking is a bargain at $20 a day—about half the going rate of most downtown hotels.

3434 N. Broadway (at Hawthorne Place), Chicago, IL 60657. ℂ **888/401-8781** or 773/244-3434. Fax 773/244-3435. www.hawthorneterrace.com. 59 units. $139–$229 double and suites. Rates include continental breakfast. Kids 12 and under stay free in parent's room. Rollaways free (sofa beds provided in junior suites); cribs free. AE, DC, DISC, MC, V. Subway/El: Red Line to Belmont. **Amenities:** Concierge; exercise room with hot tub and sauna. *In room:* A/C, TV w/pay movies, fridge, hair dryer, microwave, Wi-Fi.

★ **Days Inn Chicago**   This is an older hotel (in the 1920s, it was known as the Diversey Arms Hotel), with a modern facelift. Often called the Rock-'N'-Roll Days Inn, the website features a list of bands who have stayed here to play nearby music venues. Rooms are sleek, clean, and impeccable, particularly for the price (often under $100). You're in a superb location in a cozy neighborhood filled with great bars and restaurants. Free breakfast of waffles, cereal, fruit, and pastries is a nice extra for the price, and there's also a Starbucks across the street. Free wireless, microwave, and minifridge make it possible to stay connected and cook your own meals. Bathrooms are small but clean and feature large bathtubs; linens are fresh. The elevator feels small and old, but really, it's hard to complain about this at the price. The hotel is ideally suited for enjoying the North Side.

644 W. Diversey Pkwy. (at the intersection of Diversey, Lincoln, and Broadway), Chicago, IL 60614. ℂ **800/DAYS-INN** or 773/525-7010. Fax 773/525-6998. www.days inn.com or www.daysinnchicago.net. 133 units. $99 double. Rates include complimentary continental breakfast. Kids under 17 stay free in parent's room. Rollaways and cribs free. AE, DC, DISC, MC, V. Valet parking $20 with in/out privileges. Subway/El: Brown Line to Diversey; walk 4 blocks west to hotel. No pets. **Amenities:** Free passes to Bally's health club next door. *In room:* A/C, TV w/pay movies, fridge, hair dryer, Wi-Fi.

# WORTH A SPLURGE

**Windy City Urban Inn**    This grand 1886 home is located on a tranquil side street just blocks away from busy Clark Street and Lincoln Avenue—both chock-full of shops, restaurants, and bars. The inn is charming enough, but the true selling point of the Windy City Inn is hosts Andy and Mary Shaw. He's a well-known political reporter, and she has 20 years of experience in the Chicago bed-and-breakfast business. Together, they are excellent resources for anyone who wants to get beyond the usual tourist sites. Subtle Chicago touches give guests a distinctive experience: Blues and jazz play during the buffet breakfast, and local food favorites offered to guests include the famous cinnamon buns from Ann Sather's restaurant and beer from Goose Island Brewery. The remodeled building has a more open feel than the typical Victorian home. The five rooms in the main house and three apartments in a coach house are each named after Chicago writers. Two coach-house apartments can sleep four: two in an upstairs bedroom and two on a bed that folds up against the wall. (Custom-made for the Shaws, these feature top-quality mattresses, making them much more comfortable than the Murphy beds of old.) These apartments have kitchens and are wonderfully cozy with their fireplaces and Jacuzzi tubs. In good weather, guests are invited to eat breakfast on the back porch or in the garden between the main house and the coach house. There, you can sit back and imagine that you're living in your very own Chicago mansion—the type of home that many Chicagoans wish they could live in themselves. FINE PRINT As with many bed & breakfasts, this Inn is happy to accommodate children age 10 and up.

607 W. Deming Place, Chicago, IL 60614. (&#x2461; **877/897-7091** or 773/248-7091. Fax 773/529-4183. www.windycityinn.com. 8 units. $125–$255 double; $175–$325 coach-house apts. Kids age 10–18 stay free in parent's room (coach-house apts only). No rollaways or cribs. Rates include buffet breakfast. AE, DC, DISC, MC, V. Parking $6 in nearby lot with in/out privileges. Subway/El: Red Line to Fullerton. *In room:* A/C, TV, hair dryer upon request, kitchenette, Wi-Fi.

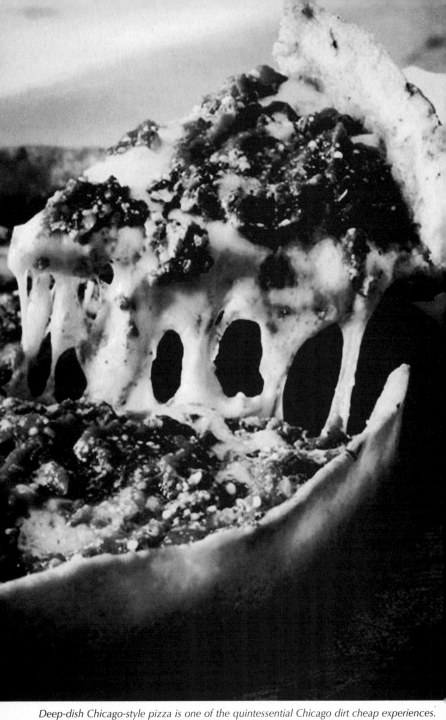

*Deep-dish Chicago-style pizza is one of the quintessential Chicago dirt cheap experiences.*

# CHEAP EATS

If you're looking for a no-frills spot to dig in to some inexpensive eats, well, you've come to the right town. Chicago has an embarrassment of riches when it comes to low-cost dining. The city is particularly strong on Mexican and Thai restaurants, in addition to a large concentration of Indian restaurants on the North Side on Devon Street, and Chinese restaurants on the opposite end of town. All you need to join the dinner party is a little money and an adventurous palate, because half the fun of visiting Chicago is the opportunity to sample the flavors of the world in one fell swoop. Best of all, many of the city's greatest eating experiences are its small, affordable neighborhood haunts, the kind where you'll get to mingle with the locals—another real treat.

We've tried to list places that offer a good meal for $10 or less per person (not including drinks), as well as a couple of good-value splurges. And that's what the prices were at press time; as everyone knows, pretty much everyone was looking for reasonable restaurants meals in late 2009, so a lot of places were dealing with the economic downturn by keeping prices steady or even lowering them. At the same time, the economy was forcing far too many small businesses, including restaurants, out of business. If you're making a special trip to a small, off-the-beaten-track restaurant, it's always a good idea to call or check online first. Two particularly good websites for locating cheap dining are www.metromix.com, the *Chicago Tribune*'s online entertainment and dining guide, and www.wttw.com, the local PBS television station's website. Under the programs list, you can watch episodes of the "Check, Please" show, a very popular Friday-night staple here, in which Chicago natives pick their favorite local restaurants, and the three diners at their table review them. You'll always find great dirt cheap options here, with reliable reviews.

And, before you head out on the streets of Chicago to your culinary destiny, there are a few things you should keep in mind:

- **Note to smokers:** The Chicago City Council has banned smoking in all restaurants; those with a separate bar area can choose to allow smoking there, but only if they have installed an air filtration system. If you want to light up when you go out, call first to see if smoking is permitted.

- Plan on dining early. Most restaurants close their kitchens around 10pm.

- If there's a long wait for a table, ask if you can order at the bar, which often has faster service and a more affordable menu.

- Note that a lot of the places we list are smaller "mom-and-pop" style and may not take credit cards (and, some of the neighborhoods are, um, up-and-coming, and may not have a plethora of ATMs nearby). So make sure you have some cash on you *before* you order.

- If you're driving to a restaurant, add extra time into your itinerary to find parking, which can be an especially infuriating exercise in the Loop, Lincoln Park, River North, and most everywhere else for that matter.

# 1 The Loop & West Loop

**Heaven on Seven**    *AMERICAN/CAJUN* Hidden on the seventh floor of an office building opposite Macy's, this is truly an insider's spot (you'll find it by following the office workers who line up for lunch during the week). Loud, crowded, and casual, it's a no-frills spot that buzzes with energy. Chef/owner Jimmy Bannos's Cajun and Creole specialties come with a cup of soup and include such Louisiana staples as red beans and rice, a catfish po' boy sandwich, and jambalaya. If you don't have a taste for Tabasco, the extensive coffee-shop-style menu covers all the traditional essentials: grilled-cheese sandwiches, omelets, tuna—the works. Indulge in chocolate peanut butter pie or homemade rice pudding for dessert. FINE PRINT Although Heaven on Seven is usually open only for breakfast and lunch, they do serve dinner on the third Friday of the month from 5:30 to 9pm.

Heaven also has another downtown location just off the Mag Mile at **600 N. Michigan Ave.** (© **312/280-7774**); unlike the original location, they accept reservations and credit cards and are open for dinner. The ambience is more lively than gritty, making it a popular spot for families.

111 N. Wabash Ave. (at Washington St.), 7th floor. © **312/263-6443.** www.heavenon seven.com. Reservations not accepted. Sandwiches $8–$12; main courses $10–$14. No credit cards. Mon–Fri 8:30am–5pm; Sat 10am–3pm; 3rd Fri of each month 5:30–9pm. Subway/El: Red Line to Washington.

**Russian Tea Time**    *EASTERN EUROPEAN/RUSSIAN* Very popular with Chicago Symphony Orchestra patrons and musicians, Russian Tea Time is far from being the simple tea cafe that its name implies. Reading through this family-owned restaurant's extensive menu is like taking a tour through the cuisine of czarist Russia and the former Soviet republics (for Russian neophytes, all the dishes are well described). For budget diners, the attraction is the borscht, the sweet and sour soup made of beets, cabbage, carrots, potatoes, onions, and tomatoes, and topped with sour cream. A big, satisfying bowl will keep you going during an afternoon-long tour of the nearby Art Institute for a mere $8. A stack of five latkes, the equally-as-filling potato pancakes, are accompanied by sour cream and applesauce, all for $8.95. The atmosphere is old-world and cozy, with lots of woodwork and a friendly staff.

77 E. Adams St. (btw. Michigan and Wabash aves.). ⓒ **312/360-0000.** www.russian teatime.com. Reservations recommended. Main courses $15–$27. AE, DC, DISC, MC, V. Sun–Thurs 11am–9pm; Fri–Sat 11am–midnight (the restaurant sometimes closes earlier during the summer months). Tea service daily 2:30–4:30pm. Subway/El: Brown, Purple, Green, or Orange line to Adams; or Red Line to Monroe or Jackson.

**South Water Kitchen**   *AMERICAN* Because Loop restaurants cater to office workers and business travelers, there aren't a lot of budget-friendly options other than fast food. So while South Water Kitchen isn't breaking any new culinary ground, it deserves a mention as one of the few places in the area that won't break the bank. It's especially good if you're a family on a budget, because the menu sticks to modern twists on familiar favorites. At lunch, grown-ups should try one of the daily "TV Dinners," which range from meatloaf, mashed potatoes, and green beans to a Wisconsin Fish Fry on Fridays. Each dinner comes with a butterscotch blondie (a chocolate chip cookie in the form of a bar), for a slight splurge of $15. The restaurant provides not only kids' menus but also games to keep the little ones occupied. Best of all, half the proceeds of all children's meals go to the Chicago Coalition for the Homeless.

In the Hotel Monaco, 225 N. Wabash Ave. (at Wacker Dr.). ⓒ **312/236-9300.** www. southwaterkitchen.com. Main courses $9–$19 lunch, $16–$26 dinner. AE, DC, MC, V. Mon–Fri 7–10:30am and 11am–3pm; Sat–Sun 7am–2:30pm; daily 5–10pm. Subway/ El: Red Line to State/Lake.

★ **Trattoria No. 10**   *ITALIAN* Elegant but not pretentious, Trattoria No. 10 is a favorite with Chicagoans who work in the Loop. This is one of the best-looking restaurants in the city: The burnt-orange tones, ceramic floor tiles, and gracefully arched ceilings set a dining-in-Italy mood. The regular menu will run you $15 to $33 for entrees; but we budget-conscious diners don't bother with the regular menu. Psst: I'll let you in on the best-kept dining secret in the Loop. Trattoria No. 10 has a fabulous happy-hour buffet. Stop by between 5 and 8pm on weekdays for an all-you-can-eat buffet at the bar; $12 (plus a $6 drink minimum) gets you tastes of beef tenderloin, shrimp, and various pasta specials. It's an absolutely huge spread of food. Along with McCormick and Schmick's, this gets my vote for best happy hour buffet in town.

10 N. Dearborn St. (btw. Madison and Washington sts.). ⓒ **312/984-1718.** www. trattoria10.com. Reservations recommended. Main courses $15–$33. AE, DC, DISC,

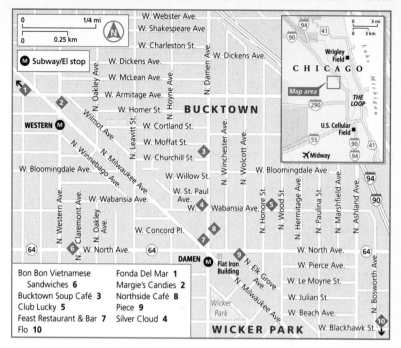

0 | 1/4 mi
0 | 0.25 km

Ⓜ Subway/El stop

W. Webster Ave.
W. Shakespeare Ave.
W. Charleston St.
W. Dickens Ave.
W. Dickens Ave.
W. McLean Ave.
W. Armitage Ave.
W. Homer St.
W. Cortland St.
W. Moffat St.
W. Churchill St.
W. Bloomingdale Ave.
W. Willow St.
W. Bloomingdale Ave.
W. St. Paul Ave.
W. Wabansia Ave.
W. Wabansia Ave.
W. Concord Pl.
W. North Ave.
W. North Ave.
W. Pierce Ave.
W. Le Moyne St.
W. Julian St.
W. Beach Ave.
W. Blackhawk St.

WESTERN Ⓜ
BUCKTOWN
DAMEN Ⓜ
Flat Iron Building
Wicker Park
WICKER PARK

N. Oakley Ave.
Wilmot Ave.
N. Leavitt St.
N. Hoyne Ave.
N. Damen Ave.
N. Winnebago Ave.
N. Milwaukee Ave.
N. Winchester Ave.
N. Wolcott Ave.
N. Honore St.
N. Wood St.
N. Hermitage Ave.
N. Paulina St.
N. Marshfield Ave.
N. Ashland Ave.
N. Western Ave.
N. Claremont Ave.
N. Oakley Ave.
N. Elk Grove Ave.
N. Milwaukee Ave.
N. Bosworth Ave.

CHICAGO
Wrigley Field
Map area
THE LOOP
U.S. Cellular Field
Midway
0 | 3 mi
0 | 3 km
Lake Michigan

| | |
|---|---|
| Bon Bon Vietnamese Sandwiches **6** | Fonda Del Mar **1** |
| Bucktown Soup Café **3** | Margie's Candies **2** |
| Club Lucky **5** | Northside Café **8** |
| Feast Restaurant & Bar **7** | Piece **9** |
| Flo **10** | Silver Cloud **4** |

MC, V. Mon–Fri 11:30am–2pm and 5:30–9pm; Sat 5:30–10pm. Subway/El: Red line to Madison.

**The Village** *ITALIAN* Part of an old-time, three-restaurant complex known as the Italian Village, this is the most casual and affordable of the three restaurants. Be prepared for its, um, "charming" interpretation of alfresco dining in a small Italian town, complete with a midnight-blue ceiling, twinkling stars, and banquettes tucked into private, cavelike rooms. It's the kind of Pan-Chicago place where you might see one man in a tux and another in shorts. This is old-school Italian: Keep it authentic (and cheap) by ordering the meatball sandwich, with mushrooms, meat sauce, and cottage fries ($9.95), or on the healthier side, a bowl of minestrone soup ($4.95) accompanied by an order of pizza bread ($5.50). The food is good rather than great, but what sets The Village apart is the bordering-on-corny faux-Italian atmosphere. The service is outstanding, from the Italian maitre d' who flirts with all the ladies to the ancient waiters who manage somehow to keep up with the nonstop flow. And if you manage to score some half-price theater tickets (see Hot Tix, p. 173), the staff here are pros at handling pretheater dining.

## Family (and Budget) Friendly Restaurants

One of the city's first "theme" restaurants, **Ed Debevic's,** 640 N. Wells St., at Ontario Street ((C) **312/664-1707**), is a temple to America's hometown lunch-counter culture. The burgers-and-milkshakes menu is kid-friendly, but it's the staff shtick that makes this place memorable. The waitstaff plays the part of gum-chewing toughies who make wise-cracks, toss out good-natured insults, and even sit right down at your table. It's all a performance—but it works. A cheeseburger will run you $9.45, which lets this restaurant eek by, just under our $10 limit.

One of the best all-around options, and a homegrown place as well, the Southern-style restaurant **Wishbone** (p. 64) has much to recom-mend it. Children can be kept busy looking at the large and surrealistic farm-life paintings on the walls or reading a picture book, *Floop the Fly,* loaned to diners (written and illustrated by the parents of the owners). The food is diverse enough that both adults and kids can find some-thing to their liking (entrees $9–$15), but there's also a menu geared just toward children. Another all-American choice in the Loop is **South Water Kitchen** (p. 58), which offers a kids' menu and coloring books.

A fun breakfast-and-lunch spot in Lincoln Park, **Toast,** 746 W. Web-ster St., at Halsted Street ((C) **773/935-5600**), serves up all-American favorites (pancakes, eggs, sandwiches) and employs an age-old restaurateur's device for keeping idle hands and minds occupied:

71 W. Monroe St. (btw. Clark and Dearborn sts.). (C) **312/332-7005.** www.italian village-chicago.com. Reservations recommended (accepted for parties of 3 or more). Main courses (including salad) $9–$23 lunch, $13–$24 dinner. AE, DISC, MC, V. Mon–Thurs 11am–1am; Fri–Sat 11am–2am; Sun noon–midnight. Subway/El: Red Line to Monroe.

## WEST LOOP

**Avec** *FRENCH* A casual wine bar, Avec keeps things simple: top-quality ingredients in simple preparations that take inspiration from Ital-ian, French, and Spanish cuisines. The menu focuses on a variety of "small plates" meant for sharing, which is why Avec can qualify for those on a budget—with the caveat that it's more of a very high-quality

Tables at this neighborhood spot are covered with blank canvases of butcher-block paper on which kids of all ages can doodle away with crayons. FINE PRINT **This is a very popular spot for weekend brunch, so showing up with ravenous kids at 11am on Saturday—only to be told there's an hour wait—is not the best idea.** Egg dishes and omelettes range from $8 to $13; pancakes from $6 to $8.

At **Gino's East** (p. 68), the famous Chicago pizzeria, long waits can also be an issue during the prime summer tourist season. But once you get your table, the kids can let loose: Patrons are invited to scrawl all over the graffiti-strewn walls and furniture. (A large deep-dish sausage pizza costs $27 and serves 4.)

With heaping plates of pasta served up family style, **Maggiano's,** 516 N. Clark St. (© **312/644-7700**), in River North, and **Buca di Beppo,** 521 N. Rush St., right off Michigan Avenue (© **312/396-0001**), are good choices for budget-conscious families. Just make sure not to over-order: That's a sure-fire way to blow your budget. Better to start small and order more if you're still hungry. These Italian-American restaurants (both parts of national chains) serve up huge portions of pasta and meat to be passed and shared. At Maggiano's you can get a large salad and large spaghetti with meatballs for $25 that will serve 4; likewise, the same order at Buca di Beppo will cost about $40 to serve 4.

snack and appetizer deal than a gigantic, stomach-filling meal, if you want to stay within budget. Communal dining is reflected in the restaurant's design; the long, narrow dining room, with its wood walls and floors, will strike you as either cramped or cozy, and tables sit so close together you can't help overhearing your neighbors' conversations. If you're on a budget, you'll have to carefully pick and choose your small plates; if you've got a big appetite, this place will break your budget. The small plates include salads and appetizer-style dishes such as smoked lamb and quail brochettes, dates stuffed with chorizo sausage, and spicy meatballs with Spanish rice and chickpeas. There's also a good selection of specialty cheeses.

# Ethnic Dining near the Loop

## CHINATOWN

Chicago's Chinatown is about 20 blocks south of the Loop—restaurants there are cheap, the food delicious and a bit adventuous too. The district is strung along two thoroughfares, Cermak Road and Wentworth Avenue as far south as 24th Place. On weekends in seasonable weather, the **Water Taxi** will transport you for only $2 one-way (℗ **312/337-1446;** www.wendellaboats.com). Board the Water Taxi at Madison Street at the Chicago River, just east of Ogilvie Transportation Center.

Open since 1927, **Won Kow,** 2237 S. Wentworth Ave. (btw. 22nd Place and Alexander St.; ℗ **312/842-7500**), is the oldest continually operating restaurant in Chinatown. You can enjoy dim sum in the mezzanine-level dining room from 9am to 3pm daily. Most of the items cost around $2.

The spacious, fairly elegant **Phoenix,** 2131 S. Archer Ave. (btw. Wentworth Ave. and Cermak Rd.; ℗ **312/328-0848**), has plenty of room for big tables of family or friends to enjoy the Cantonese (and some Szechuan) cuisine (entrees $9–$15). A good sign: The place attracts lots of Chinatown locals. It's especially popular for dim sum brunch, so come early to avoid the wait. Late night, stop by the more casual **Saint's Alp Teahouse** downstairs (℗ **312/842-1886**), an outpost of the Hong Kong chain, which is open until midnight daily.

## LITTLE ITALY

Convenient to most downtown locations, a few blocks' stretch of Taylor Street is home to a host of time-honored, traditional, hearty Italian restaurants. If you're staying in the Loop (an easy cab ride away), the area makes a good destination for dinner.

Your best dirt cheap meal in Little Italy is **Pompei on Taylor,** 1531 W. Taylor St. (℗ **312/421-5179**), which has been making traditional thick, square, Italian bakery-style pizza since 1909. You can fill up for about $8.

**The Rosebud on Taylor,** 1500 W. Taylor St. (at Laflin St.; ℗ **312/942-1117**) is a mainstay of the neighborhood. Go for the eggplant parmesan, an excellent dish for only $9.95. Italian Wedding Soup, with meatballs, escarole, carrots, and pasta, is completely filling for $3.95, and can be accompanied by Rosebud's famed panzanella salad for $7.95.

## GREEKTOWN

A short cab ride across the south branch of the Chicago River will take you to a row of moderately priced and inexpensive Greek restaurants on Halsted Street between Van Buren and Washington streets.

To be honest, there's not much here to distinguish one restaurant from the other: They're all standard Greek restaurants with similar looks and menus, and you should be able to get an entree and share an appetizer for under $20, including tip. That said, **Greek Islands,** 200 S. Halsted St. (at Adams St.; ✆ **312/782-9855**); **Santorini,** 800 W. Adams St. (at Halsted St.; ✆ **312/829-8820**); **Parthenon,** 314 S. Halsted St. (btw. Jackson and Van Buren sts.; ✆ **312/726-2407**); and **Costas,** 340 S. Halsted St. (btw. Jackson and Van Buren sts.; ✆ **312/263-0767**), are all good bets for gyros, Greek salads, shish kabobs, and the classic moussaka. On warm summer nights, opt for either **Athena,** 212 S. Halsted St. (btw. Adams and Jackson sts.; ✆ **312/655-0000**), which has a huge outdoor seating area, or **Pegasus,** 130 S. Halsted St. (btw. Monroe and Adams sts.; ✆ **312/226-3377**), with its rooftop patio serving drinks, appetizers, and desserts. Both have wonderful views.

## PILSEN

Just south of the Loop, Pilsen is a colorful blend of Mexican culture, artists, and bohemians, and the local fare is decidedly casual.

**Nuevo Leon,** 1515 W. 18th St. (at Laflin St.; ✆ **312/421-1517**), is a popular Mexican restaurant serving the standard offerings. *Pollo ranchero,* a half-chicken smothered in salsa ranchera and served with refried beans and rice, is $8; a *chile relleno,* a roasted poblano pepper filled with melted cheese, is $6. Across the street, **Playa Azul,** 1514 W. 18th St. (at Laflin St.; ✆ **312/421-2552**), serves authentic Mexican seafood dishes, salads, and soups at equally reasonable prices.

615 W. Randolph St. ℂ **312/377-2002.** www.avecrestaurant.com. Reservations not accepted. Small plates $5–$12; large plates $15–$20. AE, DC, DISC, MC, V. Mon–Thurs 3:30pm–midnight; Fri–Sat 3:30pm–1am; Sun 3:30–10pm. The West Loop is best reached by taxi, which will cost about $5 from the Loop.

**La Sardine**   *FRENCH/BISTRO* A very reasonable and completely worthwhile way to splurge is the fantastic $22 three-course lunch served daily at this charming bistro. Sister to Jean-Claude Poilevey's popular Le Bouchon (and named after a critic's description of that tiny Bucktown bistro), this more spacious destination is bathed in a honeyed glow and is filled with sensual aromas from the open kitchen and rotisserie. La Sardine has a classic bistro look and warm, friendly service.

If you go for the $22 lunch, choose from an abbreviated menu of appetizers and salads, soups, sandwiches, and entrees, or opt for a hearty *plat du jour,* perhaps tuna Niçoise on Monday, or duck legs braised in red wine with mushrooms and potato purée on Thursday. The lunch features soup or salad and your choice of entree and dessert.

111 N. Carpenter St. ℂ **312/421-2800.** http://frenchrestaurantschicago.com. Reservations recommended. Main courses $13–$15 lunch, $16–$20 dinner. AE, DC, DISC, MC, V. Mon–Fri 11:30am–2:30pm; Mon–Thurs 5–10pm; Fri–Sat 5–11pm. The West Loop is best reached by taxi, which will cost about $5 from the Loop.

★ **Wishbone**   *CAJUN/AMERICAN* This down-home, casual spot inspires intense loyalty (even if the food is only good rather than outstanding). Known for Southern food and big-appetite breakfasts, Wishbone's extensive, reasonably priced menu blends hearty, homestyle choices with healthy and vegetarian items. Brunch is the 'Bone's claim to fame, when an eclectic crowd of bedheads packs in for the plump and tasty salmon cakes, omelets, and red eggs (a lovely mess of tortillas, black beans, cheese, scallions, chile-ancho sauce, salsa, and sour cream). However, brunch at Wishbone can be a mob scene, so I suggest lunch or dinner; offerings include "yardbird" (charbroiled chicken with sweet red-pepper sauce), blackened catfish, and hoppin' John, the classic Southern dish of brown rice, black-eyed peas, and ham (there's also a vegetarian version, hoppin' Jack). The tart key lime pie is one of my favorite desserts in the city. The casual ambience is a good bet for families (plus a children's menu is available).

There's a newer location at 3300 N. Lincoln Ave. (at W. School St.; ℂ **773/549-2663**), but the original location has more character.

## A Spot of Tea

High tea at any of the major hotels will cost you a pretty penny (we're talking $25 and up for tea, finger sandwiches, and pastries). But, after about 5 o'clock in the evening, you can have a lovely pot of tea minus the finger sandwiches in the same atmosphere, for about $6.50. And you'll come away feeling just as civilized. My favorite evening tea spot is The Greenhouse at the Ritz Carlton ℂ 312/266-1000, with its lovely atrium setting, views of the lakefront and downtown, and huge selection of tea. It's open Sunday from 2:30 to 11pm, Monday through Thursday from 3:30 to 11pm, and Friday and Saturday from 2:30pm to midnight.

1001 Washington St. (at Morgan St.). ℂ **312/850-2663.** www.wishbonechicago. com. Reservations accepted, except for weekend brunch. Main courses $5–$10 breakfast and lunch, $6–$15 dinner. AE, DC, DISC, MC, V. Mon–Fri 7am–3pm; Tues–Thurs 5–9pm; Fri–Sat 5–10pm; brunch Sat–Sun 8am–3pm. The West Loop is best reached by taxi, which will cost about $5 from the Loop.

# 2 Magnificent Mile, River North, Gold Coast & Old Town

★ Billy Goat Tavern    *AMERICAN* "Cheezeborger, Cheezeborger—No Coke . . . Pepsi." Viewers of the original *Saturday Night Live* will certainly remember the classic John Belushi routine, a moment in the life of a crabby Greek short-order cook. The comic got his material from the Billy Goat Tavern, located under North Michigan Avenue near the bridge that crosses to the Loop (you'll find it by walking down the steps across the street from the *Chicago Tribune* building). Just butt in anytime, says the sign on the red door. The tavern is a classic dive: dark, seedy, and no-frills. But unlike the *Saturday Night Live* skit, the guys behind the counter are friendly ("Double cheezeborger is the best!" one shouted out cheerfully to me when I couldn't decide what to order on my last visit). The menu is pretty basic (mostly hamburgers and hot dogs), but yes, the cheeseburgers are pretty good. Billy Goat is a hangout for newspaper workers and writers, so you might overhear the latest media buzz. After work this is a good place to watch a game, chitchat at the bar, and down a few beers. And, if you're out late at night, you can satiate your grease and salt cravings here until 2am.

For the same "cheezeborgers" in less grungy (but less authentic) surroundings, head to the Billy Goat's outpost on Navy Pier (② **312/ 670-8789**).

430 N. Michigan Ave. ② **312/222-1525.** www.billygoattavern.com. Reservations not accepted. Menu items $4–$7. No credit cards. Mon–Fri 6am–2am; Sat 10am–2am; Sun 11am–2am. Subway/El: Red Line to Chicago.

**Café Iberico**   *SPANISH* This no-frills tapas spot won't win any points for style, but the consistently good food and festive atmosphere make it a longtime local favorite for singles in their 20s and 30s. Café Iberico gets very loud, especially on weekends, so it makes a fun group destination—but plan your romantic tête-à-tête elsewhere. You should be able to dine here for about $15 per person. I'd suggest starting with the *queso de cabra* (baked goat cheese with fresh tomato-basil sauce), then continue ordering rounds of hot and cold tapas as your hunger demands. A few standout dishes are the vegetarian Spanish omelet, spicy potatoes with tomato sauce, chicken brochette with caramelized onions and rice, and grilled octopus with potatoes and olive oil. There are a handful of entrees on the menu, and a few desserts if you're still not sated.

739 N. LaSalle St. (btw. Chicago Ave. and Superior St.). ② **312/573-1510.** www.cafe iberico.com. Reservations accepted for parties of 6 or more; no reservations for Fri– Sat dinner. Tapas $4–$7; main courses $7–$10. DC, DISC, MC, V. Mon–Thurs 11am–11:30pm; Fri 11am–1:30am; Sat noon–1:30am; Sun noon–11pm. Subway/El: Red or Brown Line to Chicago.

★ **Cyrano's Bistrot & Wine Bar**   *FRENCH* Warm and welcoming, Cyrano's represents a haven of authentic bistro charm in the congested River North restaurant scene, due in no small part to the friendly presence of chef Didier Durand and his wife, Jamie. The cheery blue-and-red wood exterior, eclectic artwork, and charming personal asides on the menu ("Use of cellular phones may interfere with the stability of our whipped cream") all signal the owner's hands-on touch. The budget way to experience Cyrano's is at lunchtime. My advice is to order the moules mariniere and a side of pommes frites served with three condiments (Dijon mustard, homemade ketchup,

# CHEAP EATS IN THE MAGNIFICENT MILE, GOLD COAST & RIVER NORTH

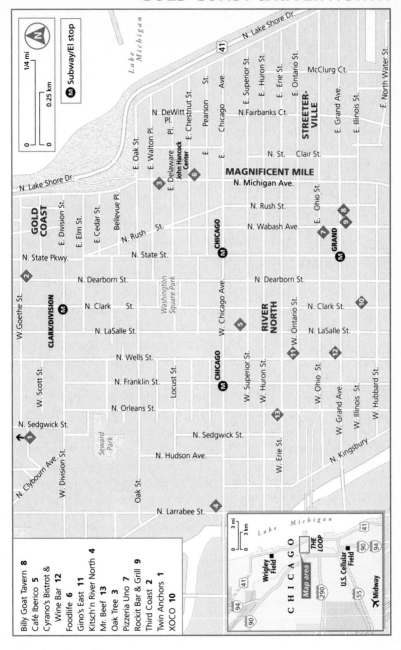

Billy Goat Tavern **8**
Café Iberico **5**
Cyrano's Bistrot &
  Wine Bar **12**
Foodlife **6**
Gino's East **11**
Kitsch'n River North **4**
Mr. Beef **13**
Oak Tree **3**
Pizzeria Uno **7**
Rockit Bar & Grill **9**
Third Coast **2**
Twin Anchors **1**
XOCO **10**

M Subway/El stop

and mayonnaise), which in total will cost about $15. (That's a splurge, to be sure, but not a bank-busting one.) If mussels aren't your thing, you might try one of Durand's sensationally flavorful soups (the lobster bisque is a highlight). Service is knowledgeable and friendly. You'll also find an outpost of Cyrano's on the south side of the Chicago riverwalk, west of Michigan Avenue—a fine choice in warm weather.

546 N. Wells St. (btw. Ohio St. and Grand Ave.). ℂ **312/467-0546.** www.cyranos bistrot.com. Main courses $14–$28; 3-course prix-fixe dinner $29. AE, DC, DISC, MC, V. Mon–Fri 11:30am–2:30pm; Mon–Sat 5:30–10:30pm. Subway/El: Brown Line to Merchandise Mart.

**foodlife**   *AMERICAN*  Taking the standard food court up a few notches, foodlife consists of a dozen or so kiosks offering both ordinary and exotic specialties on the mezzanine of Water Tower Place mall. Seats are spread out cafe style, in a pleasant environment under boughs of (realistic) artificial trees festooned with strings of lights. A hostess will seat you, give you an electronic card, and then it's up to you to stroll around and get whatever food strikes your fancy (each purchase is recorded on your card, and you pay on the way out).

The beauty of a food court, of course, is that it offers something for everybody, and you can pick and choose based on your budget. At foodlife, diners can choose from burgers, pizza, south-of-the-border dishes, an assortment of Asian fare, and veggie-oriented, low-fat offerings. A lunch or snack is usually inexpensive, but make sure to mentally tally your total as you go along: The payment method makes it easy to build up a big tab while holding a personal taste-testing session at each kiosk.

In Water Tower Place, 835 N. Michigan Ave. ℂ **312/335-3663.** Reservations not accepted. Most items $8–$15. AE, DC, DISC, MC, V. Breakfast kiosk daily 7:30–10:30am. All other kiosks Mon–Thurs 11am–8pm; Fri–Sun 11am–9pm. Subway/El: Red Line to Chicago.

**Gino's East**   *ITALIAN*  Gino's—once the quintessential dive restaurant—now occupies a cavernous space that's a testament to its enduring popularity with both Chicago natives and tourists. (The original restaurant's graffiti-covered booths were brought along to keep the "authentic" flavor.) Despite the restaurant's size, be prepared to wait for a table during peak hours, because Gino's pizza—with good reason—is still a major draw.

Many Chicagoans consider Gino's the quintessential deep-dish Chicago-style pizza (I know transplanted Midwesterners who come here for their cheesy fix whenever they're back in town). True to its reputation, the pizza is heavy (a small cheese pizza is enough for two), so work up an appetite before chowing down. Specialty pizzas include the supreme, with layers of cheese, sausage, onions, green pepper, and mushrooms; and the vegetarian, with cheese, onions, peppers, asparagus, summer squash, zucchini, and eggplant. Gino's also offers salads, sandwiches, and pastas—but I've never seen anyone order them. A warning to the famished: Pizzas are cooked to order, so you'll have to wait about 45 minutes for your food (I highly recommend calling ahead to preorder, which will save you about a half-hour of waiting time, but preorders aren't accepted Fri–Sat).

If you want to take a pizza home on the plane, call a day in advance and Gino's will pack a special frozen pie for the trip.

633 N. Wells St. (at Ontario St.). ☎ **312/943-1124.** www.ginoseast.com. Reservations not accepted. Pizza $12–$29. AE, DC, DISC, MC, V. Mon–Thurs 11am–10pm; Fri–Sat 11am–11pm; Sun noon–9pm. Subway/El: Red Line to Grand.

★ **Kitsch'n River North** *AMERICAN* This '70s-inspired diner features shag carpeting and one of the best kids' menus in the city (and Tang martinis for the grown-ups!). Comfort foods like fried chicken and waffles, puff pastry pot pies, and green eggs and ham (the green is actually provided by spinach pesto) should keep everyone happy. If the weather's fine, sit on the large outdoor patio, enjoy a Twinkie tiramisu dessert, and imagine this huge riverside building as the former home of retailing giant Montgomery Ward. The original location, in the neighborhood of Roscoe Village (near Lakeview), is smaller but just as kitschy (2005 W. Roscoe St.; ☎ **773/248-7372**).

600 W. Chicago Ave. ☎ **312/644-1500.** Reservations not accepted. Main courses $9–$15; kids' menu under $5. AE, DISC, MC, V. Mon–Thurs 8am–7pm; Fri 8am–8pm; Sat–Sun 9am–3pm. Bus: Bus No. 66.

**Mr. Beef** *AMERICAN* Calling Mr. Beef a restaurant may be a stretch: The place is basically a fast-food stand, without much atmosphere or room for seating. Despite these drawbacks, Mr. Beef is a much-loved Chicago institution. Its claim to fame is the classic Italian beef sandwich, the Chicago version of a Philly cheese steak. The Mr. Beef variety is made of sliced beef dipped in jus, piled high on a chewy bun, and topped with sweet or hot peppers. Heavy, filling, and *very*

# Only in Chicago

## PIZZA

We have three pizza styles in Chicago: Chicago style, also known as deep-dish, which is thick-crusted and often demands a knife and fork; stuffed, which is similar to a pie, with a crust on both top and bottom; and thin crust. Many pizzerias serve both thick and thin, and some make all three kinds. One benefit of ordering deep-dish pizza: You can get your pizza cooked well-done or gooey, exactly the way you want it. A large cheese deep-dish pizza will cost about $16, with each extra ingredient (onions, mushrooms, green peppers, sliced tomatoes, and the like) costing about $2.

Three of Chicago's best gourmet deep-dish restaurants are **Pizzeria Uno** (p. 74), **Pizzeria Due** (p. 75), and **Gino's East** (p. 68). In River North, **Lou Malnati's Pizzeria,** 439 N. Wells St. (at Hubbard St.; ℂ 312/828-9800), bakes both deep-dish and thin-crust pizza and even has a low-fat-cheese option. **Edwardo's** is a local pizza chain that serves all three varieties, but with a wheat crust and all-natural ingredients; locations are in the Gold Coast at 1212 N. Dearborn St. (at Division St.; ℂ 312/337-4490); in the South Loop at 521 S. Dearborn St. (btw. Congress Pkwy. and Harrison St.; ℂ 312/939-3366); and in Lincoln Park at 2622 N. Halsted St. (at Wrightwood Ave.; ℂ 773/871-3400). Not far from Lincoln Park Zoo is **Ranalli and Ryan's,** 1925 N. Lincoln Ave. (btw. Wisconsin St. and Armitage Ave.; ℂ 312/642-4700), whose biggest selling point is a large open-air patio and extensive selection of beers.

In Wrigleyville, just off Belmont Avenue, is **Leona's Pizzeria,** 3215 N. Sheffield Ave. (btw. Belmont Ave. and School St.; ℂ 773/327-8861), which serves all three kinds of pizza. Leona's also has a location in Little Italy at 1419 W. Taylor St. (btw. Bishop and Loomis sts.; ℂ 312/850-2222).

For a unique take on the deep-dish phenomenon, try the "pizza potpie" at **Chicago Pizza & Oven Grinder,** 2121 N. Clark St., steps from the Lincoln Park Zoo (btw. Webster and Dickens aves.; ℂ 773/248-2570). The pizzas are baked in a bowl and then turned over when served. This neighborhood spot stays popular year after year, so plan on showing up early for dinner.

## HOT DOGS

The classic Chicago hot dog includes a frankfurter by Vienna Beef (a local food processor and hallowed institution), heaps of chopped onions and green relish, a slather of yellow mustard, pickle spears, fresh tomato wedges, a dash of celery salt, and, for good measure, two or three "sport" peppers, those thumb-shaped holy terrors that turn your mouth into its own bonfire. Generally speaking, the going rate for a Chicago dog these days is about $2.

Chicago is home to many standout hot-dog spots but one, **Hot Doug's,** 3324 N. California Ave. (at Roscoe St.; © **773/279-9550**), takes encased meats to a new level, featuring several gourmet sausages on a bun every day except Sunday (plan on standing in line no matter which day you show up—and it's always worth it). A beer-soaked bratwurst costs $3.50, and a large order of fries, $2.25. Hot Doug's also serves a great classic Chicago dog ($1.75) just like many other stands in town. Other standout hot dog restaurants include **Gold Coast Dogs,** 159 N. Wabash Ave., at Randolph Street (© **312/917-1677**), in the Loop just a block from Michigan Avenue. **Fluky's,** in The Shops at North Bridge mall, 520 N. Michigan Ave. (© **312/245-0702**), is part of a local chain that has been serving great hot dogs since the Depression (Dan Aykroyd and Jay Leno are fans). **Portillo's,** 100 W. Ontario St. (at Clark St.; © **312/587-8930**), is another local chain that specializes in hot dogs but also serves tasty pastas and salads. **Murphy's Red Hots,** 1211 W. Belmont Ave. (at Racine Ave.; © **773/935-2882**), is a neighborhood spot not too far from Wrigley Field, while **The Wieners Circle,** in Lincoln Park at 2622 N. Clark St. (btw. Wrightwood Ave. and Drummond Place; © **773/477-7444**), is a late-night favorite where rude order-takers are part of the shtick.

If you've got a car, head to **Superdawg Drive-In,** 6363 N. Milwaukee Ave. (at Devon Ave.; © **773/763-0660**), on the northwest side of the city (look for the giant hot dogs dressed as Tarzan and Jane on the roof). This classic 1950s-style flashback has been run by the same family for three generations, and, yes, they still have carhops who bring out your order.

## Breakfast & Brunch

### NEAR THE LOOP & MAGNIFICENT MILE

A local breakfast favorite since 1923 is **Lou Mitchell's,** 565 W. Jackson Blvd. (© **312/939-3111**), across the south branch of the Chicago River from the Loop, a block farther west than Union Station. You'll be greeted at the door with a basket of doughnut holes and milk duds so that you can nibble while waiting for a table. A jumbo omelette, which will definitely feed two and potentially keep you both fueled until you grab a late lunch, costs $9.95 and comes stuffed with everything from apple and cheese to sour cream, bacon bits, and tomato.

For a Southern-style breakfast of spicy red eggs, cheese grits, or biscuits and gravy, head over to **Wishbone,** a homespun dining hall in a warehouse district west of the Loop.

### LINCOLN PARK & THE NORTH SIDE

A perfect breakfast or brunch spot if you're heading up to Wrigleyville for a Cubs game or a walk through Lincoln Park is **Ann Sather,** the restaurant that's famous for its homemade cinnamon rolls. To-die-for Swedish pancakes are $6.50 (make sure to get lingonberries as accompaniment); if you're interested in venturing into slightly more daring culinary territory, order a side of Swedish potato sausage ($2.95).

The **Nookies** restaurants are Chicago favorites for all the standard morning fare. Locations include 2114 N. Halsted St., in Lincoln Park (© **773/327-1400**); 1748 N. Wells St., in Old Town (© **312/337-2454**); and 3334 N. Halsted St., in Lakeview (© **773/248-9888**).

Chicago, Mr. Beef really hops during lunchtime, when dusty construction workers and suit-clad businessmen crowd in for their meaty fix. While you're chowing, check out the celebrity photos and newspaper clippings covering the walls, and you'll see why this place is considered a local monument.

666 N. Orleans St. (at Erie St.). © **312/337-8500.** Sandwiches $6–$8.50. No credit cards. Mon–Thurs 8am–9pm; Fri 8am–5am; Sat 10:30am–3:30pm and 10:30pm–5:30am. Subway/El: Red Line to Grand.

Go to **Orange,** 3231 N. Clark St., at Belmont (© **773/549-4400**), for a fun twist on breakfast foods. Try the Green Eggs and Ham ($8.95)— eggs scrambled with pesto, tomatoes, mozzarella, and pancetta. There's a kids' menu, too, making this a popular choice for families. Huevos Rancheros get your morning off to a spicy start for $7.95. Of course, Orange is known for its pancake flights ($11) with a theme that changes weekly. Come early or late; the line for a table winds outside during prime weekend brunch hours.

## WICKER PARK/BUCKTOWN

The brightly colored **Bongo Room,** 1470 N. Milwaukee Ave. (btw. Evergreen Ave. and Honore St.; © **773/489-0690**), is a neighborhood gathering place for the hipsters of Wicker Park/Bucktown, but the restaurant's tasty, creative breakfasts have drawn partisans from all over the city who feel right at home stretching out the morning with a late breakfast. FINE PRINT Don't bother trekking over here for weekend brunch, when you'll have to wait an hour or more for a table; it's much more pleasant eating here during the week. Try the vegetarian croissant sandwich, with melted Muenster cheese, spinach, tomatoes, mushrooms, cucumber, alfalfa sprouts, and scallions, with one egg any style and hash browns, all for $8.95. If you're being bad, go for Raspberry Oreo Pancakes or White Chocolate and Caramel-Covered Pretzel pancakes ($9.25). The same owners also run **Room 12,** 1152 S. Wabash Ave. (btw. 11th St. and Roosevelt Rd.; © **312/291-0100**), in the South Loop; the food is just as good as at the Wicker Park location, and it tends to be less crowded.

**Oak Tree** *AMERICAN* Though it's located on the sixth floor of the ritzy 900 N. Michigan indoor mall (home of Bloomingdale's, Gucci, and Michael Kors), Oak Tree isn't exactly high profile. But it's popular with the younger ladies-who-lunch crowd and is one of my favorite places to have brunch before a day of downtown touring. The cafe decor is bright and cheery, which helps you momentarily forget that you're inside a mall. If you can, get a table along the windows that

## ★ McDonald's Gets Glitzy

A longstanding free and dirt cheap dining option (and a real, true Chicago original—well, suburban Des Plaines, to be exact), McDonald's is on most budget diners' lists. If you're going to go the fast-food route, head for the McDonald's at the corner of Grand Avenue and Clark Street, which was unveiled for the company's 50th anniversary in 2005. The gleaming, glass-enclosed building looks like something out of *The Jetsons*, and it's filled with stylish amenities that would look right at home in a luxury airport lounge. You can chow down while relaxing in a reproduction of Mies van der Rohe's famous Barcelona chair, check out the exhibit of collectible Happy Meal toys from inside a 1960s-style egg chair, or order a cappuccino and gelato at the upstairs cafe.

look down on Michigan Avenue—but be aware that everyone else coming to eat here wants those tables, too. Oak Tree's real draw is the enormous, varied menu. You'll find something to satisfy every taste: a large salad selection, Asian noodles, sandwiches that range from trendy (duck breast with mango chutney) to manly (meatball with roasted bell peppers), Mexican quesadillas, even blue-plate specials such as turkey hash or a patty melt. The breakfast menu is just as extensive. Oak Tree can get crowded during prime weekend lunch hours, but it's relatively calm by mid-afternoon—just about the time you've toured all your energy away and need a break.

900 N. Michigan Ave. (at Delaware Place), 6th floor. ✆ **312/751-1988.** Reservations not accepted. Main courses $8–$15. AE, DC, DISC, MC, V. Mon–Fri 7:30am–6:30pm; Sat–Sun 7:30am–5:30pm. Subway/El: Red Line to Chicago.

**Pizzeria Uno** *ITALIAN* Pizzeria Uno invented Chicago-style pizza, and many deep-dish aficionados still refuse to accept any imitations. Uno's is now a chain of restaurants throughout the country, but this location is the original. You can eat in the restaurant itself on the basement level or, weather permitting, on the outdoor patio right off the sidewalk. Salads, sandwiches, and a house minestrone are also available, but let's be honest—the only reason to come here is for the pizza. As with Gino's East (see p. 68), pizzas take about 45 minutes to make, so if you're starving, order an appetizer or salad.

Uno was so successful that the owners opened **Pizzeria Due** in a lovely gray-brick Victorian town house nearby at 619 N. Wabash Ave., at Ontario Street (© **312/943-2400**). The menu is exactly the same; the atmosphere just a tad nicer (with more outdoor seating).

29 E. Ohio St. (at Wabash Ave.). © **312/321-1000**. www.unos.com. Reservations not accepted Fri–Sat. Pizzas $7–$22. AE, DC, DISC, MC, V. Mon–Fri 11am–1am; Sat 11:30am–2am; Sun 11:30am–11:30pm. Subway/El: Red Line to Grand.

**Rockit Bar & Grill**   *AMERICAN* Take your standard American burger joint, give it an upscale, urban makeover, and you've got Rockit. The current hot spot for well-heeled 20- and 30-something singles, Rockit is definitely a scene after work and on weekends, with loud music and plenty of flirting at the busy front bar. The dining room is a trendy take on traditional tavern decor, where exposed-brick walls and distressed-wood tables combine with sleek metallic accents and chocolate-brown leather booths. The menu is fairly predictable, but a few notches above your standard bar fare. The Rockit Burger is a complete splurge at $19, but then again, it was named "best burger" in America by ABC-TV's Good Morning, America. A mix of Kobe beef and foie gras, the burger is served with french fries cooked in truffle oil. Slightly more in range with our budget is the excellent pulled pork sandwich ($11). The Chopped Salad ($12) —a signature dish—is a hearty mix of salami, olives, tomatoes, provolone, hot cherry peppers, corn, and egg with balsamic dressing. Rockit is no gourmet destination, but if you're looking to chow down on better-than-decent food in a high-energy setting, Rockit fits the bill. (Bonus: The waitstaff range from good-looking to gorgeous.)

22 W. Hubbard St. (btw. Wabash and State sts.). © **312/645-6000**. www.rockitbar andgrill.com. Reservations accepted for parties of 6 or more. Main courses $9–$19 lunch, $12–$29 dinner. AE, DC, DISC, MC, V. Sun–Fri 11:30am–1:30am; Sat 11:30am–2:30am. Subway/El: Red Line to Grand.

**Third Coast** *CAFE*   Just steps from the raucous frat-boy atmosphere of Division Street is this laid-back, classic, independent coffeehouse. The below-ground space is a little shabby, but it attracts an eclectic mix of office workers, students, and neighborhood regulars. The full menu is available late, and the drinks run the gamut from lattes to cocktails. There's often some kind of folk music on weekends.

1260 N. Dearborn St. (north of Division St.). © **312/649-0730**. Baked goods, sandwiches, $9 and under. AE, DISC, MC, V. Daily 7 a.m.–midnight. Subway/El: Red Line to Clark/Division.

# Dining Alfresco

Cocooned for 6 months of the year, with furnaces and electric blankets blazing, Chicagoans revel in the warm months of late spring, summer, and early autumn. For locals and visitors alike, dining alfresco is an ideal way to experience the sights, sounds, smells, and social fabric of this multifaceted city. Just be prepared to wait on a nice night, because you'll be fighting a lot of other diners for a coveted outdoor table.

## LOOP & VICINITY

**Park Grill** Millennium Park's restaurant serves upscale versions of American comfort food with panoramic views of Michigan Avenue. In good weather, save money by picking up a sandwich ($5) and grabbing a seat on the large patio. 11 N. Michigan Ave., at Madison Street (© **312/521-PARK** [7275]).

## MAGNIFICENT MILE & GOLD COAST

**Charlie's Ale House at Navy Pier** One of several outdoor dining options along Navy Pier, this outpost of the Lincoln Park restaurant has lip-smacking pub fare ($9–$15) and a great location overlooking the lakefront and Loop skyline. It's located at 700 E. Grand Ave., near the entrance to the Pier (© **312/595-1440**).

**Oak Street Beachstro** Suit up and head for this warm-weather-only beachfront cafe—literally on the sands of popular Oak Street Beach—which serves inventive cafe fare (fresh seafood, sandwiches, and pastas for $9–$15). Alcohol is also available. The address is 1000 N. Lake Shore Dr., at Oak Street Beach (© **312/915-4100**).

**Puck's at the MCA** This cafe—run by celebrity chef Wolfgang Puck—is tucked in the back of the Museum of Contemporary Art, where you'll get a view of the museum's sculpture garden. Take in the art, the fresh air, and a shrimp club sandwich, Chinois salad, or wood-grilled pizza. The signature barbecue chicken pizza is $11. (Restaurant-only patrons bypass museum admission.) The address is 220 E. Chicago Ave., at Fairbanks Court (© **312/397-4034**).

## LINCOLN PARK

**Charlie's Ale House**  A true neighborhood hangout, this Lincoln Park pub's wonderful beer garden is spacious and buzzing with activity and good vibes. It's located at 1224 W. Webster Ave., at Magnolia Avenue (© **773/871-1440**).

**O'Brien's Restaurant**  Wells Street in Old Town is lined with several alfresco options, but the best belongs to O'Brien's, the unofficial nucleus of neighborhood life. The outdoor patio has teakwood furniture, a gazebo bar, and a mural of the owners' country club on a brick wall. Order the dressed-up chips ($9), a house specialty. Located at 1528 N. Wells St., 2 blocks south of North Avenue (© **312/787-3131**).

## WRIGLEYVILLE & VICINITY

**Arco de Cuchilleros**  The tapas and sangria at this cozy Wrigleyville restaurant can compete with other, better-known Spanish spots, and the intimate, leafy terrace out back glows with lantern light. Located at 3445 N. Halsted St., at Newport Avenue (© **773/296-6046**).

**Moody's**  For 30 years, Moody's has been grilling some of the best burgers in Chicago ($7.50 for a $1/2$ lb. burger). It's ideal in winter for its dark, cozy dining room, but it's better still in summer for its awesome outdoor patio, a real hidden treasure. The address is 5910 N. Broadway Ave., between Rosedale and Thorndale avenues (© **773/275-2696**).

## WICKER PARK/BUCKTOWN

**Northside Café**  On a sunny summer day, Northside seems like Wicker Park's town square, packed with an eclectic mix of locals catching up and checking out the scene. The entire front of the restaurant opens onto the street, making it relatively easy to get an "outdoor" table. Located at 1635 N. Damen Ave., just north of North Avenue (© **773/384-3555**).

★ **Twin Anchors**    *BARBECUE/GRILL* A landmark in Old Town since the end of Prohibition, Twin Anchors manages to maintain the flavor of old Chicago. It's a friendly, family-owned pub with Frank Sinatra songs on the jukebox and pictures of Ol' Blue Eyes on the walls (he apparently hung out here on swings through town in the 1960s). But rather than striking a self-consciously retro pose, this feels like the real deal, with a long mahogany bar up front and a modest dining room in back with red Formica-topped tables crowded close. Go for the barbecue pork sandwich ($9.50) or a bowl of their acclaimed homemade chili and a basket of onion rings. For dessert, there's a daily cheesecake selection.

1655 N. Sedgwick St. (1 block north of North Ave.). ✆ **312/266-1616.** www.twin anchorsribs.com. Reservations not accepted. Sandwiches $6–$10; main courses $11–$24. AE, DC, DISC, MC, V. Mon–Thurs 5–11pm; Fri 5pm–midnight; Sat noon–midnight; Sun noon–10:30pm. Subway/El: Brown Line to Sedgwick.

★ **XOCO**    *MEXICAN* A new concept from famed chef Rick Bayless (who owns Topolobampo and Frontera Grill, located adjacent to XOCO—both superb restaurants, and both out of a budget diner's reach), this Mexican marketplace rocks some big flavors for small prices. Here you'll sample Bayless' contemporary take on Mexico's most beloved street food and snacks. Churros, breakfast empanadas (filled with eggs or roasted poblanos), tortas (Mexican submarine sandwiches—they are becoming a new, hot item around town), and made-to-order caldos (meal-in-a-bowl soups) that feature everything from roasted vegetables to seafood and pork belly. All are downright mouth-watering. You can eat your meal at a communal table or take it to go. The ambiance XOCO (pronounced *Sho*-ko) is trying to conjure is that of a street food stall, complete with a wood-burning oven where tortas are crisped and suckling pig and lamb are braised. Everything—and I mean everything, including the chocolate—is made from scratch. Not to be missed!

449 N. Clark St. ✆ **312/334-3688.** www.xocochicago.com. Reservations not accepted. Main courses $9–$15. AE, DC, DISC, MC, V. Mon–Sat 7am–10pm; closed Sun. Subway/El: Red Line to Grand.

# 3  Lincoln Park, Wrigleyville, Lincoln Square & the North Side

**Ann Sather**    *SCANDINAVIAN* A sign hanging by Ann Sather's door bears the following inscription: "Once one of many neighborhood

Swedish restaurants, Ann Sather's is the only one that remains." This is a real Chicago institution, where you can enjoy Swedish meatballs with buttered noodles and brown gravy, or the Swedish sampler of duck breast with lingonberry glaze, meatball, potato-sausage dumpling, sauerkraut, and brown beans. All meals are full dinners, including appetizer, main course, vegetable, potato, and dessert. Sticky cinnamon rolls are a highlight of Sather's popular (and very affordable) weekend brunch menu (it can get frenzied, but you should be okay if you get here before 11am). The people-watching is priceless: a cross section of gay and straight, young and old, from club kids to elderly couples and families with toddlers.

There are smaller cafes with similar menus at 3411 N. Broadway (© 773/305-0024) and 3416 N. Southport Ave. (© 773/404-4475).

929 W. Belmont Ave. (btw. Clark St. and Sheffield Ave.). © 773/348-2378. www. annsather.com. Reservations accepted for parties of 6 or more. Main courses $6–$12. AE, DC, MC, V. Mon–Fri 7am–3pm; Sat–Sun 7am–4pm. Free parking w/validation. Subway/El: Brown or Red Line to Belmont.

★ Anteprima    ITALIAN This neighborhood gem features rustic Italian home cooking. Local and organic food are features, and while this place would normally be out of the free and dirt cheap price range, the three-course fixed price menu for $29 is one of our choices for a splurge. This is a fantastic restaurant that really provides a good value for the higher price, and the fixed price menu of simple, rustic Italian meals is very much worth your while: Available Sunday through Thursday nights, you can choose any combination of starter, entree, and dessert off the regular menu or specials, or starter, half pasta, and entrée, with no dessert. FINE PRINT There is a $5 upcharge on steak, lamb chops, or whole fish. Call ahead to book a table on the back patio. Standout dishes include the grilled octopus appetizer, the chianti-braised pork entree, and the orange cake or lemon panna cotta desserts.

5316 N. Clark St. © 773/506-9990. Main courses $16–$25. AE, DISC, MC, V. Sun–Thurs 5:30–10pm; Fri–Sat 5:30pm–midnight. Subway/El: Red Line to Berwyn.

The Bagel Restaurant and Deli    AMERICAN/DELI The Bagel has been a popular Chicago delicatessen since 1950. You can count on The Bagel for delicious takeout (grab a potato knish for quick energy when you're on the go), or classic Jewish comfort food like chicken soup and corned beef. Belly up to the long lunch counter, or grab a seat in a cozy booth. In addition to a huge selection of bagels, there are cold cuts, cheeses, and deli salads. Most items can be bought to eat as meals in the deli, or to take home (soups by the pint or quart, bulk salads, and pastries are popular choices). A meal will cost you around $8.

3107 N. Broadway. ℭ **773/477-0300.** Sandwiches $7–$11. AE, DC, DISC, MC, V. Sun–Thurs 8am–10pm, Fri–Sat 8am–11pm. Subway/El: Brown, Purple, or Red Line to Belmont.

★ Bourgeois Pig    *AMERICAN* Eclectic antiques fill this brownstone that's become a mecca for DePaul University students and neighborhood families. Bookshelves are packed with literature, and the atmosphere is cluttered and comfy. The menu makes it clear that the Bourgeois Pig caters to an intellectual crowd: "The Sun Also Rises," "Hamlet," and "The Old Man and the Sea" are among the menu's 25 gourmet sandwiches. Kids will enjoy the "build your own sandwich" menu, and staff will accommodate kids' tastes with less-than-gourmet fare such as American cheese. Baked goods, including ginger molasses cookies, are homemade. The Pig always ranks high in surveys for best cup of coffee in Chicago, so don't miss one of the four varieties brewed daily, or one of a mind-bending array of espresso drinks. Juices, shakes, and root beer made here are also great bets. You'll feel comfortable bringing kids in, as there are often a couple sets of parents with strollers parked inside. (If you do have kids in tow, treat them to an ice cream for dessert.)

738 W. Fullerton Pkwy. (at Burling). ℭ **773/883-5282.** Main courses under $10. AE, DISC, MC, V. Mon–Fri 6:30am–11pm; Sat–Sun 8am–11pm. Subway/El: Red or Brown Line to Fullerton. Bus: 8, 11, or 74.

Café Ba-Ba-Reeba!    *SPANISH* One of the city's first tapas restaurants, Café Ba-Ba-Reeba! is still going strong, thanks to its location on bustling Halsted Street, near the Armitage Avenue shopping strip. The clientele tends to be young and comes to the restaurant in groups. Tapas lovers will see plenty of favorites, including garlic potato salad, roasted eggplant salad with goat cheese, beef and chicken empanadas, and roasted dates wrapped in bacon (which have been a popular menu item for years). The menu has also been updated with miniversions of more upscale fare, including a spicy devil's lobster tail dish, a cured pork lomo with frisee salad, and a flavorful plate of seared Spanish sausages.

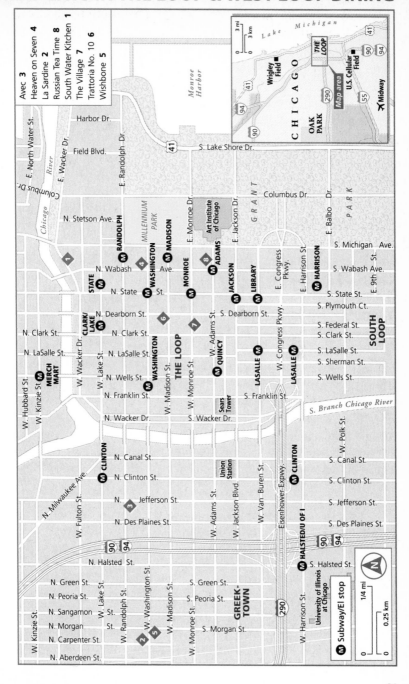

Avec **3**
Heaven on Seven **4**
La Sardine **2**
Russian Tea Time **8**
South Water Kitchen **1**
The Village **7**
Trattoria No. 10 **6**
Wishbone **5**

**Subway/El stop**

2024 N. Halsted St. (at Armitage Ave.). © **773/935-5000.** www.cafebabareeba.com.
Reservations recommended on weekends. Tapas $4–$13; main courses $9–$30. AE,
DC, DISC, MC, V. Mon–Thurs 5–10pm; Fri 5pm–midnight; Sat 11am–midnight; Sun
11am–10pm. Subway/El: Red or Brown line to Fullerton, or Brown Line to Armitage.

**Café Luigi**    *ITALIAN* Here's a real New York–style pizzeria, where
you can grab a slice, fold it in half, and go. This might just be the best
Big Apple–style pizza in the City of Big Shoulders. Slices come piled
with toppings including spinach, artichokes, ricotta, and fresh tomato.
Your second option is stuffed pizza, but why bother? The NY slice is
the best. Other options include salads, garlic bread, subs, and aran-
cini (rolls stuffed with rice, green peas, beef, and cheese).

2548 N. Clark St. © **773/404-0200.** Main courses average $4. MC, V. Mon–Thurs
11am–11pm, Fri–Sat 11am–midnight, Sun 11am–9pm. Subway/El: Brown or Purple
Line to Diversey.

**Café Selmarie**    *AMERICAN* Café Selmarie is a long-standing institution in the Lincoln Square neighborhood, and the cozy atmosphere
will make you feel as if you're eating at some darling, quirky relative's
house (if your relative were an amazing cook, that is). One look at the
baked goods in the case and you'll find it hard to stick to your diet.
The real draw here is the weekend brunch, which is a good value.
The breakfast burrito ($9), followed by a purchase of raspberry heart
cookies to go, is an inexpensive and yummy way to start your Saturday (brunch is such a big Saturday tradition here that it's served from
8am–4pm). Sugar-dusted cookies, cupcakes, éclairs, and the house
specialty rum balls are also worth taking home with you. Salads,
sandwiches, egg dishes, and other simple but healthful meals are on
offer. In good weather, make sure to eat on the patio while watching
the world go by.

4729 N. Lincoln Ave. © **773/989-5595.** Sandwiches $8–$11; main courses $10–$16.
AE, DC, DISC, MC, V. Mon 11am–3pm; Tues–Thurs 8am–9pm; Fri–Sat 8am–10pm; Sun
9am–10pm. Subway/El: Brown Line to Western.

★ **Flat Top Grill**    *ASIAN* This create-your-own-stir-fry restaurant
often has lines, but never fear, they move quickly. If you've never
been here before, you might want to follow the suggested recipes on
the giant blackboards. Or, experiment away! Choose from over 25
homemade sauces and 70 fresh ingredients including rice, noodles,
seafood, chicken, beef, veggies, and sauces—all for one low price.

## Dining Alfresco on the Cheap

Picnic, anyone? When the weather is fine, there's no cheaper way to dine. Sure, you can pick up a sandwich from a chain restaurant, but why not take it up a notch with take-out from someplace special like the **Bourgeois Pig** (738 W. Fullerton Pkwy.; ℂ **773/883-5282;** www. bpigcafe.com)? For $7.45, you can head for a Lincoln Park picnic spot with a nice fat bag containing a Peppernini or one of their classic sandwiches (named after classic pieces of literature) like *The Sun Also Rises*. A little farther north in Boystown, check out **Wally & Agador's Gourmet Deli** (3310 N. Halsted St.; ℂ **773/325-9664;** www.wally-agadors. com), where you can choose from one of a dozen sandwiches named after Hollywood divas like The Mama Cass, made of shaved black forest ham, gruyere cheese, butter lettuce, heirloom tomato, and Dijon mayo on multi-grain wheat ($8) or The Marilyn Monroe, with country-style duck pâté, chicken liver mousse, shaved red onion, and a schmear of brie on a toasted baguette with Dijon mayo and baby frisee ($9). Add a side of the roasted Yukon Gold, Italian sausage, and spring pea salad to share ($7/pound) and you have a hearty meal.

Best yet, the price includes multiple visits to the food line (a lifesaver if your brilliant culinary combination has gone awry).

3200 N. Southport Ave. (just south of Belmont Ave.). ℂ **773/665-8100.** www.flat topgrill.com. Main courses lunch around $9, dinner around $12; kids' stir-fry (under age 11) $5. AE, DC, DISC, MC, V. Mon–Thurs 11:30am–10pm; Fri–Sat 11:30am–11pm; Sun 9am–10pm. Bus: 76.

★ **Goose Island Brewing Company**    *AMERICAN* Some of the best beer in Chicago is manufactured at this comfy, award-winning microbrewery on the western edge of Old Town (an impressive cast of professional beer critics agrees). In the course of a year, Goose Island produces about 100 varieties of lagers, ales, stouts, pilsners, and porters that change with the seasons. If you don't want to commit to a full pint ($6), order some 3-ounce sampler glasses for your very own tasting session (4 glasses for $8). For a behind-the-scenes look, you can tour the brewing facility Sunday at 3pm ($5, which includes tastings afterward).

The food here is far more than an afterthought. If you prefer to chow down in a restaurant atmosphere (rather than sitting at the large bar), there's a separate, casual dining area. Cut-above bar food includes burgers (including a killer, dragon-breath-inducing Stilton burger with roasted garlic), sandwiches (pulled pork, blackened catfish po' boy, chicken Caesar), and some serious salads. Most sandwiches will run you $10. Goose Island is also known for its addictive homemade potato chips, doughy Bavarian pretzels, fresh-brewed root beer, and orange cream soda. The zero-attitude, come-as-you-are ambience is very refreshing for a lazy afternoon pit stop or a casual lunch or dinner. A second location, at 3535 N. Clark St. (near W. Eddy St.) in Wrigleyville (✆ **773/832-9040**), has an enclosed beer garden.

1800 N. Clybourn Ave. (at Sheffield Ave.). ✆ **312/915-0071.** www.gooseisland.com. Reservations accepted. Sandwiches $7.50–$10; main courses $11–$17. AE, DC, DISC, MC, V. Sun–Thurs 11am–1am; Fri–Sat 11am–2am; main dining room closes at 10pm daily, but a late-night menu is available in the bar. Subway/El: Red Line to North/ Clybourn.

★ **I Monelli Trattoria Pizzeria**   *ITALIAN* Thin-crust pizza is the focus of this casual trattoria in Lincoln Square (the name literally translates to "those rascals"), where you can get your pizza topped with tasty combos such as eggplant and zucchini; potato and rosemary; or diced ham, fresh mushrooms, artichokes, and black olives. It's BYOB, and in addition to the thin-crust pizza, the menu includes antipasti, salads, pasta, panini, and pizza; highlights include spicy pancetta-laced *bucatini all'Amatriciana,* and *dell' ortolano,* a roasted eggplant, zucchini, red pepper, and mozzarella panini. The atmosphere is warm and welcoming, and at $7 for a super-delicious individual pizza, who can go wrong? (If you decide you need a bottle of wine at the last minute, there's a liquor store across the street.)

5019 N. Western Ave. ✆ **773/561-8499.** Whole pizzas average $15. AE, DC, DISC, MC, V. Sun, Mon, Wed, Thurs 11am–10pm; Fri–Sat 11am–11pm. Closed Tues. Subway/El: Brown Line to Western.

★ **Intelligentsia**   *CAFE* A down-to-earth San Francisco married couple set up this coffee-roasting operation in the heart of Lakeview. A French roaster dominates the cafe, and the owners also make their own herbal and black teas. Warm drinks are served in handsome cups nearly too big to get your hands around, and tea sippers receive their own pots and brew timers. Sit at the window or in an Adirondack chair on the sidewalk, or decamp to the homey back seating area.

3123 N. Broadway (btw. Belmont Ave. and Diversey Pkwy.). ℂ **773/348-8058.** Sandwiches, baked goods all under $9. AE, DC, DISC, MC, V. Mon–Thurs 6am–10pm; Fri 6am–11pm; Sat 7am–11pm; Sun 7am–10pm. Subway/El: Red Line to Addison.

★ **Julius Meinl**    *CAFE* Austria's premier coffee roaster chose Chicago—and, even more mysteriously, a location near Wrigley Field—for its first U.S. outpost. The result is a mix of Austrian style (upholstered banquettes, white marble tables, newspapers hanging on wicker frames) and American cheeriness (lots of natural light, smiling waitstaff, smoke-free air). The excellent coffee and hot chocolate are served European-style on small silver platters with a glass of water on the side, but it's the desserts that keep the regulars coming back. Try the apple strudel or millennium torte (glazed with apricot jam and chocolate ganache), and for a moment you'll swear you're in Vienna.

3601 N. Southport Ave. (at Addison St.). ℂ **773/868-1857.** Baked goods, salads, sandwiches, soups, and desserts under $9. Mon–Thurs 6am–10pm, Fri 6am–midnight, Sat 7am–midnight, Sun 7am–10pm. Subway/El: Brown Line to Southport.

**La Creperie**    *FRENCH* Germain and Sara Roignant have run this intimate gem of a cafe since 1972, never straying from the reasonably priced crepes that have won them a loyal following. The decor is heavy on '70s-era brown, but if you find the main dining room too dark, head to the back patio (enclosed in colder months), which sparkles with strings of white lights. Onion soup, pâté, and escargot are all good starters, but the highlights here are the whole-wheat crepes—each prepared on a special grill that Germain imported from his native Brittany. Single-choice fillings include cheese, tomato, egg, or ham; tasty duets feature chicken and mushroom or broccoli and cheese. Beef bourguignon, coq au vin, and curried chicken are the more adventurous crepe combinations. Crepe prices range from $6 to $11. Don't leave without sharing one of the dessert crepes, which tuck anything from apples to ice cream within their warm folds.

2845 N. Clark St. (½ block north of Diversey Pkwy.). ℂ **773/528-9050.** www.la creperieusa.com. Reservations accepted for groups of 6 or more. Main courses $5–$14. AE, DC, DISC, MC, V. Tues–Fri 11:30am–11pm; Sat 11am–11pm; Sun 11am–9:30pm. Subway/El: Brown Line to Diversey.

**Little Brother's**    *ASIAN* This quick-serve Korean-Asian restaurant is located near the DePaul University campus in Lincoln Park, where the signature dish is the Big Brother, a generous scoop of white rice accompanied by your choice of lemon-and-garlic-marinated chicken

($7.99), Korean barbecue-style steak ($8.99), or cubes of lightly fried tofu ($7.99). You can add one of three sauces, including a sweet Thai chili sauce with a hint of cilantro, or a smoky, Korean chili paste sauce. Plus, you get two sides, with options ranging from wasabi coleslaw to veggie dumplings. My favorite is the Little Brother bowl (a slightly smaller version of the Big Brother), with steak and cucumber salad, a bargain at $6.99. Iced green tea will cost an additional $1.49.

818 W. Fullerton Ave. ✆ **773/661-6482.** Main courses $9 and under. No credit cards. Mon–Sat 11am–10pm; closed Sun. Subway/El: Red, Brown, or Purple line to Fullerton.

★ **M. Henry**    *AMERICAN* Upscale twists on classics abound at this popular eatery, which manages to be simultaneously mod *and* earthy. Dulce banana rumba French toast, blackberry bliss cakes, and fresh fruit crepes draw long lines for brunch. At lunch, try the fire-grilled jerk chicken or baby spinach and warm chevre salad with pomegranate vinaigrette. Menu items will run you between $9 and $15; an equally delicious alternative to dining in is picking up a treat from their bakery case and market. Dinner is BYOB with no corkage fee.

5707 N. Clark St. ✆ **773/561-1600.** Average main course $12. AE, DC, DISC, MC, V. Tues–Fri 7am–2:30pm; Sat–Sun 8am–3pm. Bus: 22 to Clark.

**Mamacita's**    *MEXICAN* This Lincoln Park Mexican restaurant, owned by two brothers, offers fresh, healthy Mexican food (as in, no lard is used), with the added bonus of offering some of the best vegan and vegetarian Mexican food in the city. With its Spanish tiles and heavy wooden tables, the restaurant has an authentic Mexican feel, and serves up a great chicken taco salad. Menu standards include the usual fajitas, burritos, and enchiladas, with a few unique items thrown in (the duck breast quesadilla is a winner). An extensive array of pancakes also makes this a popular breakfast spot. Evenings, the place is BYOB (no corkage fee).

2439 N. Clark St. ✆ **773/404-7788.** Main courses under $9. AE, MC, V. Mon–Thurs 10am–9pm; Fri 10am–10pm; Sat 9am–10pm; Sun 9am–9pm. Subway/El: Red or Brown lines to Fullerton.

**Penny's Noodle Shop**    *ASIAN* Predating many of Chicago's Pan-Asian noodle shops, Penny's has kept its loyal following even as others have joined the fray. Penny Chiamopoulous, a Thai native, has assembled a concise menu of delectable dishes, all of them fresh and made to order—and all at prices that will make you do a double take. The two

## ★ Dessert Tour (Complete with Free Dessert)

Eli's cheesecake is a Chicago icon—the rich, creamy cakes have been served at presidential inaugurations and numerous other high-profile events. For a behind-the-scenes peek at Chicago's most famous dessert, take a tour of Eli's bakery on the northwest side of the city. After watching the cooking and decorating processes, you get to enjoy a full-size slice of your favorite flavor (for free with the price of the tour). Tours are given Monday through Friday at 1pm (although reservations aren't necessary, call to make sure the bakery isn't closed for periodic maintenance). The 40-minute tour costs $3 for adults and $2 for children 11 and under; special packages are available for groups of 10 or more. Eli's bakery is at 6701 Forest Preserve Dr., at the corner of Montrose Avenue (© **800/ELI-CAKE** [354-2253]; www.elischeesecake.com).

dining rooms are clean and spare; single diners can usually find a seat along the bar that wraps around the grill. The Thai spring roll, filled with seasoned tofu, cucumber, bean sprouts, and strips of cooked egg, makes a refreshing starter. Of course, noodles unite everything on the menu, so your main decision is choosing among the options (crispy wide rice, rice vermicelli, Japanese udon, and so on) served in a soup or spread out on a plate. There are several barbecued pork and beef entrees, and plenty of options for vegetarians as well.

The original Penny's, tucked under the El tracks at 3400 N. Sheffield Ave., near Wrigley Field (© **773/281-8222**), is small and often has long waits. You stand a better chance of scoring a table at the Diversey Avenue location or the one in Wicker Park at 1542 N. Damen Ave. (at W. Pierce Ave.; © **773/394-0100**). The original location is BYOB; the Diversey Avenue and Wicker Park locations have decent beer and wine lists.

950 W. Diversey Ave. (at Sheffield St.). © **773/281-8448.** Reservations not accepted. Main courses $5–$8. MC, V. Sun–Thurs 11am–10pm; Fri–Sat 11am–10:30pm. Subway/El: Brown Line to Diversey.

**Potbelly Sandwich Works**   *AMERICAN*  It doesn't seem to matter what time I stop by Potbelly; there's invariably a line of hungry 20- and 30-somethings waiting to get their sandwich fix. Yes, there's a potbelly stove inside, as well as a player piano and other Old West saloon-type memorabilia, but come here for the made-to-order grilled sub sandwiches (that's all they serve). Prepared on homemade rolls stuffed with your choice of turkey, Italian meats, veggies, pizza ingredients, and more, and layered with lettuce, tomato, onion, pickles, and Italian seasonings, they're warmed in a countertop toaster oven. Even with all the fixin's, each is under $5 (unlike the massive subs found at many other spots, Potbelly's are more the size of normal sandwiches). Tempting milkshakes keep the blender busy. And the good news about those lines: The behind-the-counter staff are experts at keeping things moving, so you never end up waiting too long. Potbelly has close to 30 locations throughout the city, including 190 N. State St. (© **312/683-1234**) and in the Westfield North Bridge shopping center, 520 N. Michigan Ave. (© **312/664-1008**), both of which are convenient to the Loop and Mag Mile.

2264 N. Lincoln Ave. (btw. Belden Ave. and Webster St.). © **773/528-1405.** www. potbelly.com. Reservations not accepted. Sandwiches $3.50–$5.50. MC, V. Daily 11am–11pm. Subway/El: Brown or Red line to Fullerton.

**RoseAngelis**   *ITALIAN* What keeps me coming back to RoseAngelis when there's not exactly a shortage of Italian restaurants in this city? The reliably good food, cozy ambience, and very reasonable prices— this is neighborhood dining at its best. Hidden on a residential side street in Lincoln Park, the restaurant fills the ground floor of a former private home with a charming series of cozy rooms and a garden patio. The menu emphasizes pasta (my favorites are the rich lasagna and the ravioli al Luigi, filled with ricotta and served with a sun-dried-tomato cream sauce). The garlicky chicken Vesuvio is also excellent, but it's not offered on Friday or Saturday nights because of preparation time. While RoseAngelis is not a vegetarian restaurant per se, there's no red meat on the menu, and many of the pastas are served with vegetables rather than meat. Finish up with the deliciously decadent bread pudding with warm caramel sauce, one of my favorite desserts in the city (and big enough to share). I suggest stopping by on a weeknight to avoid fighting crowds of locals on Friday and Saturday nights (when you'll wait up to 2 hr. for a table).

1314 W. Wrightwood Ave. (at Lakewood Ave.). © **773/296-0081.** www.roseangelis. com. Reservations accepted for parties of 8 or more. Main courses $10–$16. DISC, MC, V. Tues–Thurs 5–10pm; Fri–Sat 5–11pm; Sun 4:30–9pm. Subway/El: Brown or Red line to Fullerton.

## Taste of Thai

Thai restaurants are to Chicago what Chinese restaurants are to many other American cities: ubiquitous, affordable, and perfect for a quick meal that offers a taste of the exotic. If you've never tried Thai, Chicago is a great place to start. Good introductory dishes are pad thai noodles topped with minced peanuts or the coconut-based mild yellow curry.

Most entrees at these spots don't cost much more $10. A staple of the River North dining scene is the bright and airy **Star of Siam,** 11 E. Illinois St., at North State Street (© 312/670-0100). On the north end of the Gold Coast where it meets Old Town, **Tiparos,** 1540 N. Clark St. at North Avenue (© 312/712-9900), is a very friendly place that features Thai textiles on its brick interior walls and serves delicious specialties such as mussaman curry. **Thai Classic,** 3332 N. Clark St., at Roscoe Street (© 773/404-2000), conveniently located between the busy Belmont/Clark intersection and Wrigley Field, offers an excellent all-you-can-eat buffet on weekends if you want to try a taste of everything. While wandering the Lakeview neighborhood, a good stop is the **Bamee Noodle Shop,** 3120 N. Broadway, at Wellington Street (© 773/281-2641), which offers a good selection of "Noodles on Plates" and "Noodles in Bowls," as well as a number of soups and fried-rice combinations.

**Thai Pastry & Restaurant**   *ASIAN* Argyle Street is packed with Thai and Vietnamese restaurants, and this one stands out. You can't miss the dessert case, displayed prominently in front, with a rainbow of colors of gelatin and chewy desserts. If you're in for a meal, try the fish cake appetizer, classic pad thai, or any of 12 other rice or noodle dishes. The lunch special is a great value—lunch is prepared to order, unlike at many of the area restaurants, which serve buffet style.

4925 N. Broadway. © 773/784-5399. AE, DC, MC, V. Main courses under $9. Mon–Thurs 9am–10pm; Fri–Sat 9am–11pm. Subway/El: Red Line to Argyle, walk 1 block west and 1 block south.

★ **Tre Kronor**   *SCANDINAVIAN* Healthy, delicious, and inexpensive Scandinavian food makes this a fabulous choice on the north side of the city, in the neighborhood that surrounds North Park University. (After your meal, walk around and check out the classic Chicago bungalows that make up this charming neighborhood.) You won't find a better piece of salmon in the city (or, for that matter, a better Swedish meatball sandwich, served on limpa bread—a rye bread flavored with anise—and topped with slices of hard-boiled egg and tomato). Omelets are practically bursting with a generous filling of *falukorv* sausage and dill. If you've never had a lacy, thin Swedish pancake topped with tart, bright red lingonberry preserves, this is the place to indulge.

3259 W. Foster Ave. ✆ **773/267-9888.** Average main course $8. AE, DC, DISC, MC, V. Mon–Sat 7 am–10 pm; Sun 9 am–3 pm. Subway/El: Brown Line to Kedzie.

★ **Uncommon Ground** *AMERICAN/BRUNCH*   When you're looking for refuge from Cubs game days and party nights in Wrigleyville, Uncommon Ground offers a dose of laid-back, vaguely bohemian civility. Just off busy Clark Street, the cafe has a fireplace in winter (when the cafe's bowl—yes, bowl—of hot chocolate is a sight for cold eyes) and a spacious sidewalk operation in more temperate months. Breakfast is served all day; plus there's a full lunch and dinner menu. Music figures strongly; the late Jeff Buckley and ex-Bangle Susanna Hoffs are among those who've played the place. Open until 2am daily.

1214 W. Grace St. (at Clark St.). ✆ **773/929-3680.** Average main course: $9–$15. AE, DC, DISC, MC, V. Mon–Fri 9 am–2 am; Sat–Sun 8 am–2 am. Subway/El: Red Line to Addison.

## 4  Wicker Park & Bucktown

**Bon Bon Vietnamese Sandwiches**   *ASIAN* This place only serves one item: *bahn mi,* the traditional Vietnamese sandwich, served on a French-style roll. Ginger chicken, minced pork, *char siu* pork (a sweet, barbecued pork), and roasted portobello are among the fillings, all made in house. The chewy, flaky rolls come from well-known Lincoln Square Vietnamese bakery Nhu Lan. Each sandwich is topped with julienned carrots, cucumber, daikon radish, and fresh cilantro. For $3.95, you'll get a big, filling sandwich. A wide variety of packaged Asian sweets and beverages are available. But for the $6.50 sandwich-and-coffee combo deal, you can pair your sandwich with a

# CHEAP EATS IN LINCOLN PARK, WRIGLEYVILLE & NORTH SIDE

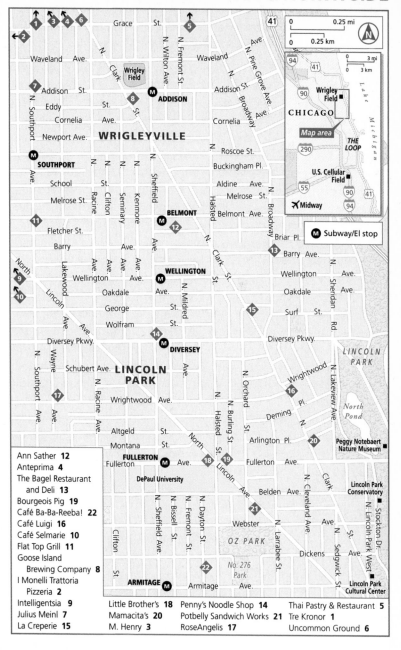

Ann Sather 12
Anteprima 4
The Bagel Restaurant and Deli 13
Bourgeois Pig 19
Café Ba-Ba-Reeba! 22
Café Luigi 16
Café Selmarie 10
Flat Top Grill 11
Goose Island Brewing Company 8
I Monelli Trattoria Pizzeria 2
Intelligentsia 9
Julius Meinl 7
La Creperie 15

Little Brother's 18
Mamacita's 20
M. Henry 3

Penny's Noodle Shop 14
Potbelly Sandwich Works 21
RoseAngelis 17

Thai Pastry & Restaurant 5
Tre Kronor 1
Uncommon Ground 6

Vietnamese coffee, icy and thick with sweetened condensed milk. If you really want to break the bank, go for the $2.95 bubble tea.

2333 W. North Ave. ⓒ **773/278-5800.** Sandwiches $3.95. No credit cards. Tues–Sun 11am–8pm; closed Mon. Subway/El: Blue Line to Western.

**Bucktown Soup Café** *AMERICAN* If you're looking to fill up for a minimal cost, soup is one of your best bets (and, it's a particularly attractive option, given Chicago's winters). Perhaps that's why Chicagoans have flocked to this cafe, with a rotating menu of 90 soups (you'll find nine varieties on offer daily). Soups come in 12-ounce and 16-ounce sizes, and average about $7.50 with a couple of slices of yummy whole-grain bread from nearby Red Hen Bakery. Tomato-basil bisque, lobster bisque, kickin' crab (with crabmeat and sweet corn), chicken tortilla, and chicken and cheese enchilada are some of the best options. At this price, you and a friend can lunch for under $20.

184 N. Damen Ave. ⓒ **773/904-8364.** Soup meals $9 and under. AE, DC, MC, V. Mon– Fri 10:30am–9pm; Sat noon–6pm; closed Sun. Subway/El: Blue Line to Damen.

**Club Lucky** *ITALIAN* Club Lucky seems to have been carved from a local 1950s-era corner tavern with an Italian mamma cooking up family recipes in the back. The Naugahyde banquettes, Formica-topped bar and tables, and Captain Video ceiling fixtures give the place a fun retro flair. The scene here changes throughout the evening: Young families gradually give way to stylish couples posing with glasses of the restaurant's signature martinis (be prepared to wait on weekends).

You might or might not take to the scene, but the food does not disappoint. Prices overall are moderate, especially considering the generous family-style portions. The large calamari appetizer—"for two," the menu says—will almost certainly keep you in leftover land for a day or two. The menu offers real Italian home-style cooking such as *pasta e fagioli* (thick macaroni-and-bean soup—really a kind of stew). Or try the rigatoni with veal meatballs, served with steamed escarole and melted slabs of mozzarella, or the spicy grilled boneless pork chops served with peppers and roasted potatoes. The lunch menu, where the best deals are found, includes about a dozen Italian sandwiches, such as scrambled eggs and pesto, meatball, and Italian sausage.

1824 W. Wabansia Ave. (1 block north of North Ave., btw. Damen and Ashland aves.). ⓒ **773/227-2300.** www.clubluckychicago.com. Reservations accepted for parties of

6 or more. Sandwiches $8–$11; main courses $10–$36. AE, DC, DISC, MC, V. Mon–Thurs 11:30am–11pm; Fri 11:30am–midnight; Sat 5pm–midnight; Sun 4–10pm; cocktail lounge open later. Subway/El: Blue Line to Damen.

**Feast Restaurant & Bar** *GLOBAL* Perusing this menu is like traveling around the world and picking the best comfort food from each culture. You'll find Indian, Mediterranean, and Mexican influences on the menu. Butternut squash ravioli with goat cheese, balsamic, and brown butter; chipotle barbecue salmon; and the wonton Napoleon stacked with tuna sashimi and tartare are all favorites of the neighborhood regulars. Choose a side—wasabi mashed potatoes and caramelized green beans are both superb—and wind up your meal with a bread pudding. The dining room is cozy in the wintertime with a real fireplace, and sidewalk seating plus a spacious patio provide cool seating in the summer.

1616 N. Damen Ave. ℂ 773/772-7100. Main courses $9–$25. AE, DISC, MC, V. Mon–Thurs 5:30–10pm; Fri–Sat 5:30–11pm; Sun 5–9pm. Brunch Mon–Fri 11am–3pm; Sat–Sun 9am–3pm. Subway/El: Blue Line to Damen.

**Flo** *AMERICAN/SOUTHWESTERN* A funky, casual dining room and interesting meals inspired by New Mexico, plus locally grown and organic ingredients, make this reasonable restaurant a real find. Brunch and breakfast include green-chile enchiladas and huevos rancheros, while the lunch menu features grilled shrimp enchiladas. For dinner, try the tacos filled with catfish, stewed chicken, or portabello mushrooms. Cheese quesadillas, chorizo meat loaf, and roasted chicken mole are also hugely popular. (Make sure you can take the heat—Flo gets its peppers directly from a farmer in New Mexico, and many of these dishes pack a spicy wallop!) Wash it all down with homemade sangria or fresh lime margaritas.

1434 W. Chicago Ave. ℂ 312/243-0477. Main courses $10–$13. AE, MC, V. Tues–Fri 8:30am–2:30pm, brunch Sat–Sun 8:30am–2:30pm, dinner Tues–Thurs 5:30–10pm, Fri–Sat 5:30–11pm. Subway/El: Blue Line to Chicago.

★ **Fonda Del Mar** *MEXICAN* A seafood-centric Mexican spot in Logan Square, the decor at this restaurant place will make you feel as if you've just spent the day surfing (photos of Puerto Escondido, a Mexican resort town known for its great surfing, line the walls). Marlin ceviche, poblano pepper stuffed with smoked salmon and mushrooms, grilled tilapia with a grilled tomatillo-serrano sauce, and arroz a la tumbada, a paella-esque dish with an abundance of seafood, are all stellar. Finish with a chocolate Maya (flan) or a lime tart. On Mondays and Tuesdays, house and sabor (flavored) margaritas (sometimes including a really terrific passion fruit margarita) are $5.

3749 W. Fullerton St. ⓒ **773/489-3748.** Entrees $9–$15. MC, V. Mon–Thurs 5–9pm; Fri–Sat 5–10pm; Sun 4–9pm. Bus: No. 74 Fullerton Bus.

★ **Margie's Candies**    *AMERICAN* Kitschy and cool, Margie's is a trip back in time . . . to 1921, the year this ice cream shop opened, to be exact. Still a family-owned and -operated business, Chicagoans flock here for a dose of nostalgia, and the homemade chocolates and candies, plus a wonderful selection of sundaes, banana splits, and shakes. Don't miss out on the homemade butterscotch and caramel sauces! The third generation of family running the place still pride themselves on making their own ice cream. Yes, there is diner food, but don't let that get in the way of the main attraction: Make sure you leave room for one of Margie's sundaes, which cost $3.95–$7.95, served in a giant conch-shell dish.

1960 N. Western Ave. ⓒ **773/384-1035.** Diner meals $9 and under. AE, DC, MC, V. Mon–Thurs 9am–10pm; Fri 9am–11pm; Sat 9am–midnight. Subway/El: Brown Line to Montrose.

**Northside Café**    *AMERICAN* Among the best cheap eats in the neighborhood, Northside cooks up great burgers, sandwiches, and salads—all for about $10 or less. This is strictly neighborhood dining, without attitude and little in the way of decor; the back dining room looks like a rec room circa 1973, complete with a fireplace, pinball machines, and a pool table. In nice weather, Northside opens up its large front patio for dining, and a sky-lit cover keeps it in use during the winter. You're always sure to be entertained by people-watching here, as Northside attracts all sorts. During the week, the cafe is more of a neighborhood hangout, while on weekends a touristy crowd from Lincoln Park and the suburbs piles in. A limited late-night menu is available from 10pm to 1am.

1635 N. Damen Ave. (at North and Milwaukee aves.). ⓒ **773/384-3555.** Reservations not accepted. Menu items $6–$15. AE, DC, DISC, MC, V. Sun–Fri 11:30am–2am; Sat 11am–3am. Subway/El: Blue Line to Damen.

**Piece**    *ITALIAN* Piece proves to deep-dish-loving Chicagoans that thin-crust pizza deserves respect. A casual, welcoming hangout,

Piece makes a good lunch stop for families with older kids; at night it becomes a convivial scene full of young singles sipping one of the restaurant's seasonal microbrew beers. The large, airy dining room—a former garage that's been outfitted with dark wood tables and ceiling beams—is flooded with light from the expansive skylights overhead; even when it's crowded (as it gets on weekend evenings), the soaring space above keeps the place from feeling claustrophobic.

Piece offers a selection of salads and sandwiches on satisfyingly crusty bread, but pizza in the style of New Haven, Connecticut (hometown of one of the owners), is the house specialty. Pick from three styles—plain (tomato sauce, Parmesan cheese, and garlic), red (tomato sauce and mozzarella), or white (olive oil, garlic, and mozzarella), then add on your favorite toppings. Sausage and/or spinach work well with the plain or red, but the adventurous should sample a more offbeat choice: clam and bacon on white pizza. Large pizzas that serve three to five people will cost about $17 and up.

1927 W. North Ave. (at Milwaukee Ave.). ℂ **773/772-4422.** www.piecechicago.com. Reservations accepted for groups of 10 or more. Pizza $11–$17. AE, DISC, MC, V. Mon–Thurs 11:30am–11pm; Fri–Sat 11:30am–12:30am; Sun 11am–10pm. Subway/El: Blue Line to Damen.

★ **Silver Cloud** *AMERICAN* The motto of this casual cafe is "Food like Mom would make if she was gettin' paid." Indeed, Silver Cloud is comfort-food central, with a laid-back pub-meets-diner decor and suitably attitude-free clientele. If intimate conversation is your priority, try to snag one of the roomy red-leather booths. While the food isn't extraordinary, the restaurant does deliver consistently reliable home-style favorites: chicken potpie, grilled-cheese sandwiches, pot roast, sloppy Joes with a side of tater tots, s'mores, and root beer floats. While Silver Cloud attracts a mix of families, couples, and groups of friends during the day and early-evening hours, it becomes more of a cocktail lounge at night. A warning for those with sensitive ears: The jukebox volume gets turned up at night, too. The Sunday brunch is especially popular; the "Hangover Helpers" attract a fair number of hip young things recovering from nightly adventures.

1700 N. Damen Ave. (at Wabansia St.). ℂ **773/489-6212.** www.silvercloudchicago. com. Main courses $6–$10 lunch, $10–$16 dinner. AE, DC, MC, V. Mon–Thurs 11:30am–11pm; Fri 11:30am–midnight; Sat–Sun 10am–midnight. Bar stays open later every night except Sun. Subway/El: Blue Line to Damen.

# 5 Hyde Park

**The Medici on 57th** *AMERICAN* This casual restaurant located near the University of Chicago campus has fed generations of students (you'll find some of their names carved into the tables, and graffittied onto the walls, tables, and chairs). The house specialty is pizza: Try the personal-size garbage pizza, complete with sausage, ground beef, pepperoni, fresh mushrooms, green peppers, onions, and Canadian bacon for $9.25. Strawberry-banana and fudge-banana-nut milkshakes are another favorite ($3.89). In the evening, it's BYOB.

1327 E. 57th St. ✆ **773/667-7394.** www. medici57.com. Entrees $9–$15. MC, V. Mon–Thurs 11am–11pm; Fri 11am–midnight; Sat 9am–midnight; Sun 9am–11pm. Subway/El: No. 6 Bus to 57th and Stony Island.

★ **The Nile Restaurant** *MIDDLE EASTERN* Located on the University of Chicago campus in Hyde Park, this restaurant makes an ideal stop if you're visiting the Robie House or checking out Rockefeller Chapel. Huge portions mean you can fill up for about $10 per person. Fresh, warm pita bread is filled with shaved, roasted chicken, tomatoes, onions, and a spicy sauce to make their popular chicken shawarma sandwich. You'll want to start with the red lentil soup and hummus (if hummus isn't your thing, the mashwiya is a delicious

---

### ★ An All-You-Can-Eat Taste of Poland

Chicago has long been a popular destination for Polish immigrants (currently, about one million Chicagoans claim Polish ancestry). It's somewhat mystifying, then, why they haven't made much of an impact on the city's dining scene. There are Polish restaurants here, but they tend to be small, casual, family-run affairs in residential neighborhoods far removed from the usual tourist attractions. If you'd like to try some hearty, stick-to-your-ribs Polish food, the best-known restaurant is **Red Apple** (Czerwone Jabluszko), 3121 N. Milwaukee Ave. (✆ **773/588-5781;** http://redapplebuffet.com). Dining here is strictly buffet, and the lineup includes Polish specialties such as pierogi (meat- or cheese-stuffed dumplings) and blintzes, as well as a huge selection of roast meats, salads, and bread (there's even fruit, should you feel nutrient-starved). Best of all is the price: $8.50 on weekdays and $9.50 on weekends for all you can eat.

## Corkage-Free BYOB

No one wants to bring your own bottle to a licensed restaurant only to be slapped with a large corkage fee. At these restaurants, there's no corkage fee when you BYOB. Make sure to look beyond the traditional Italian or pizza places to excellent Mexican restaurants that will blend your margaritas with BYOB tequila, and down-home barbecue joints that serve up ribs that demand a big red wine. Here are a few favorites:

- **Smoke Shack:** Specializing in slow-cooked brisket and ribs, you can grab a stool at the counter or cozy up in a booth with a bottle of your own choosing (no corkage fee). A half-slab of ribs is a deal at $9.95, and brisket platter with coleslaw and a side, $8.95. 800 W. Altgeld St. (just west of Halsted); ℂ **773/248-8886.**

- **Dorado:** Grab a bottle of shiraz at the **Claddagh Ring** bar across the street, and head to **Dorado**, a Lincoln Square Latin eatery known for its fabulous Dorado nachos, a big pile of corn chips topped with Chihuahua cheese, shredded smoked duck, onions, guacamole, and jalapenos and topped with lime cream sauce ($9.95). 2301 W. Foster Ave.; ℂ **773/561-3780;** www.dorado restaurant.com.

- **Istanbul:** Pick up a bottle at **The Gourmet Grape** (3530 N. Halsted; ℂ **773/388-0942;** www.gourmetgrape.com) and head around the corner to **Istanbul** for a satisfying meal of kiymali pide, a bread roll (baked fresh on the premises) stuffed with Turkish mozzarella cheese, ground lamb, and onion ($10.95). 3613 N. Broadway; ℂ **773/525-0500.**

alternative to hummus, made with zucchini and yogurt). The kibbeh are not to be missed: a small, football-shaped crust of bulgar wheat, filled with spicy ground lamb and pine nuts. The restaurant is comfortable, but don't expect much in terms of atmosphere—the food is the reason to visit. No alcohol is served here, but it's BYOB for wine and beer. Finish your meal with a Turkish coffee.

1611 E. 55th St. ℂ **773/324-9499.** Entrees $9–$15. AE, DC, MC, V. Mon–Sat 11:30am–9pm; Sun noon–8pm. Bus: 6 to 55th St. in Hyde Park. Walk east 2 blocks.

*Chicago has every kind of attraction you can imagine, from neighborhood festivals to sights that are truly out of this world (see p. 118).*

# EXPLORING CHICAGO

**E**xperiencing the best of Chicago does not necessarily mean parting with your hard-earned money. You don't see the natives lining up for overpriced chain restaurants and paying ridiculous prices for tacky attractions, do you? Instead, you'll find us flying a kite in Grant Park, or taking in a concert under the Pritzker Pavilion, and that's exactly what you should do. We'll show up in droves for Venetian Night, when dozens of boats are lit up and decorated according to a theme (2009's was "Hollywood on the Lake"), floating by as we cheer. And even though we live in the midst of great architecture, we never tire of admiring the gorgeous skylines. The more and more I've learned about Chicago's architecture, the more interesting the buildings become.

Within this chapter are dozens and dozens of cool places and activities, all there for the experiencing—from mind-broadening talks, readings, and lectures to cheap bleacher seats at the Cubs' and White Sox's ballparks—all of which are only-in-Chicago experiences that fit my "cheap *and* priceless" criteria. Stick with these recommendations and you're guaranteed to have a big adventure in Chicago at very little expense.

# 1 Chicago's Top 10 Free Attractions

**1. The Lakefront**   Chicago was blessed to have forefathers with foresight. Thanks to them, in 1836, our lakefront was declared public ground "to remain forever open, clear, and free" from construction—that's why you won't find warehouses, docks, stinky factories, electric plants, or private businesses along our beautiful lakeshore. Instead, join Chicagoans in reveling in 30 miles of sand beaches, green lawns, flower beds, and bicycle paths. More than half of the 2,800 acres of lakefront were created by filling in the lake and building a string of splendid lakeshore parks (from north to south, Lincoln, Grant, Burnham, Jackson, Rainbow, and Calumet). Chicagoans take full advantage of the lakefront to walk, rollerblade, bike, run, swim, picnic, and play volleyball. Most activity takes place around Oak Street Beach (just north of the Magnificent Mile) and North Avenue Beach (several blocks north of Oak St. at North Ave. and Lake Shore Dr.). Sitting on a bench at the beach and watching the world go by is enough to entertain me, and apparently about half of the city's population, on any given night. It's just that simple: Entertainment doesn't always have to come with a price.

Lake Shore Dr., north of Oak St. and at North Ave. www.chicagoparkdistrict.org. Bus: 151 Michigan Ave.

**2. Millennium Park**   One of Chicago's grandest-ever public works projects produced Millennium Park, which opened to huge fanfare in 2004 (4 years late, but it was worth the wait). It's not easy to create new icons for a major city, but many of Millennium Park's installations have already come to symbolize Chicago. In fact, I dare you to stand with your toes in the water at the Crown Fountain, surveying the spectacular cityscape of South Michigan Avenue, and not feel an irrepressible urge to uproot yourself and move into a condo overlooking the park.

The park has been a strikingly beautiful success, and thank goodness Chicago's donors and government saw fit to overspend the budget by leaps and bounds and go far beyond the deadline to ensure a place like this. It's really an example of what a modern park can be. Compare the Crown Fountain, Millennium Park's interactive fountain, with the grande dame of Chicago fountains, Buckingham Fountain (just to the south in Grant Park), which is lovely but untouchable, and you'll see how far we've come. Even the sculpture is interactive—the "bean" (properly titled "Cloud Gate") by Anish Kapoor is essentially a gigantic 3-D mirror. Kids and adults are equally attracted to its reflective surface and house-of-mirrors qualities. The Crown Fountain is another kid favorite, with its two 50-foot glass-brick towers facing each other across a black granite plaza, with water cascading down their sides. Faces of Chicagoans are projected through the glass blocks and change at regular intervals—and watch out, because water spews from their mouths when you least expect it. Don't you love public art with a sense of humor? The Jay Pritzker Pavilion, with its Frank Gehry–designed band shell, is a sight to behold, and the BP Pedestrian Bridge, also designed by Gehry, curves and winds its way over Columbus Drive, providing changing views of the cityscape as you walk. Gardens of native plants are starting to flourish, and you will feel that you are walking through a Midwestern prairie as you stroll the Lurie Garden, with 250 varieties of native perennial plants. All in all, this is a must-see, must-experience park.

For a small splurge, you can lunch at the **Park Grill** (© **312/521-7275;** www.parkgrillchicago.com; daily 11am–10:30pm), an eatery overlooking the McCormick Tribune Plaza ice-skating rink. Dining on the cheap today? Skip the indoor restaurant. Next door to the grill, Park Café offers takeout salads and sandwiches. If you're driving, parking is easy, too, with plentiful underground lots at reasonable rates of around $14/day.

Free walking tours of the park are offered daily from Memorial Day through October at 11:30am and 1pm, starting at the Park's Welcome Center, 201 E. Randolph St. (© **312/742-1168**).

Michigan Ave., from Randolph Dr. on the north to Monroe Dr. on the south, and west to Columbus Dr. © **312/742-1168.** www.millenniumpark.org. Daily 6am–11pm. El: Blue line to Washington; Red Line to Lake; Brown, Green, Orange, or Purple Line to Randolph.

**3. Chicago SummerDance**   In an informal poll of Chicago friends, this annual summer event ranked as the number-one free event in the city. From July through late August, the City's Department of Cultural Affairs transforms a patch of Grant Park into a lighted outdoor dance venue. The 4,600-square-foot dance floor provides ample room for throwing down moves while live bands play music—from ballroom and klezmer to samba and zydeco.

East side of S. Michigan Ave. btw. Balbo and Harrison sts. ✆ **312/742-4007.** www. explorechicago.org. Free admission. SummerDance takes place on Thurs, Fri, and Sat 6–9:30pm; Sun 4–7pm. 1-hour lessons offered 6–7pm.

**4. Navy Pier Fireworks**   Some of the best views of the city can be had from the tip of Navy Pier. If you are a runner or walker, you can get a traffic-free early-morning jog or stroll in by heading to the end of the pier, circling around its far end, and then heading west to the city—but do it very early, say, 6 or 7am. It's about ¾-mile in length, so out and back will give you a nice 1½-mile route. Don't attempt to take a walk or run here any later in the day, as you will find yourself tripping over tourists. Another way to take in the view is to check out the regular free evening fireworks displays. From Memorial Day through Labor Day, Navy Pier hosts twice-weekly fireworks shows Wednesday nights at 9:30pm and Saturday nights at 10:15pm.

**5. Lincoln Park Zoo**   One of Chicago's don't-miss attractions for kids, Lincoln Park Zoo occupies a scant 35 acres, and its landmark Georgian Revival brick buildings and modern structures sit among gently rolling pathways, verdant lawns, and a kaleidoscopic profusion of flower gardens. The zoo is so compact that a tour of the various habitats takes all of 2 or 3 hours—a convenience factor even more enticing when you consider that the nation's oldest zoo (it was founded in 1868) stays open 365 days a year and is one of the last free zoos in the country. Lincoln Park Zoo has held a special place in the hearts of Chicagoans since the days of Bushman, the mighty lowland gorilla who captivated the world in the 1930s and 1940s and now suffers the ignominious fate of being a stuffed exhibit at The Field Museum of Natural History. The late Marlon Perkins, legendary host of the *Mutual of Omaha's Wild Kingdom* TV series, got his start here as the zoo's director, and filmed a pioneering TV show called *Zoo Parade* (*Wild Kingdom's* predecessor) in the basement of the old Reptile House.

The zoo has taken on an ambitious modernization, renovating and expanding exhibits to reflect natural habitats. For years, the star attraction has been the lowland gorillas at the Regenstein Center for African Apes. The zoo has had remarkable success in breeding both gorillas and chimpanzees, and watching these ape families is mesmerizing. Regenstein African Journey, a series of linked indoor and outdoor habitats, is home to elephants, giraffes, rhinos, and other large mammals; large glass-enclosed tanks allow visitors to go face-to-face with swimming pygmy hippos and (not for the faint of heart) a rocky ledge filled with hissing cockroaches from Madagascar.

The Small Mammal–Reptile House is a state-of-the-art facility, housing 200 species and featuring a glass-enclosed walk-through ecosystem simulating river, savanna, and forest habitats. The popular Sea Lion Pool, home to harbor seals, gray seals, and California sea lions, features an underwater viewing area spanning 70 feet and an amphitheater.

The Park Place Café food court is in a historic building that originally housed Chicago's first aquarium, but beware, because the food here is expensive. If you bring a picnic, you can eat outside on the rolling green slope that borders the large patio area, and watch the nearby monkeys doing acrobatics. Or, walk west into Lincoln Park where there's a **Cosi Sandwich Bar** located nearby (2200 N. Clark St. at Webster; ✆ **773/472-2674**). The Mahon Theobold Pavilion features a sprawling indoor gift shop and a unique rooftop eatery called Big Cats Café that opens at 8am (1 hr. before the exhibits do) and serves fresh-baked muffins and scones, focaccia sandwiches, salads, and flatbreads. FINE PRINT For best animal viewing, go on a temperate-weather day—in really hot weather, the animals tend to be lethargic. Allow 3 hours.

2200 N. Cannon Dr. (near Lake Shore Dr. at Fullerton Pkwy.). ✆ **312/742-2000.** www.lpzoo.com. Free admission. Buildings daily 10am–5pm (until 6:30pm Sat–Sun Memorial Day to Labor Day); grounds 9am–6pm (until 7pm Memorial Day to Labor Day and 5pm Nov 1–Mar 31). Parking $14 for up to 3 hours in on-site lot. Bus: 151 or 156.

**6. Grant Park Music Festival**   Chicago is one of the last cities in America to still present a free, open-air, professional series of orchestral concerts each summer. The Grant Park Symphony Orchestra and Chorus puts on its popular series at the centerpiece of Millennium Park, the dramatic Frank Gehry–designed **Pritzker Music Pavilion,** featuring massive curved ribbons of steel. Concerts take place most Wednesday through Sunday evenings in the summer. For a schedule of concert times and dates, call or check the website. I caught part of a rehearsal one morning at about 10:30am, and it was just as good as hearing the concert—a volunteer even handed us programs. Plus, I scored a prime seat right up front. You won't believe how fantastic the sound system is until you hear it with your own ears. FINE PRINT Lawn and general seating is free—no tickets necessary. Get there an hour before the concert starts to claim a good spot on the lawn.

Michigan Ave. at Randolph St. ℂ **312/742-7638.** www.grantparkmusicfestival.org. Free admission. Bus/El: 151 Michigan Ave. to Randolph; Red Line to Randolph.

**7. Neighborhood Festivals and Garden Walks**   Summer finds Chicagoans ready to get out and about, and celebrate. Each weekend, there are multiple festivals to choose from. Garden Walks, basically a neighborhood festival with the added benefit of being able to peer inside some of Chicago's most gorgeous backyards, are hugely popular, and—you guessed it—touring the gardens is free. Two of the best are the **Sheffield Garden Walk,** starting at Sheffield and Webster avenues (ℂ **773/929-9255;** www.sheffieldfestivals.org), where you can snoop in the lush backyards of Lincoln Park homeowners. The walk isn't just for garden nuts; the bands, children's activities, and food and drink tents attract lots of singles and young families.

A slightly more upscale affair is the **Dearborn Garden Walk & Heritage Festival,** North Dearborn and Astor streets (ℂ **312/632-1241;** http://dearborngardenwalk.com). Regular folks can check out private gardens on the Gold Coast, one of the most expensive and exclusive neighborhoods in the city. As you'd expect, many yards are the work of the best landscape architects, designers, and art world luminaries that old money can buy. There's also live music, a marketplace, and a few architectural tours. Both garden walks take place in mid-July; check websites or call for information.

If you're in for a straightforward neighborhood street fair, your best bet is **Taste of Lincoln Avenue,** Lincoln Park, between Fullerton Avenue and Wellington Street (ℂ **773/868-3010;** www.wrightwood neighbors.org). This is one of the largest and most popular of Chicago's many neighborhood street fairs; it features 50 bands performing music on five stages. Neighborhood restaurants staff the food stands, and there's also a kids' carnival. Last weekend in July.

## Money-Saving Tourist Passes

If you're the type who loves to cram as many attractions as possible into one trip, then purchasing a **Chicago CityPass** or **GO Chicago Card** could be a real money-saver. The CityPass includes five Chicago attractions: the Shedd Aquarium, Field Museum, Adler Planetarium, Museum of Science and Industry, and either the John Hancock or Willis Tower (formerly the Sears Tower) Skydeck, for $69 (adults) or $59 (children). The pass is valid for 9 days. For more information, check out www.city pass.com or call ☎ **888/330-5008.**

I think the better deal, however, is the GO Chicago Card (☎ **800/ 887-9103;** www.gochicagocard.com). The GO Chicago Card provides you access to over 30 of Chicago's top attractions and tours for a single low price on a single ticket. Take a trip to the top of the Willis (Sears) Tower, visit the Shedd Aquarium, enjoy a Shoreline cruise, experience the Field Museum, have fun at Navy Pier—these and 25 other options are all included in the cost of a GO Chicago Card. The card is available in 1-, 2-, 3-, 5-, and 7-day increments over a 14-day period, and you can save up to 55% over the cost of individual attractions. In addition, some stores and restaurants offer discounts of up to 20% to GO Chicago Card holders. The GO Cards are smart-technology enabled, which means they operate by calendar day and are activated the first time they are swiped, so you'll want to start your touring early in the morning to get the most value. The 2-day card costs $93 for adults ($70 for kids 3–12), and it doesn't need to be used on consecutive days, but try to pick attractions in close proximity so you have time to visit three attractions in a single day for the best value. You can purchase the GO Cards via their website or at multiple locations in the city, including the Macy's visitor center (111 N. State St. at Washington St., 7th floor), or Water Tower Place concierge desk (835 N. Michigan Ave., at Chestnut St.).

**8. Venetian Night**    This carnival of illuminated boats on the lake is complete with fireworks and synchronized music by the Grant Park Symphony Orchestra. Shoreline viewing is fine, but you'll have to get there early to snag a prime viewing spot; the best way to take it in, if you can swing it, is from another boat nearby. Each year brings another crazy theme and even crazier revelers who dress up in full costume and party on the boats. Last Saturday in July.

Lakefront, Monroe Harbor to Adler Planetarium. ⓒ **312-744-3315.** www.explore chicago.org. Bus/El: 151 Michigan Ave.; Red Line to Randolph.

**9. Garfield and Lincoln Park Conservatories**   Just beyond the zoo's northeast border is Lincoln Park Conservatory, a lovely botanical garden housed in a soaring glass-domed structure. Inside are four great halls filled with thousands of plants. If you're visiting Chicago in the wintertime, I can't think of a better prescription for free mood elevation than this lush haven of greenery. The Palm House features giant palms and rubber trees (including a 50-ft. fiddle-leaf rubber tree dating back to 1891); the Fernery nurtures plants that grow close to the forest floor; and the Tropical House is a symphony of flowering trees, vines, and bamboo. The fourth environment is the Show House, where seasonal flower shows take place. Even better than the plants inside, however, might be what lies outside the front doors. The expansive lawn, with its French garden and lovely fountain on the conservatory's south side, is one of the best places in town for an informal picnic.

The Lincoln Park Conservatory has a sister facility on the city's West Side, in Garfield Park, that is much more remarkable. In fact, the 2-acre **Garfield Park Conservatory,** 300 N. Central Park Ave. (ⓒ **312/ 746-5100**), designed by the great landscape architect Jens Jensen in 1907, is one of the largest gardens under glass in the world. It's open 365 days a year from 9am to 5pm. FINE PRINT Unfortunately, a rather blighted neighborhood with a high crime rate surrounds the conservatory. I recommend driving rather than using public transportation. (Free parking manned by security guards is adjacent to the conservatory).

Fullerton Ave. (at Stockton Dr.). ⓒ **312/742-7736.** Free admission. Daily 9am–5pm. Bus: 73, 151, or 156.

**10. Oak Park**   West suburban Oak Park has the highest concentration of Frank Lloyd Wright–designed and –built houses or buildings anywhere. People come here from all over the world to marvel at the work of a man who saw his life as a twofold mission: to wage a single-handed battle against excessively ornamental architecture (Victorian, in particular), and to create in its place a new form that would be at the same time functional, appropriate to its natural setting, and stimulating to the imagination.

Oak Park has 25 homes and buildings by Wright, constructed between 1892 and 1913, which constitute the core output of his Prairie School period. You can drop some serious dollars if you take the formal guided tours and buy the tchotchkes in the gift shop. But that's not the free and dirt cheap way: Instead, set out and explore the Historic District surrounding the Home and Studio at your own pace. Marvel at the exteriors of a wide selection of Wright-designed, Prairie-style homes and the same Victorian buildings that drove Frank Lloyd Wright to distraction. You can walk the gorgeous neighborhood surrounding Wright's Home and Studio for free. It would be worthwhile, however, to stop in the Ginkgo Tree bookstore (part of the Home & Studio) in order to buy a $3 neighborhood map. For more details on what's available in Oak Park, including the birthplace of Ernest Hemingway, check out the "Dirt Cheap (or Thereabouts)" section (p. 132).

## 2 Other Attractions & Museums

### ALWAYS FREE

★ **Chicago Cultural Center**   The Chicago Cultural Center was built in 1897 as the city's public library, and in 1991, it was transformed into a showplace for visual and performing arts. Today, it's an overlooked civic treasure with a basic Beaux Arts exterior and a sumptuous interior of rare marble, fine hardwood, stained glass, and mosaics of Favrile glass, colored stone, and mother-of-pearl inlaid in white marble. The crowning centerpiece is Preston Bradley Hall's majestic Tiffany dome, said to be the largest of its kind in the world. If nothing else, stop inside and check out this gorgeous piece of free public art.

The building also houses one of the Chicago Office of Tourism visitor centers, which makes it an ideal place to kick-start your visit. If you stop in to pick up tourist information and take a quick look around, your visit won't take longer than 15 minutes, but the Cultural Center also schedules an array of art exhibitions, concerts, films, lectures, and other special events (many free), which might convince you to extend your time here. A long-standing tradition is the 12:15pm Dame Myra Hess Memorial classical concert every Wednesday in the Preston Bradley Hall. (Free!)

Free, guided architectural tours of the Cultural Center run at 1:15pm on Wednesday, Friday, and Saturday.

# EXPLORING CHICAGO

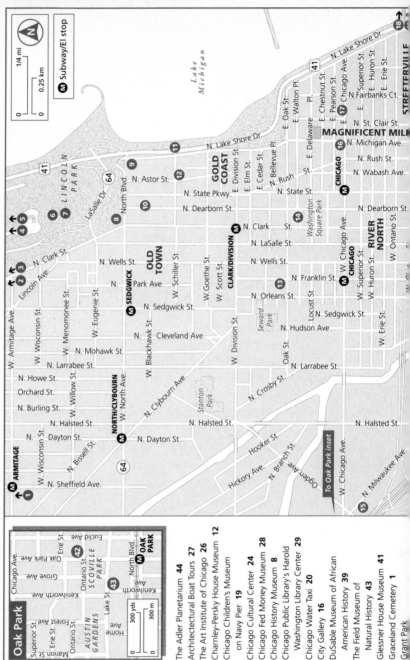

The Adler Planetarium **44**
Architectural Boat Tours **27**
The Art Institute of Chicago **26**
Charnley-Persky House Museum **12**
Chicago Children's Museum
  on Navy Pier **19**
Chicago Cultural Center **24**
Chicago Fed Money Museum **28**
Chicago History Museum **8**
Chicago Public Library's Harold
  Washington Library Center **29**
Chicago Water Taxi **20**
City Gallery **16**
DuSable Museum of African
  American History **39**
The Field Museum of
  Natural History **43**
Glessner House Museum **41**
Graceland Cemetery **1**
Grant Park

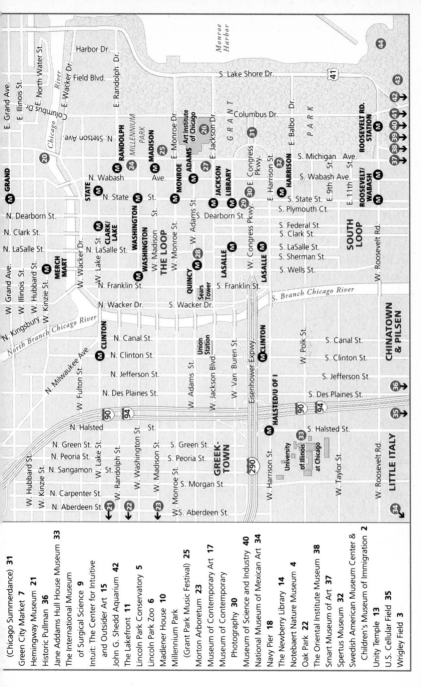

(Chicago Summerdance) **31**

Green City Market **7**

Hemingway Museum **21**

Historic Pullman **36**

Jane Addams Hull House Museum **33**

The International Museum
of Surgical Science **9**

Intuit: The Center for Intuitive
and Outsider Art **15**

John G. Shedd Aquarium **42**

The Lakefront **11**

Lincoln Park Conservatory **5**

Lincoln Park Zoo **6**

Madlener House **10**

Millennium Park

(Grant Park Music Festival) **25**

Morton Arboretum **23**

Museum of Contemporary Art **17**

Museum of Contemporary
Photography **30**

Museum of Science and Industry **40**

National Museum of Mexican Art **34**

Navy Pier **18**

The Newberry Library **14**

Notebaert Nature Museum **4**

Oak Park **22**

The Oriental Institute Museum **38**

Smart Museum of Art **37**

Spertus Museum **32**

Swedish American Museum Center &
Children's Museum of Immigration **2**

Unity Temple **13**

U.S. Cellular Field **35**

Wrigley Field **3**

78 E. Washington St. ⓒ **312/744-6630,** or 312/FINE-ART (347-3278) for weekly events. www.cityofchicago.org/exploringchicago. Free admission. Mon–Thurs 10am–7pm; Fri 10am–6pm; Sat 10am–5pm; Sun 11am–5pm. Closed major holidays. Bus: 3, 4, 20, 56, 145, 146, 147, 151, or 157. Subway/El: Brown, Green, Orange, or Purple line to Randolph, or Red Line to Washington/State.

**Chicago Fed Money Museum**   The visitor center at the Federal Reserve Bank of Chicago is worth a quick stop if you're wandering around the Loop. More than just the standard history-of-banking displays, the center has a giant cube that holds a million dollars and an exhibit that lets you try detecting counterfeit bills. There's even a section where visitors can pretend to be Ben Bernanke for a moment; it shows how changes in interest rates affect the economy. Free guided tours begin at 1pm on weekdays. Allow a half-hour.

230 S. LaSalle St. (at Quincy St.). ⓒ **312/322-2400.** www.chicagofed.org. Free admission. Mon–Fri 9am–4pm. Closed federal holidays. Bus: 134, 135, 136, or 156. Subway/El: Brown Line to Quincy/Wells.

**Chicago Public Library's Harold Washington Library Center**   A massive, hulking building that looks like an Italian Renaissance fortress, Chicago's main public library is the largest public library in the world. Named for the city's first and only African-American mayor, who died of a heart attack in 1987 at the beginning of his second term in office, the building fills an entire city block at State Street and Congress Parkway. The interior design has been criticized for feeling cold (you have to go up a few floors before you even see any books), but the stunning, 52-foot glass-domed Winter Garden on the top floor is worth a visit. On the second floor is another treasure: the vast Thomas Hughes Children's Library, which makes an excellent resting spot for families traveling with kids. The library also offers an interesting array of free events and art exhibitions that are worth checking out. A 385-seat auditorium is the setting for a unique mix of dance and music performances, author talks, and children's programs. Want to check your e-mail for free? Stop by the third-floor Computer Commons, which has about 75 terminals available for public use. Allow a half-hour.

400 S. State St. ⓒ **312/747-4300.** www.chipublib.org. Free admission. Mon–Thurs 9am–7pm; Fri–Sat 9am–5pm; Sun 1–5pm. Closed major holidays. Bus: 2, 6, 11, 29, 36, 62, 145, 146, 147, or 151. Subway/El: Red Line to Jackson/State, or Brown Line to Van Buren/Library.

**City Gallery at the Historic Water Tower**   Along with the pumping station across the street, the Chicago Water Tower is one of only a handful of buildings to survive the Great Chicago Fire of 1871. It has long been a revered symbol of the city's resilience and fortitude, although today the building is dwarfed by the high-rise shopping centers and hotels of North Michigan Avenue. The Gothic-style limestone building is now an art gallery. The spiffed-up interior is intimate and sunny, and it's a convenient, quick pit stop of culture on your way to the Water Tower shopping center or the tourist information center across the street in the pumping station. Exhibits focus mostly on photography, usually featuring Chicago-based artists such as the fashion photographer Victor Skrebneski. Allow 15 minutes.

806 N. Michigan Ave. (btw. Chicago Ave. and Pearson St.). © 312/742-0808. Free admission. Mon–Sat 10am–6:30pm; Sun 10am–5pm. Bus: 3, 145, 146, 147, or 151.

★ Graceland Cemetery   Don't be scared away by the creepy connotations. Some of Chicago's cemeteries are as pretty as parks, and they offer a variety of intriguing monuments that are a virtual road into the city's history. One of the best is **Graceland,** the Victorian-era cemetery that stretches along Clark Street in the Swedish neighborhood of Andersonville. Here, you can view the tombs and monuments of many Chicago notables.

When Graceland was laid out in 1860, public parks were rare. The elaborate burial grounds that were constructed in many large American cities around that time had the dual purpose of relieving the congestion of the municipal cemeteries closer to town and providing pastoral recreational settings for the Sunday outings of the living. Indeed, cemeteries like Graceland were the precursors of such great municipal green spaces as Lincoln Park. Much of Lincoln Park, in fact, had been a public cemetery since Chicago's earliest times. (Many who once rested there were re-interred in Graceland when the building of Lincoln Park went forward.)

You can pick up a free map and list of notable graves at the administrative office and stroll the cemetery on your own. Be aware, however, that the area is huge, and if you are intent on seeing a number of famous graves, you might find it worthwhile to drop $10 on the Chicago Architecture Foundation's walking tours of Graceland (© 312/922-TOUR [8687]; www.architecture.org). The tours take place on select Sundays during August, September, and October. For $10, you get a 2-hour tour—not a bad deal. Among the points of interest in these 121 beautifully landscaped acres are the Ryerson and Getty tombs, famous architectural monuments designed by Louis Sullivan.

Sullivan himself rests here in the company of several of his distinguished colleagues: Daniel Burnham, Ludwig Mies van der Rohe, and Howard Van Doren Shaw. Chicago giants of industry and commerce buried at Graceland include Potter Palmer, Marshall Field, and George Pullman. The Chicago Architecture Foundation offers tours of other cemeteries including Rosehill Cemetery, suburban Lake Forest Cemetery, and Oak Woods Cemetery, the final resting place for many famous African-American figures, including Jesse Owens, Ida B. Wells, and Mayor Harold Washington.

4001 N. Clark St. (at Irving Park Rd.). ℂ **773/525-1105.** www.gracelandcemetery.org. Open daily 8 am–4:30 pm. El: Red Line to Sheridan.

★ **Green City Market**    On Wednesday and Saturday mornings in Lincoln Park, you can sample some of the Midwest's best farm-grown foods at the Chicago Green City Market. Founded by prominent Chicago chefs, this market allows regular folks to buy the same organic and sustainably grown foods that will appear on plates in the best restaurants in town. In July, you're likely to find fresh goat cheese and blueberries picked in Michigan just hours before you can pop them in your mouth. There's music, live cooking demonstrations, and a chance to sample French-style crepes, made to order with market ingredients. Trust me, you'll love this market.

In Lincoln Park, btw. 1750 N. Clark St. and Stockton Dr. (in cooler or inclement weather, the market moves into the Kovler Lion House in Lincoln Park Zoo). www. chicagogreencitymarket.org. May–Oct Wed and Sat 7am–1:30pm. Bus: 151.

**Historic Pullman**    Railway magnate George Pullman may have been a fabulously wealthy industrialist, but he fancied himself more enlightened than his 19th-century peers. So when it came time to build a new headquarters for his Pullman Palace Car Company, he dreamed of something more than the standard factory surrounded by tenements. Instead, he built a model community for his workers, a place where they could live in houses with indoor plumbing and abundant natural light—amenities almost unheard of for industrial workers in the 1880s. Pullman didn't do all this solely from the goodness of his heart: He hoped that the town, named after him, would attract the most skilled workers (who would be so happy that they wouldn't go on strike). As one of the first "factory towns," Pullman caused an international sensation and was seen as a model for other companies to follow. The happy workers that Pullman envisioned did go on strike in 1894, however, frustrated by the company's control of every aspect of their lives.

Today the Pullman district makes a fascinating stop for anyone with a historical or architectural bent. While most of the homes remain private residences, a number of public buildings (including the lavish Hotel Florence, the imposing Clock Tower, and the two-story colonnaded Market Hall) still stand. You can walk through the area on your own (stop by the visitor center for a map), or take a guided tour at 1:30pm on the first Sunday of the month from May through October ($5 adults, $4 seniors, $3 students). Allow 1½ hours for the guided tour.

11141 S. Cottage Grove Ave. ⓒ **773/785-8901.** www.pullmanil.org. Visitor center Tues–Sun 11am–3pm. Free admission. Train: Metra Electric line to Pullman (111th St.), turn right on Cottage Grove Ave., and walk 1 block to the visitor center.

**Intuit: The Center for Intuitive and Outsider Art**    Chicago is home to an active community of collectors of "outsider art," a term attached to a group of unknown, unconventional artists who do their work without any formal training or connection to the mainstream art world. Often called folk or self-taught artists, they produce highly personal and idiosyncratic work using a range of media, from bottle caps to immense canvases. Intuit was founded in 1991 to bring attention to these artists through exhibitions and educational lectures. It's in the warehouse district northwest of the Loop, and has two galleries and a performance area. The museum offers a regular lecture series, films, and more. Allow 1 hour.

756 N. Milwaukee Ave. (at Chicago and Ogden aves.). ⓒ **312/243-9088.** www.art. org. Free admission. Tues–Sat 11am–5pm (Thurs until 7:30pm). Bus: 56 or 66. Subway/El: Blue Line to Chicago.

**Jane Addams Hull House Museum**    Three years after the 1886 Haymarket Riot, a young woman named Jane Addams bought a mansion on Halsted Street that had been built in 1856 as a "country home" but was surrounded by the shanties of poor immigrants. Here, Addams and her co-worker, Ellen Gates Starr, launched the American settlement-house movement with the establishment of Hull House, an institution that endured on this site in Chicago until 1963. (It continues today as a decentralized social-service agency known as Hull House Association.) In that year, all but two of the settlement's 13 buildings, along with the entire residential neighborhood in its immediate vicinity, were demolished to make room for the University of

Illinois at Chicago campus, which now owns the museum buildings. Of the original settlement, what remain today are the Hull-House Museum, the mansion itself, and the residents' dining hall, snuggled among the ultramodern, poured-concrete buildings of the university campus. Inside are the original furnishings, Jane Addams' office, and numerous settlement maps and photographs. Rotating exhibits re-create the history of the settlement and the work of its residents, showing how Addams was able to help transform the dismal streets around her into stable inner-city environments worth fighting over.

University of Illinois at Chicago, 800 S. Halsted St. (at Polk St.). ℂ **312/413-5353.** www. uic.edu/jaddams/hull. Free admission. Tues–Fri 10am–4pm; Sun noon–4pm. Closed university holidays. Bus: 8. Subway/El: Blue Line to Halsted/University of Illinois.

**Museum of Contemporary Photography**  Ensconced in a ground-floor space at Columbia College—a progressive arts- and media-oriented institution that boasts the country's largest undergraduate film department and a highly respected photojournalism-slanted photography department—the Museum of Contemporary Photography is the only museum in the Midwest of its kind. As the name indicates, it exhibits, collects, and promotes modern photography, with a special focus on American works from 1959 to the present. Rotating exhibitions showcase images by both nationally recognized and "undiscovered" regional artists. Related lectures and special programs take place during the year. Allow 1 hour.

600 S. Michigan Ave. ℂ **312/663-5554.** www.mocp.org. Free admission. Mon–Fri 10am–5pm (Thurs until 8pm); Sat 10am–5pm; Sun noon–5pm. Bus: 6, 146, or 151. Subway/El: Red Line to Harrison.

**National Museum of Mexican Art**  Chicago's vibrant Pilsen neighborhood, just southwest of the Loop, is home to one of the nation's largest Mexican-American communities. A stop at this museum, followed by a meal at one of the completely cheap and delicious Mexican restaurants (for suggestions, see chapter 3, "Cheap Eats") that dot the neighborhood can add up to a very cheap and worthwhile experience. In Pilsen, ethnic pride emanates from every doorstep, taqueria, and bakery, and colorful murals splash across building exteriors and alleyways. This institution—the only Latino museum accredited by the American Association of Museums—may be the neighborhood's most prized possession. That's quite an accomplishment, given that it was founded in 1987 by a passel of public-school teachers who pooled $900 to get it started.

Exhibits showcase Mexican and Mexican-American visual and performing artists, often drawing on the permanent collection of more than 5,000 works, but the visiting artists, festival programming, and community participation make the museum really shine. Its Day of the Dead celebration, which runs for about 8 weeks beginning in September, is one of the most ambitious in the country. The Del Corazon Mexican Performing Arts Festival, held in the spring, features programs by local and international artists here and around town, and the Sor Juana Festival, presented in the fall, honors Mexican writer and pioneering feminist Sor Juana Ines de la Cruz with photography and painting exhibits, music and theater performances, and poetry readings by Latina women.

The museum has an excellent gift shop (cheap souvenirs!) and stages a holiday market, featuring items from Mexico, on the first weekend in December. Allow 1 hour.

1852 W. 19th St. (a few blocks west of Ashland Ave.). ℂ 312/738-1503. www.national museumofmexicanart.org. Free admission. Tues–Sun 10am–5pm. Closed major holidays. Bus: 9. Subway/El: Blue Line to 18th St.

Navy Pier    Built during World War I, this 3,000-foot-long pier was a Navy training center for pilots during World War II. The military aura is long gone and replaced with a combination of carnival attractions, a food court, and boat dock, making it a bustling tourist mecca and a place for a fun stroll (if you don't mind the crowds). If you dread tourist scenes, you might skip Navy Pier altogether. If you have kids in tow, you might find yourself here for the Children's Museum or a boat ride.

Midway down the pier are the Crystal Gardens, with 70 full-size palm trees, dancing fountains, and other flora in a glass-enclosed atrium; a carousel and kiddie carnival rides; and a 15-story Ferris wheel, a replica of the original that made its debut at Chicago's 1893 World's Fair. The 50 acres of pier and lakefront property are also home to the Chicago Children's Museum (p. 123), a 3-D IMAX theater (ℂ 312/595-5629), a small ice-skating rink, and the Chicago Shakespeare Theatre (p. 178). The shops tend to be bland and touristy, and dining options include a food court (McDonald's and the like are about the only dirt cheap option here), an outpost of Lincoln Park's popular Charlie's Ale House, and the white-tablecloth seafood restaurant Riva. You'll also find a beer garden with live music; Joe's Be-Bop Cafe & Jazz Emporium, a Southern-style barbecue restaurant with live music; and Bubba Gump Shrimp Co. & Market, a casual family seafood joint. (Be forewarned: None of these sit-down restaurants are cheap. Even a slushie from a kiosk will run you $6. This is full-on tourist central, after all). Summer is one long party at the pier, with fireworks on Wednesday and Saturday evenings.

The free attractions within Navy Pier that I can recommend are the Smith Museum of Stained Glass Windows and Olive Park. A museum of stained glass may sound incredibly dull, but decorative-art aficionados shouldn't miss this remarkable installation of more than 150 stained-glass windows set in illuminated display cases. Occupying an 800-foot-long expanse on the ground floor of Navy Pier, the free museum features works by Frank Lloyd Wright, Louis Sullivan, John LaFarge, and Louis Comfort Tiffany.

And if nothing else, you can enjoy the Pier for free by taking the ¾-mile stroll to the end of the pier, east of the ballroom, where you can find a little respite and enjoy the wind, the waves, and the city view, which is the real delight of a place like this. Or, unwind in Olive Park, a small sylvan haven with a sliver of beach just north of Navy Pier.

You'll find more than half a dozen sailing vessels moored at the south dock, including a couple of dinner-cruise ships, the pristine white-masted tall ship *Windy,* and the 70-foot speedboats *Seadog I, II,* and *III.* In the summer months, water taxis speed between Navy Pier and other Chicago sights ($4 a person and much cheaper than a land taxi).

600 E. Grand Ave. (at Lake Michigan). ℭ **800/595-PIER** (7437) (outside 312 area code) or 312/595-PIER (7437). www.navypier.com. Free admission. Summer Sun–Thurs 10am–10pm, Fri–Sat 10am–midnight; fall–spring Mon–Thurs 10am–8pm, Fri–Sat 10am–10pm, Sun 10am–7pm. Parking: $19/day weekdays; $23/day weekends. Lots fill quickly. Bus: 29, 65, 66, 120, or 121. Subway/El: Red Line to Grand/State; transfer to city bus or board a free pier trolley bus.

**The Newberry Library** The Newberry Library is a bibliophile's dream. Established in 1887 thanks to a bequest by Chicago merchant and financier Walter Loomis Newberry, the noncirculating research library contains many rare books and manuscripts (such as Shakespeare's first folio and Jefferson's copy of *The Federalist Papers*), housed in a comely five-story granite building. The library is also a major destination for genealogists digging at their roots, with holdings that are open free to the public (over the age of 16 with a photo ID).

The collections include more than 1.5 million volumes and 75,000 maps, many of which are on display during an ongoing series of public exhibitions. For an overview, take a free 1-hour tour Thursday at 3pm or Saturday at 10:30am. The Newberry operates a fine bookstore and also sponsors a series of concerts (including those by its resident early-music ensemble, the Newberry Consort), lectures, and children's story hours throughout the year. One popular annual event is the free Bughouse Square debates. Held across the street in Washington Square Park, the debates re-create the fiery soapbox orations of the left-wing agitators in the 1930s and 1940s. The late, great, Pulitzer Prize–winning oral historian Studs Terkel used to emcee the hullabaloo. His spirit lives on in the debates today.

60 W. Walton St. (at Dearborn Pkwy.). © **312/943-9090,** or 312/255-3700 for programs. www.newberry.org. Free admission. Reading room Tues–Thurs 10am–6pm; Fri–Sat 9am–5pm. Exhibit gallery Mon, Fri, and Sat 8:15am–5:30pm; Tues–Thurs 8:15am–7:30pm. Bus: 22, 36, 125, 145, 146, 147, or 151. Subway/El: Red Line to Chicago/State.

**The Oriental Institute Museum**    Near the midpoint of the campus, a few blocks from Rockefeller Memorial Chapel, is the Oriental Institute, which houses one of the world's major collections of Near Eastern art. Although most of the galleries have been renovated within the last few years, this is still a very traditional museum: lots of glass cases and very few interactive exhibits (in other words, there's not much to interest young children). It won't take you long to see the highlights here, and a few impressive pieces make it worth a stop for history and art buffs.

Your first stop should be the Egyptian Gallery, which showcases the finest objects among the museum's 35,000 Egyptian artifacts. At the center stands a monumental, 17-foot solid-quartzite statue of the boy king Tutankhamen; the largest Egyptian sculpture in the Western Hemisphere, it tips the scales at 6 tons. The surrounding exhibits, which document the life and beliefs of Egyptians from 5000 B.C. to the 8th century A.D., have a wonderfully accessible approach that emphasizes themes, not chronology. Among them are mummification (there are 14 mummies on display—five people and nine animals), kingship, society, and writing (including a deed for the sale of a house, a copy of the Book of the Dead, and a schoolboy's homework).

The Oriental Institute also houses important collections of artifacts from civilizations that once flourished in what are now Iran and Iraq. The highlight of the Mesopotamian Gallery is a massive 16-foot-tall sculpture of a winged bull with a human head, which once stood in the palace of Assyrian king Sargon II. The gallery also contains some of the earliest man-made tools ever excavated, along with many other pieces that have become one-of-a-kind since the destruction and looting of the National Museum in Baghdad in 2003. Artifacts from Persia, ancient Palestine, Israel, Anatolia, and Nubia fill other galleries.

The small but eclectic gift shop, called the Suq, stocks many unique items, including reproductions of pieces in the museum's collection.

1155 E. 58th St. (at University Ave.). ℂ **773/702-9514.** http://oi.uchicago.edu. Free admission; suggested donation $5 adults, $2 children. Tues–Sat 10am–6pm (Wed until 8:30pm); Sun noon–6pm. Bus: 6 or Metra Electric train to 57th St. and Lake Park Ave.

**Smart Museum of Art** The University of Chicago's fine-arts museum looks rather modest, but packs a lot of talent into a compact space. Its permanent collection of more than 7,000 paintings and sculptures spans Western and Eastern civilizations, ranging from classical antiquity to the present day. Bona fide treasures include ancient Greek vases, Chinese bronzes, and Old Master paintings; Frank Lloyd Wright furniture; Tiffany glass; sculptures by Degas, Matisse, and Rodin; and 20th-century paintings and sculptures by Mark Rothko, Arthur Dove, Diego Rivera, Henry Moore, and Chicago sculptor Richard Hunt. Built in 1974, the contemporary building doesn't really fit in with the campus's Gothic architecture, but its sculpture garden and outdoor seating area make a nice place for quiet contemplation. The museum also has a gift shop and cafe. Allow 1 hour.

5550 S. Greenwood Ave. (at E. 55th St.). ℂ **773/702-0200.** http://smartmuseum. uchicago.edu. Free admission. Tues–Fri 10am–4pm (Thurs until 8pm); Sat–Sun 11am–5pm. Closed major holidays. Bus: 6.

## SOMETIMES FREE

We of the free and dirt cheap bent know how to take advantage of museum free days. What are museum free days? Well, most of these institutions, which have a regular admission fee that can run over $20 (like the Shedd Aquarium), have 1 day per month, per week, whenever, on which you can enter gratis (or for a "suggested donation"). So mark your calendars for the money-saving times, and check out the box on p. 130, which lists the institutions and their free days.

**The Adler Planetarium** The building may be historic, but some of the attractions here will captivate the most jaded video-game addict.

## mp3 Audiotours—for Free

Scanning the websites of museums and other attractions before you visit can enhance your trip when you get here. At the **Field Museum of Natural History** website (www.fieldmuseum.org), you can download an mp3 audiotour of the museum's permanent collection; you can also print out a Family Adventure Tour, which sends kids on a scavenger hunt throughout the museum. The **Millennium Park** mp3 audiotour (available at www.millenniumpark.org) includes interviews with the artists who created the park's eye-catching artwork. And if you're intimidated by the massive size of the **Museum of Science and Industry,** check out the website's Personal Planner, which will put together a customized itinerary based your family's interests (www.msichicago.org).

The first planetarium in the Western Hemisphere was founded by Sears, Roebuck and Co. executive Max Adler, who imported a Zeiss projector from Germany in 1930.

The good news for present-day visitors is that the planetarium has been updated since then. Your first stop should be the modern Sky Pavilion, where the don't-miss experience is the StarRider Theater. Settle down under the massive dome, and you'll take a half-hour interactive virtual-reality trip through the Milky Way and into deep space, featuring a computer-generated 3-D-graphics projection system and controls in the armrest of each seat. Six high-resolution video projectors form a seamless image above your head—you'll feel as if you're literally floating in space. If you're looking for more entertainment, the Sky Theater shows movies with an astronomical bent. Recent shows have included *Secrets of Saturn* and *Mars Now!,* both of which are updated as new discoveries are made.

The planetarium's exhibition galleries feature a variety of displays and interactive activities. If you're only going to see one exhibit (and have kids in tow), check out Shoot for the Moon, an exhibit on lunar exploration that's full of interactive stations (it also showcases the personal collection of astronaut Jim Lovell, captain of the infamous Apollo 13 mission, who now lives in the Chicago suburbs). Other

# Gangster Landmarks—Free for the Viewing

Chicago infamously was home base for many of the most notorious criminals of the 1920s and 1930s, and there's no sign of interest abating, with a movie about John Dillinger's life making headlines as this book is being written. You can pay for a bus tour that will take you to some of the notorious sites of crimes and hideouts, but you can also check out many of them on foot.

- **The Alley Where Dillinger Was Killed:** Notorious bank robber John Dillinger was ambushed by the FBI, shot, and killed in the alley outside of the Biograph Theater, 2433 N. Lincoln, after watching a movie on July 22, 1934. Today, the building is Victory Gardens Theater.

- **St. Valentine's Day Massacre:** Seven men from the Moran gang were killed by Al Capone's men in a garage at 2122 N. Clark St. on Feb. 14, 1929. The former S-M-C Cartage Company garage has since been torn down, and is now a fenced-in lawn adjacent to a nursing home.

exhibits include Bringing the Heavens to Earth, which traces the ways different cultures have tried to make sense of astronomical phenomena, and From the Night Sky to the Big Bang, which includes artifacts from the planetarium's extensive collection of astronomical instruments (although suitable for older children, these can get a bit boring for little ones unless they're real astronomy nuts).

The museum's cafe provides views of the lakefront and skyline. On the first Friday evening of the month, visitors can view dramatic close-ups of the moon, the planets, and distant galaxies through a closed-circuit monitor connected to the planetarium's Doane Observatory telescope.

Allow 2 hours, more if you want to see more than one show.

1300 S. Lake Shore Dr. ⓒ **312/922-STAR** (7827). www.adlerplanetarium.org. Admission $10 adults, $8 seniors, $6 children 4–17, free for children 3 and under; admission including 1 show and audiotour $19 adults, $17 seniors, $15 children. Free admission Mon–Tues Oct–Nov and Jan–Feb. Memorial Day to Labor Day daily 9:30am–6pm;

early Sept to late May daily 9:30am–4:30pm; 1st Fri of every month until 10pm. Star-Rider Theater and Sky Shows run throughout the day; call main number for current times. Bus: 12 or 146.

★ **The Art Institute of Chicago**    You can't—and shouldn't—miss the Art Institute, particularly since the opening of the fantastic Modern Wing in May 2009. (You really have no excuse, since the museum is conveniently located right on Michigan Ave. in the heart of downtown.) I have to say up front, though, that admission is steep at $18. In the free and dirt cheap spirit, try to take advantage of the free Thursday evenings (5–9pm) and the fact that the museum charges no admission for the entire month of February.

No matter what medium or century interests you, the Art Institute has something in its collection to fit the bill. Japanese *ukiyo-e* prints, ancient Egyptian bronzes, Greek vases, 19th-century British photography, masterpieces by most of the greatest names in 20th-century sculpture, and modern American textiles are just some of the works on display, but for a general overview of the museum's collection, take the free "Highlights of the Art Institute" tour, offered at 2pm on Tuesday, Saturday, and Sunday.

If time is limited, head straight to the museum's renowned anthology of Impressionist art, which includes one of the world's largest collections of Monet paintings; this is one of the most popular areas of the museum, so arriving early pays off. Among the treasures, you'll find Seurat's pointillist masterpiece *Sunday Afternoon on the Island of La Grande Jatte.* The galleries of European and American contemporary art include paintings, sculptures, and mixed-media works by Pablo Picasso, Henri Matisse, Salvador Dalí, Willem de Kooning, Jackson Pollock, and Andy Warhol. Visitors are sometimes surprised when they discover many of the icons that hang here. (Grant Wood's *American Gothic* and Edward Hopper's *Nighthawks* are two that often get double takes.)

Other recommended exhibits are the collection of delicate mid–19th-century glass paperweights in the famous Arthur Rubloff collection, and the great hall of European arms and armor dating from the 15th to 19th centuries. Composed of more than 1,500 objects, including armor, horse equipment, swords and daggers, polearms, and maces, the collection is one of the most important assemblages of its kind in the country. (If you do head down here, don't miss Marc Chagall's stunning stained-glass windows at the end of the gallery.)

Designed by Renzo Piano, the Modern Wing houses the museum's world-renowned collections of modern European painting and sculpture, contemporary art, architecture, design, and photography. It's a worthwhile splurge if you love contemporary art. You can check out works by Roy Lichtenstein, Jackson Pollack, Andy Warhol, and Pablo Picasso. Stop for coffee at the second-floor lounge area. (There's also a bistro, Terzo Piano, part of the deck overlooking the Pritzker Pavillion.) While you're there, don't miss traversing the spectacular pedestrian bridge that connects the Modern Wing to Millennium Park. (You can check out the bridge for free if you're hanging out in Millennium Park, too.)

**FREE** Good news for families: Families can enter the new Ryan Education Center without paying museum admission. The kids' area takes up the entire first floor of the East pavilion of the Modern Wing, and includes studio space, classrooms, a library, teacher resources, and galleries.

The museum has a cafeteria and an elegant full-service restaurant, a picturesque courtyard cafe (open June–Sept), and a large shop. It offers a busy schedule of lectures, films, and other special presentations, as well as guided tours. The museum also has a research library. Allow 3 hours.

111 S. Michigan Ave. (at Adams St.). ✆ **312/443-3600.** www.artic.edu. Admission $18 adults, $12 seniors and students with ID, free for children 14 and under. Chicago residents receive a $2 discount with proof of residency. Additional cost for special exhibitions. Free admission Thurs 5–8pm. Mon–Fri 10:30am–5pm (Thurs until 8pm; until 9pm Thurs–Fri Memorial Day to Labor Day); Sat–Sun 10am–5pm. Closed Jan 1, Thanksgiving, and Dec 25. Bus: 3, 4, 60, 145, 147, or 151. Subway/El: Green, Brown, Purple, or Orange line to Adams; or Red Line to Monroe/State or Jackson/State.

**Charnley-Persky House Museum**   A Gold Coast mansion designed by Frank Lloyd Wright and Louis Sullivan in 1891, this is a worthwhile stop and one of the few homes open for tours in this old-money neighborhood. Free 45-minute tours of the interior are given on Wednesday at noon. A 90-minute tour of the home and the surrounding neighborhood is offered Saturdays at 10am year-round ($15); an additional tour is offered at 1pm from April through November ($15). FINE PRINT Tours are limited to 15 people and are available on a first come, first served basis.

1365 N. Astor St. ✆ **312/915-0105** or 312/573-1365; www.charnleyhouse.org. Subway/El: Red Line to Clark/Division, walk two blocks north on Clark, turn right onto Schiller and walk three blocks to Astor Street.

# Do-It-Yourself Sightseeing Tours

An inexpensive and relaxing way to tour the city is by hopping aboard one of Chicago's El trains or buses. Do-it-yourselfers can take their own tour for the cost of subway or bus fare—$2, plus 25¢ for a transfer (good for a return trip if you use it within 2 hr.). Here are some of the city's best sightseeing routes:

- **The El: Brown Line** (trip duration 20 min.; daily). Ride from the Loop to Belmont Station. You get a bird's-eye view of downtown, gentrified loft districts, and a number of historic neighborhoods. Start at the big El station at Clark and Lake streets and get on the northbound train.

- **No. 151 Sheridan Bus** (trip duration 30 min.; daily). Pick up the 151 downtown on Michigan Avenue (the bus stops every 2 blocks on the avenue) and ride it north to Belmont. You cover Lake Shore Drive and Lincoln Park. If you take the bus south, you travel State Street and wind up at Union Station.

- **No. 146 Marine–Michigan Bus** (trip duration 20 min.; daily). This express bus allows you to take in North Michigan Avenue, State Street, and the Museum Campus. Pick up the bus on Sheridan and Diversey going south. (You can also pick up the 146 along Michigan Ave., although it has fewer stops than the 151.) You see the Harold Washington Library, the Art Institute of Chicago, the Chicago Cultural Center, and the landmark Water Tower.

- **No. 10 Museum of Science and Industry Bus** (trip duration 35 min.; weekends year-round, daily in summer and winter holiday season). From North Michigan Avenue at the Water Tower (the stop is in front of Borders on Michigan Ave. across from Water Tower Place), ride south to the Museum Campus. You see Grant Park, the Art Institute of Chicago, the University of Chicago, and Chinatown.

**Chicago Children's Museum on Navy Pier**    Located on tourist-filled Navy Pier, this museum is one of the most popular family attractions in the city. The building has areas especially for preschoolers as well as for children up to age 10, and several permanent exhibits allow

## Circle the Globe, for Free

The impressive Gothic **Tribune Tower,** just north of the Chicago River on the east side of Michigan Avenue, is home to one of the country's media giants and the *Chicago Tribune* newspaper. It's also notable for an array of architectural fragments jutting out from the exterior—kids love getting hands-on here by touching stones from all over the world. The newspaper's notoriously despotic publisher, Robert R. McCormick, started the collection shortly after the building's completion in 1925, gathering pieces during his world travels. *Tribune* correspondents then began supplying building fragments that they acquired on assignment. Each one now bears the name of the structure and country whence it came. There are 138 pieces in all, including chunks and shards from the Great Wall of China, the Taj Mahal, the White House, the Arc de Triomphe, the Berlin Wall, the Roman Colosseum, London's Houses of Parliament, the Great Pyramid of Cheops in Giza, Egypt, and the original tomb of Abraham Lincoln in Springfield, Illinois.

kids a maximum of hands-on fun. Dinosaur Expedition re-creates an expedition to the Sahara, allowing kids to experience camp life, conduct scientific research, and dig for the bones of *Suchomimus,* a Saharan dinosaur discovered by Chicago paleontologist Paul Sereno (a full-scale model stands nearby). There's also a three-level schooner that children can board for a little climbing, from the crow's nest to the gangplank; PlayMaze, a toddler-scale cityscape with everything from a gas station to a city bus that children under 5 can touch and explore; and an arts-and-crafts area where visitors can create original artwork to take home. Allow 2 to 3 hours.

Navy Pier, 700 E. Grand Ave. ✆ **312/527-1000.** www.chichildrensmuseum.org. Admission $8 adults and children, $7 seniors. Free admission Thurs 5–8pm. Mon–Fri 10am–5pm (Thurs until 8pm); Sat 10am–8pm; Sun 10am–5pm. Closed Thanksgiving and Dec 25. Bus: 29, 65, or 66. Subway/El: Red Line to Grand; transfer to city bus or Navy Pier's free trolley bus.

**Chicago History Museum**  The Chicago History Museum at the southwestern tip of Lincoln Park is one of the city's oldest cultural institutions (founded in 1856), but it's reinvented itself for the 21st century. The main, must-see exhibit is Chicago: Crossroads of America, which fills the museum's second floor. A survey of the city's history—from its founding as a frontier trading post to the riots at the 1968 Democratic Convention—it's filled with photos, artifacts, and newsreels that make the past come alive; surrounding galleries track the development of local sports teams, architecture, music, and art. Although the exhibit is geared toward families with older children (you can even download an mp3 audio tour for teenagers from the museum's website), little ones love the re-creation of an 1890s El station, where they can run inside the city's first elevated train. Another museum highlight is the hall of dioramas that re-create scenes from Chicago's past. Although they've been around for decades (and are decidedly low-tech), they're a fun way to trace the city's progression from a few small cabins to the grand World's Columbian Exposition of 1893. The Costume and Textile Gallery showcases pieces from the museum's renowned collection of historic clothing; recent exhibitions included couture gowns by French designer Christian Dior and a survey of American quilts. The Children's Gallery on the ground floor has interactive exhibits for kids, including a giant table where you can experience the "Smells of Chicago" (my personal favorite).

The History Museum also presents a wide range of lectures, seminars, and tours, including walking tours of the surrounding neighborhood; check the museum's website for details, as the schedules change frequently. Allow 1 to 2 hours.

1601 N. Clark St. (at North Ave.). © **312/642-4600.** www.chicagohistory.org. Admission $12 adults, $10 seniors and students, free for children 12 and under. Free admission Mon. Mon–Sat 9:30am–4:30pm (until 8pm Thurs); Sun noon–5pm. Research center Tues–Thurs 1–4pm; Fri 10am–4:30pm. Bus: 11, 22, 36, 72, 151, or 156.

**DuSable Museum of African American History**   The DuSable Museum is a repository of the history, art, and artifacts pertaining to the African-American experience and culture. Named for Chicago's first permanent settler, Jean Baptiste Point du Sable, a French-Canadian of Haitian descent, it is admirable not so much for its collections and exhibits as for the inspiring story behind its existence. Founded in 1961 with a $10 charter and minimal capital, the museum began in the home of Dr. Margaret Burroughs, an art teacher at the city's DuSable High School. In 1973, as a result of a community-based campaign, the museum took up residence in its present building (a former parks administration facility and police lockup) on the eastern edge of Washington Park. With no major endowment to speak of, the

## Loop Tour Train

For a distinctive downtown view at an unbeatable price—free!—hop aboard the **Loop Tour Train,** a special elevated train that runs on Saturday from May through September. Docents from the Chicago Architecture Foundation point out notable buildings along the way and explain how the El shaped the city. Riders must pick up tickets at the Chicago Cultural Center, 77 E. Randolph St., beginning at 10am on the day of the tour; tours leave at 11am, 11:40am, 12:20pm, and 1pm from the Randolph/Wabash El station. For more information, call ℂ **312/744-2400,** or visit www.cityofchicago.org/exploringchicago.

DuSable Museum has managed to accumulate a respectable collection of more than 13,000 artifacts, books, photographs, art objects, and memorabilia. Its collection of paintings, drawings, and sculpture by African-American and African artists is excellent.

In 1993, the DuSable Museum added a 25,000-square-foot wing named in honor of the city's first and only African-American mayor, Harold Washington. The permanent exhibit on Washington contains memorabilia and personal effects, and surveys important episodes in his political career. The museum also has a gift shop, a research library, and an extensive program of community-related events, such as a jazz and blues music series, poetry readings, film screenings, and other cultural events, all presented in a 466-seat auditorium. Allow 1 to 2 hours.

740 E. 56th Place. ℂ **773/947-0600.** www.dusablemuseum.org. Admission $3 adults, $2 students and seniors, $1 children 6–13, free for children 5 and under. Free admission Sun. Tues–Sat 10am–5pm; Sun noon–5pm. Closed major holidays. Bus: 6 or Metra Electric train to 57th St. and Lake Park Ave., and then a short cab ride.

**Museum of Contemporary Art**    Although the MCA is one of the largest contemporary art museums in the country, theaters and hallways seem to take up much of the space, so seeing the actual art won't take you long. The museum exhibits emphasize experimentation in a variety of media, including painting, sculpture, photography, video and film, dance, music, and performance. The gloomy, imposing building, designed by Berlin's Josef Paul Kleihues, is a bit out of place between the lake and the historic Water Tower, but the interior spaces are more vibrant, with a sun-drenched two-story central corridor, elliptical staircases, and three floors of exhibition space. The MCA has tried to raise its national profile to the level of New York's Museum of Modern Art by booking major touring retrospectives of working artists such as Cindy Sherman and Chuck Close.

You can see the MCA's highlights in about an hour, although art lovers will want more time to wander (especially if a high-profile exhibit is in town). Your first stop should be the handsome barrel-vaulted galleries on the top floor, dedicated to pieces from the permanent collection. Visitors who'd like a little guidance with making sense of the rather challenging works can rent an audio tour or take a free tour (1 and 6pm Tues; 1pm Wed–Fri; noon, 1, 2, and 3pm Sat–Sun). In addition to a range of special activities and educational programming, including films, performances, and a lecture series in a 300-seat theater, the museum features Puck's at the MCA, a cafe operated by Wolfgang Puck of Spago restaurant fame, with seating that overlooks a 1-acre terraced sculpture garden. The store, with one-of-a-kind gift items, is worth a stop even if you don't make it into the museum. The museum's First-Friday program, featuring after-hours performances, live music, and food and drink, takes place on the first Friday of every month. Allow 1 to 2 hours.

220 E. Chicago Ave. (1 block east of Michigan Ave.). © **312/280-2660.** www.mca chicago.org. Admission $10 adults, $6 seniors and students with ID, free for children 12 and under. Free admission Tues. Tues 10am–8pm; Wed–Sun 10am–5pm. Closed Jan 1, Thanksgiving, and Dec 25. Bus: 3, 10, 66, 145, 146, or 151. Subway/El: Red Line to Chicago/State.

★ **Museum of Science and Industry**    This is by no means a dirt cheap museum, but if you're going to visit one museum in Chicago, MSI will give you a lot of bang for your buck. Even if you don't plan on spending the day in Hyde Park, you'll pass through the neighborhood on your way to one of Chicago's most popular tourist attractions. The massive Museum of Science and Industry is the granddaddy of interactive museums, with some 2,000 exhibits. Schedule at least 3 hours here; a comprehensive visit can take all day, especially if you catch an OMNIMAX movie.

While the museum is constantly adding new displays to cover the latest scientific breakthroughs, you shouldn't miss certain tried-and-true exhibits that have been here for years and epitomize the museum for Chicagoans. The U-505, a German submarine that was captured in 1944 and arrived at the museum 10 years later, brings home the claustrophobic reality of underwater naval life. The sub is displayed in a dramatic indoor arena with exhibits and newsreel footage that put the U-boat in historical context. FINE PRINT A guided tour of the sub's interior costs $5 extra, but the exhibit is worth visiting even if you don't go inside. The full-scale Coal Mine, which dates back to 1934, incorporates modern mining techniques into the exhibit—but the best part is the simulated trip down into a dark, mysterious mine. Get to these exhibits quickly after the museum opens because they attract amusement-park-length lines during the day.

If you love planes, trains, and automobiles, don't miss All Aboard the Silver Streak, a refurbished Burlington Pioneer Zephyr train with onboard interactive exhibits; the massive model-train exhibit that makes up The Great Train Story; or Take Flight, an aviation exhibit featuring a full-size 727 airplane that revs up its engines and replays the voice recordings from a San Francisco–Chicago flight periodically throughout the day. Networld, which offers a flashy immersion in the Internet (with plenty of interactive screens), will entrance computer addicts. More low-tech—but fun for kids—are The Farm (where children can sit at the wheel of a giant combine) and the chick hatchery inside the exhibit Genetics: Decoding Life, where you can watch as tiny newborn chicks poke their way out of eggs. Enterprise immerses minicapitalists in the goings-on of a virtual company and includes an entire automated toy-making assembly line. If you have really little ones (under age 5), head for the Idea Factory, which is filled with hands-on play equipment (admission is limited to a set number of kids, so pick up a free timed ticket in advance).

I hate to indulge in gender stereotypes, but girls (myself included) love Colleen Moore's Fairy Castle, a lavishly decorated miniature palace filled with priceless treasures (yes, those are real diamonds and pearls in the chandeliers). The castle is hidden on the lower level. Also tucked away in an inconspicuous spot—along the Blue stairwell between the main floor and the balcony—are the Human Body Slices, actual slivers of human cadavers that are guaranteed to impress teenagers in search of something truly gross.

A major addition to the museum is the Henry Crown Space Center, which documents the story of space exploration in copious detail, highlighted by a simulated space-shuttle experience through sight and sound at the center's five-story OMNIMAX Theater. The theater offers double features on the weekends; call for show times.

When you've worked up an appetite, you can visit the museum's large food court or the old-fashioned ice-cream parlor; there's also an excellent gift shop.

Although it's quite a distance from the rest of Chicago's tourist attractions, the museum is easy enough to reach without a car; your best options are the no. 6 Jeffrey Express bus and the Metra Electric train from downtown (the no. 10 bus runs from downtown to the museum's front entrance during the summer).

57th St. and Lake Shore Dr. ✆ **800/468-6674** outside the Chicago area, 773/684-1414, or TTY 773/684-3323. www.msichicago.org. Admission to museum only $11 adults, $9 seniors, $7 children 3–11, free for children 2 and under. Free admission Mon–Tues mid-Sept through Nov and Jan–Feb. Combination museum and OMNI-MAX Theater $17 adults, $15 seniors, $12 children 3–11, free for children 2 and under on an adult's lap. Memorial Day to Labor Day Mon–Sat 9:30am–5:30pm, Sun 11am–5:30pm; early Sept to late May Mon–Sat 9:30am–4pm, Sun 11am–4pm. Closed Dec 25. Bus: 6 or Metra Electric train to 57th St. and Lake Park Ave.

**Peggy Notebaert Nature Museum**    Built into the rise of an ancient sand dune—once the shoreline of Lake Michigan—this museum bills itself as "an environmental museum for the 21st century." While that sounds pretty dull, most of the exhibits are very hands-on, making this a good stop for active kids (most exhibits are designed for children rather than adults).

Shaded by huge cottonwoods and maples, the sand-colored exterior, with its horizontal lines composed of interlocking trapezoids, resembles a sand dune. Rooftop-level walkways give strollers a view of birds and other urban wildlife below, and paths wind through gardens planted with native Midwestern wildflowers and grasses. Inside, large windows create a dialogue between the outdoor environment and the indoor exhibits designed to illuminate the outdoors. My favorite exhibit by far is the Butterfly Haven, a greenhouse habitat where about 25 Midwestern species of butterflies and moths carry on their complex life cycles (wander through as a riot of color flutters all around you). If you're traveling with little ones, I'd also recommend the Extreme Green House, a bungalow where kids can play while learning about environmentally friendly habits, and RiverWorks, a water play exhibit that gives children an excuse to splash around

# If It's Free, It's for Me!

To beef up attendance and give free and dirt cheap travelers a break, many of Chicago's public attractions and museums are open free to the public 1 day of the week (as mentioned earlier). Use the following list to plan your week around the museums' free-day schedules, then turn to the individual attraction listings earlier for more information on each museum. A word of caution: Museums change their free days constantly. If you're planning your itinerary around a certain institution's free day, it's well worth a call in advance to confirm.

**Sundays**

● DuSable Museum of African American History (p. 125)

**Mondays**

● Chicago History Museum (p. 124)

**Tuesdays**

● Museum of Contemporary Art (p. 126)

● Spertus Museum, 10 a.m.-noon (below)

● Swedish American Museum Center, second Tuesday of each month (p. 131)

while building dams and maneuvering boats along a mini river. Allow 1 to 2 hours.

2430 N. Cannon Drive (Fullerton Ave. and Cannon Dr.). ℭ **773/755-5100.** www.chias. org. Admission $7 adults, $5 seniors and students, $4 children 3–12, free for children 2 and under. Free admission Thurs. Mon–Fri 9am–4:30pm; Sat–Sun 10am–5pm. Closed Jan 1, Thanksgiving, and Dec 25. Bus: 151 or 156. Free trolley service from area CTA stations and parking garages Sat–Sun and holidays 10am–6pm Memorial Day to Labor Day. Visit the museum website for route information and schedule.

**Spertus Museum**   The Spertus Museum, an extension of the Spertus Institute of Jewish Studies, showcases intricately crafted and historic Jewish ceremonial objects, textiles, coins, paintings, and sculpture, tracing 5,000 years of Jewish heritage. In 2007, the museum moved to a new, contemporary building, with an angled glass facade that marks a welcome change from the solemn, solid structures surrounding it.

**Wednesdays**
- Charnley-Persky House Museum (p. 122)
- Clarke House Museum (p. 133)
- Glessner House Museum (p. 132)

**Thursdays**
- The Art Institute of Chicago, 5 to 8pm (p. 121)
- Chicago Children's Museum on Navy Pier, 5 to 8pm (p. 123)
- Peggy Notebaert Nature Museum (p. 129)
- Spertus Museum, 3 to 7pm (p. 130)

**Dates Vary (check websites or call)**
- The Adler Planetarium (p. 118)
- Field Museum of Natural History (p. 140)
- Museum of Science and Industry (p. 127)

Highlights of the building include a 400-seat theater for lectures and films, an interactive exhibit space designed for kids, and a kosher cafe operated by Chef Wolfgang Puck's catering company. Researchers can register to visit the Asher Library or study the Chicago Jewish Archives collection. The museum shop carries a large selection of art, books, music, videos, and contemporary and traditional Jewish ceremonial gifts. Allow 1 hour.

610 S. Michigan Ave. ② **312/322-1747.** www.spertus.edu/museum. Admission $7 adults; $5 seniors, students, and children. Free admission Tues 10am–noon and Thurs 3–7pm. Sun–Wed 10am–6pm; Thurs 10am–7pm; Fri 10am–3pm. Bus: 3, 4, 6, 145, 147, or 151. Subway/El: Red Line to Harrison; or Brown, Purple, Orange, or Green line to Adams. Validated parking in nearby lots.

★ **Swedish American Museum Center & Children's Museum of Immigration**   Chicago parents recommend a visit to this storefront museum, which chronicles the Swedish immigrant contribution to American life. The museum is a hub of activity, with cultural lectures, concerts, and classes and folk dancing geared to Swedish Americans, some of whom still live in the surrounding Andersonville neighborhood. The Children's Museum of Immigration is located on the third floor, where Swedish crafts demonstrations and classes, as well as language classes, are offered. Geared toward kindergarteners through sixth graders, the museum lets kids experience the journey from the Old World. They can step inside an authentic Swedish farmhouse and do chores on the farm, board a steamship for America, and begin a new life in a log cabin.

The permanent exhibits on display draw on a small collection of art and artifacts dating to the mass immigration of Swedes to Chicago 2 centuries ago. Temporary exhibitions (usually Swedish folk art) are mounted four times a year. There's also a nice gift shop that sells Orrefors glassware; books on Swedish folk art, decorating, and cooking; children's toys; and holiday knickknacks. Strolling down this stretch of Clark Street, where Swedish bakeries and gourmet-food stores are interspersed with an attractive mix of restaurants, bars, cafes, and theater companies, is the best reason for stopping in here.

5211 N. Clark St. (near Foster Ave.). © **773/728-8111.** www.samac.org. Admission $4 adults, $3 seniors and students, $10 family rate, free for children under 1. Free 2nd Tues of the month. Tues–Fri 10am–4pm; Sat–Sun 11am–4pm. Bus: 22. Subway/El: Red Line to Bryn Mawr, then walk several blocks west to Clark.

## DIRT CHEAP (OR THEREABOUTS)

★ **Chicago Water Taxi** Water taxis cruise the river daily April through October between a dock at Michigan Avenue, LaSalle/Clark Street, Madison Street, or Chinatown. The ride, which costs $2 each way, takes about 10 minutes and is popular with both visitors and commuters. An all-day pass is $4. The service operates about every 20 minutes from 6:30am to 7pm.

**Glessner House Museum** Prairie Avenue, south of the Loop, was the city's first "Gold Coast," and its most famous address is **Glessner House,** a must-see for anyone interested in architectural history. The only surviving Chicago building designed by Boston architect Henry Hobson Richardson, the 1886 structure represented a dramatic shift from traditional Victorian architecture (and inspired a young Frank Lloyd Wright).

The imposing granite exterior gives the home a forbidding air. (Railway magnate George Pullman, who lived nearby, complained, "I do not know what I have ever done to have that thing staring me in the face every time I go out my door.") But step inside, and the home turns out to be a welcoming, cozy retreat, filled with Arts and Crafts furnishings.

Visits to Glessner House are by guided tour only (they can also be combined with tours of the nearby Clarke House Museum, a Greek Revival home that's the oldest surviving house in the city). Tours begin at 1, 2, and 3pm Wednesday through Sunday (except major holidays); tours of the Clarke House are given at noon, 1, and 2pm. Tours are first-come, first-served, with no advance reservations except for groups of 10 or more.

1800 S. Prairie Ave. © **312/326-1480.** www.glessnerhouse.org. Admission $10 adults, $9 students and seniors, $5 children 5–12, free for children 4 and under; combination tickets for tours of the Glessner House and Clarke House $15 adults, $12 student and seniors, $8 children. Bus: 1, 3, or 4 from Michigan Ave. at Jackson Blvd. (get off at 18th St.).

**Hemingway Museum**    Frank Lloyd Wright might be Oak Park's favorite son, but the town's most famous native son is Ernest Hemingway. Hemingway had no great love for Oak Park; he moved away right after high school and later referred to his hometown as a place of "wide lawns and narrow minds." But that hasn't stopped Oak Park from laying claim to the great American writer. A portion of the ground floor of this former church, now the Oak Park Arts Center, holds a small but interesting display of Hemingway memorabilia. A 6-minute video sheds considerable light on Hemingway's time in Oak Park, where he spent the first 18 years of his life, and covers his high school experiences particularly well.

The Ernest Hemingway Birthplace Home is 2 blocks north, at 339 N. Oak Park Ave. The lovely Queen Anne house—complete with wraparound porch and turret—was the home of Hemingway's maternal grandparents, and it's where the writer was born on July 21, 1899. Its connection to Hemingway is actually pretty tenuous—he spent most of his boyhood and high school years at 600 N. Kenilworth Ave., a few blocks away (that house is still privately owned)—but the birthplace has been carefully restored to replicate its appearance at the end of the 19th century, making this an appealing stop for fans of historic house tours (whether they're Hemingway fans or not). The hours are the same as the Hemingway Museum's. Allow 1 hour.

200 N. Oak Park Ave. © **708/848-2222.** www.ehfop.org. Combined admission to Hemingway Museum and Ernest Hemingway Birthplace Home $7 adults, $5.50 seniors and children 5–12, free for children 4 and under. Sun–Fri 1–5pm; Sat 10am–5pm. Subway/El: Green Line to Oak Park.

**The International Museum of Surgical Science**    Although I lived three doors down from this museum for 7 years, I was afraid to set foot inside—maybe it was the real skeletons they put in the windows every Halloween that scared me off? Run by the International College of Surgeons, the museum is housed in a historic 1917 Gold Coast mansion designed by the noted architect Howard Van Doren Shaw, who modeled it after Le Petit Trianon at Versailles. Displayed throughout its four floors are surgical instruments, paintings, and sculpture depicting the history of surgery and healing practices in Eastern and Western civilizations. The exhibits are old-fashioned (no interactive computer displays here!) but that's part of the museum's odd appeal.

You'll look at your doctor in a whole new way after viewing the trepanned skulls excavated from an ancient tomb in Peru. The accompanying tools were used to bore holes in patients' skulls, a horrific practice thought to release the evil spirits causing their illnesses. (Some skulls show signs of new bone growth, meaning that some lucky headache-sufferers actually survived this low-tech surgery.) There are also battlefield amputation kits, a working iron-lung machine in the polio exhibit, and oddities such as a stethoscope designed to be transported inside a top hat. Other attractions include an apothecary shop and dentist's office (ca. 1900), re-created in a historical street exhibit, and the hyperbolically christened "Hall of Immortals," a sculpture gallery depicting 12 historic figures in medicine, from Hippocrates to Madame Curie. Allow 1 hour.

1524 N. Lake Shore Dr. (btw. Burton Place and North Ave.). © **312/642-6502.** www.imss.org. Admission $8 adults, $4 seniors and students. Tues–Sat 10am–4pm; May–Sept also Sun 10am–4pm. Bus: 151.

**Madlener House**    This Gold Coast mansion was designed as a private residence by Richard E. Schmidt in 1902. A National Historic Landmark, the mansion foreshadowed the Art Deco style that would not emerge in Chicago for another 20 years. The brick-and-limestone structure's clean lines and its doorways ornamented with delicate bronze grillwork offer hints of both the Prairie and Chicago schools of design. It's currently home to the Graham Foundation for Advanced Studies in the Fine Arts, which has installed a collection of fragments from famous Chicago buildings in the courtyard. It's a must for architecture buffs and historic-home fans. The Society of Architectural Historians offers a 90-minute guided tour on Saturdays, in conjunction with a tour of local historic homes. Price is $10 for adults, $5 for seniors and kids. Call ahead to book (℃ **312/573-1365**).

4 W. Burton Place. ℃ **312/787-4071.** www.grahamfoundation.org. Tours run by Society of Architectural Historians; for tour information, see www.sah.org, or call ℃ 312/573-1365. Tours $10 adults, $5 seniors and kids. Bus: 151 to Burton Place, walk west.

★ **Morton Arboretum** Should your visit to Chicago coincide with Arbor Day, here's the place to celebrate: More than 3,000 kinds of trees, shrubs, and vines grow on the 1,700-acre site in west suburban Lisle. The place has been spruced up lately (sorry for the pun), with improvements to many of the facility's buildings. Special areas include the Illinois Tree Trails' woodlands, meadows, and marshes; an area with sugar maples (colorful in the fall); a crabapple orchard (splendid when the trees are in full bloom); and a prairie with tall grasses and flowers that blossom in summer and fall. The arboretum also features trees from other countries. Most of the 13 miles of trails are covered with wood chips, so they are not stroller-friendly. If your kids are young, it's best to see the landscape by car along 11 miles of one-way roads or take a bus tour. One-hour tram tours depart at noon and 1:15pm Wednesday, Saturday, and Sunday from May to October. Cost for the tram is $4 per seat, and $3 for children ages 3 to 12. Stop by the visitor center for additional information. Light meals are available in the Ginkgo Restaurant, sandwiches and soups are served in the coffee shop, and there's a picnic area near a small lake.

4100 Illinois Hwy. 53 (at I-88, the East-West Tollway), Lisle. ℃ **630/719-2400.** www.mortonarb.org. Admission $9 adults, $8 seniors, $6 children 3–12, free for children 2 and under. Reduced admission fees on Wed. Open 365 days a year, 7am–7pm or sunset, whichever is earlier. Visitor center daily Nov–Feb 8am–5pm, Mar–Oct 8am–6pm; Gingko Tree restaurant daily 11am–3pm; coffee shop daily 9am–5pm. Free parking. Subway/El: Metra train stops at Lisle, 1¹⁄₂ miles away; cabs available.

★ **Oak Park** I've covered the free walking tours of the neighborhood surrounding the Frank Lloyd Wright Home and Studio as a no-cost way to see this lovely leafy suburb just west of Chicago. But, if you're an architecture aficionado, you'll find it worthwhile to spend a few bucks to add in two more elements to your tour of Oak Park: The Frank Lloyd Wright Home and Studio Tour and the Unity Temple Tour (and, if you're so inclined, you might also choose to drop some bucks on a guided walking tour to view the exteriors of homes throughout the neighborhood that were built by the architect, as opposed to doing it yourself).

Frank Lloyd Wright Home and Studio is ground zero for Wright fans. Start here, where Wright spent the first 20 years of his career. During that time, this remarkable complex served first and foremost as the sanctuary where he designed and executed more than 130 of an extraordinary output of 430 completed buildings. The home began as a simple shingled cottage that the 22-year-old Wright built for his bride in 1889, but it became a living laboratory for his revolutionary reinvention of interior spaces. Wright remodeled the house constantly until 1911, when he moved out permanently (in 1909, he left his wife and six children and went off to Europe with the wife of one of his clients). During Wright's fertile early period, the house was Wright's showcase, but it also embraces many idiosyncratic features molded to his own needs rather than those of a client. With many add-ons—including a barrel-vaulted children's playroom and a studio with an octagonal balcony suspended by chains—the place has a certain whimsy that others might have found less livable. This was not an architect's masterpiece but rather the master's home, and visitors can savor every room in it for the view it reflects of the workings of a remarkable mind.

Tours cannot be booked in advance by phone, but a select number of tickets for each day can be reserved online. Allow 1 hour for the tour, more time if you want to browse in the bookshop.

951 Chicago Ave. ⓒ **708/848-1976.** www.wrightplus.org. Admission $12 adults, $10 seniors and students 11–18, $5 children 4–10; combined admission for Home and Studio tour and guided or self-guided historic district tour $20 adults, $10 seniors and students 11–18, $5 children 4–10. Admission to home and studio is by guided tour only; tours depart from bookshop Mon–Fri 11am and 1 and 3pm; Sat–Sun every 20 min. 11am–3:30pm. Closed Jan 1, last week in Jan, Thanksgiving, and Dec 25. Facilities for people with disabilities are limited; please call in advance. Subway/El: Green Line to Oak Park.

**Unity Temple** After a fire destroyed its church around 1900, a Unitarian Universalist congregation asked one of its members, Frank Lloyd Wright, to design an affordable replacement. Using poured concrete with metal reinforcements—a necessity due to a small $40,000 budget—Wright created a building that on the outside seems as forbidding as a mausoleum but inside contains all the elements of the Prairie School that has made Wright's name immortal. Following the example of H. H. Richardson, Wright placed the building's main entrance on the side, behind an enclosure—a feature often employed in his houses as well—to create a sense of privacy and intimacy. Wright complained, furthermore, that the conventions of church architecture, such as the nave in the Gothic-style cathedral across the street, were overpowering. Of that particular church, he commented that he didn't feel a part of it.

Yet his vision in this regard was somewhat confused and contradictory. He wanted Unity Temple to be "democratic," but perhaps Wright was unable to subdue his own personal hubris and hauteur in the creative process, for the ultimate effect of his chapel, and much of the building's interior, is grand and imperial. This is no simple meetinghouse; instead, its principal chapel looks like the chamber of the Roman Senate. Even so, the interior, with its unpredictable geometric arrangements and its decor reminiscent of Native American art, is no less beautiful.

Wright was a true hands-on, can-do person; he knew the materials he chose to use as intimately as the artisans who carried out his plans. He added pigment to the plaster (rather than the paint) to achieve a pale, natural effect. His use of wood trim and other decorative touches is still exciting to behold; his sensitivity to grain, tone, and placement was akin to that of an exceptionally gifted woodworker. His stunning, almost-minimalist use of form is what still sets him apart as a relevant and brilliant artist. Unity Temple still feels groundbreaking 100 years later—which Wright would consider the ultimate compliment. Allow a half-hour.

875 Lake St. ✆ **708/383-8873.** http://unitytemple-utrf.org. Self-guided tours $8 adults; $6 seniors, children 6–12, and students with ID; free for children 5 and under. Free guided tours weekends at 1, 2, and 3pm. Mon–Fri 10:30am–4:30pm; Sat–Sun 1–4pm. Church events can alter schedule; call in advance.

**U.S. Cellular Field**    Despite their stunning World Series win in 2005, the Chicago White Sox still struggle to attract the same kind of loyalty (despite the fact that they regularly win more games than the Cubs). Longtime fans rue the day owner Jerry Reinsdorf (who is also majority

## Tour Wrigley for 20 Bucks

Wrigley Field is one of the last old-time baseball stadiums in the coun-try (no luxury boxes here!). For an intimate look at the historic ballpark, take one of the tours offered on various Saturdays throughout the summer; stops include the visitors' and home-team locker rooms, press box, behind-the-scenes security headquarters, and, yes, a walk around the field itself. Tours sell out, so buy tickets ($20) as far in advance as possible. Call ✆ **800/THE-CUBS** (843-2827), or stop by the box office at 1060 W. Addison St.

owner of the Bulls) replaced admittedly dilapidated Comiskey Park with a concrete behemoth that lacks the yesteryear charm of its prede-cessor. That said, sightlines at the new stadium, U.S. Cellular Field, are spectacular from every seat (if you avoid the vertigo-inducing upper deck), and the park has every conceivable amenity, including above-average food concessions, shops, and plentiful restrooms. The White Sox's endearing quality is the blue-collar aura with which so many Cubs-loathing Southsiders identify. Games rarely sell out—an effect, presumably, of Reinsdorf's sterile stadium and the blighted neighbor-hood that surrounds it. All of this makes it a bargain for bona fide base-ball fans. Tickets cost $12 to $45 and are half-price on Monday.

333 W. 35th St., in the South Side neighborhood of Bridgeport. ✆ **312/674-1000.** www.whitesox.mlb.com. To get Sox tickets, call Ticketmaster (✆ 866/SOX-GAME [769-4263]), or visit the ticket office, open Mon–Fri 10am–6pm, Sat–Sun 10am–4pm, with extended hours on game days. Subway/El: Red Line to Sox/35th St.

★ **Wrigley Field** The Chicago Cubs haven't made a World Series appearance since 1945 and haven't been world champs since 1908, but that doesn't stop people from catching games at Wrigley Field, with its ivy-covered outfield walls, its hand-operated scoreboard, its view of the shimmering lake from the upper deck, and its "W" or "L" flag announcing the outcome of the game to the unfortunates who couldn't attend. After all the strikes, temper tantrums, and other non-sense, Wrigley has managed to hold on to something like purity. Yes, Wrigley finally installed lights (it was the last major-league park to do so), but by agreement with the residential neighborhood, the Cubs still play most games in the daylight, as they should. Because Wrigley is small, just about every seat is decent.

No matter how the Cubs are doing, tickets ($15–$50) go fast; most weekend and night games sell out by Memorial Day. Your best bet is to hit a weekday game, or try your luck buying a ticket on game day outside the park (you'll often find some season-ticket holders looking to unload a few seats).

Wrigley Field, 1060 W. Addison St. ℭ **773/404-CUBS** (2827). www.cubs.mlb.com. To buy tickets in person, stop by the ticket windows at Wrigley Field, Mon–Fri 9am–6pm, Sat 9am–4pm, and on game days. Call ℭ 800/THE-CUBS (843-2827) for tickets through Tickets.com (ℭ 866/652-2827 outside of Illinois); you can also order online through the team website. Bus: No. 22. Subway/El: Red Line to Addison stop.

## WORTH THE SPLURGE

★ **Architectural Boat Tours**    When it comes to splurging on Chicago attractions, this should be first on your list, both in terms of prioritizing your splurges, and in terms of what to do first. The Chicago Architecture Foundation offers first-rate guided tours to help visitors understand what makes this city's skyline so special. And this tour will orient you to the city and its layout better than any other tour, making it a good starting point. The foundation offers walking, bike, boat, and bus tours to more than 60 architectural sites and environments in and around Chicago, led by nearly 400 trained and enthusiastic docents (all volunteers). I highly recommend taking at least one CAF tour while you're in town—they help you look at (and appreciate) the city in a new way. Tours are available year-round but are scheduled less frequently in winter.

One of the CAF's most popular tours is the 1½-hour Architecture River Cruise, which glides along both the north and the south branches of the Chicago River. Although you can see the same 50 or so buildings by foot, traveling by water lets you enjoy the buildings from a unique perspective. The excellent docents also provide interesting historical details, as well as some fun facts (David Letterman once called the busts of the nation's retailing legends that face the Merchandise Mart the "Pez Hall of Fame"). The docents generally do a good job of making the cruise enjoyable for visitors with all levels of architectural knowledge. In addition to pointing out buildings—Marina City, the Civic Opera House, the Willis (Sears) Tower—they approach the sites thematically, explaining, for example, how Chicagoans' use of and attitudes toward the river have changed over time.

Tours are $26 per person weekdays, $28 on weekends and holidays, and begin hourly every day June through October from 11am to 3pm (with more limited schedules in May and Nov). FINE PRINT The trips are extremely popular, so purchase tickets in advance through Ticketmaster (℃ 312/902-1500; www.ticketmaster.com), or avoid the service charge and buy tickets at one of the foundation's tour centers or from the boat launch on the southeast corner of Michigan Avenue and Wacker Drive.

If you want to squeeze a lot of sightseeing into a limited time, try Highlights by Bus, a 3½-hour overview tour that covers the Loop, Hyde Park—including a visit to the interior of Frank Lloyd Wright's Robie House—and the Gold Coast, plus several other historic districts. Tours start at 9:30am on Wednesday, Friday, Saturday, and Sunday April through November (Sat only Dec–Mar). Tickets are $38 per person.

Departing from the Chicago ArchiCenter, 224 S. Michigan Ave.; a few tours leave from the John Hancock Center, 875 N. Michigan Ave. ℃ **312/922-3432,** or 312/922-TOUR (8687) for recorded information. www.architecture.org. Tickets for most walking tours $10–$15. Subway/El: Brown, Green, Purple, or Orange line to Adams; or Red Line to Jackson.

★ **The Field Museum of Natural History**   Is it any wonder that Steven Spielberg thought the Field Museum of Natural History was a suitable home turf for the intrepid archaeologist and adventurer hero of his Indiana Jones movies? Spread over the museum's 9 acres of floor space are scores of permanent and temporary exhibitions— some interactive but most requiring the old-fashioned skills of observation and imagination.

Navigating all the disparate exhibits can be daunting, so start out in the grand Stanley Field Hall, which you enter from the north or south end. Standing proudly at the north side is the largest, most complete *Tyrannosaurus rex* fossil ever unearthed. The museum acquired the specimen—named Sue for the paleontologist who discovered it in South Dakota in 1990—for a cool $8.4 million after a high-stakes bidding war. The real skull is so heavy that a lighter copy had to be mounted on the skeleton; the actual one is on display nearby.

Families should head downstairs for two of the most popular kid-friendly exhibits. The pieces on display in Inside Ancient Egypt came to the museum in the early 1900s, after researchers in Saqqara, Egypt, excavated two of the original chambers from the tomb of Unis-ankh, son of the Fifth Dynasty ruler Pharaoh Unis. The *mastaba* (tomb) of Unis-ankh forms the core of a spellbinding exhibit that realistically depicts scenes from Egyptian funeral, religious, and other social practices. Visitors can explore aspects of the day-to-day world of ancient Egypt, viewing 23 actual mummies and realistic burial scenes, a living marsh environment and canal works, the ancient royal barge, a religious shrine, and a reproduction of a typical marketplace of the period. Many of the exhibits allow hands-on interaction, and there are special activities for kids, such as making parchment from living papyrus plants.

Next to the Egypt exhibit, you'll find Underground Adventure, a "total immersion environment" populated by giant robotic earwigs, centipedes, wolf spiders, and other subterranean critters. FINE PRINT The Disneyesque exhibit is a big hit with kids, but—annoyingly—carries an extra admission charge ($7 on top of regular admission).

You might be tempted to skip the "peoples of the world" exhibits, but trust me, some are not only mind-opening but also great fun. Traveling the Pacific, hidden up on the second floor, is definitely worth a stop. Hundreds of artifacts from the museum's oceanic collection re-create scenes of island life in the South Pacific (there's even a full-scale model of a Maori meetinghouse). Africa, an assemblage of African artifacts and provocative interactive multimedia presentations, takes viewers to Senegal, a Cameroon palace, the wildlife-rich savanna, and on a "virtual" journey aboard a slave ship to the Americas. Native Chicagoans will quickly name two more signature highlights: the taxidermies of Bushman (a legendary lowland gorilla that made international headlines while at the city's Lincoln Park Zoo) and the Man-Eating Lions of Tsavo (the pair of male lions that munched nearly 140 British railway workers constructing a bridge in East Africa in 1898; their story is featured in the film *The Ghost and the Darkness*). The fabulous Grainger Hall of Gems is recently renovated and glittering as ever (and free with museum admission). Check out the 3,500-year-old Egyptian garnet necklace and the famous Tiffany & Co. Sun God Opal.

The museum books special traveling exhibits (recent blockbusters included shows on King Tut and ancient Pompeii), but be forewarned: The high-profile exhibits are usually crowded and—again—have an additional admission charge. A much better deal is a free tour of the museum highlights; tours begin daily at 11am and 2pm.

When you're ready to take a break, the Corner Bakery cafe, just off the main hall, serves food a cut above the usual museum victuals (to avoid lunchtime lines, pick up a premade salad or sandwich and head for the cash register). Families also flock to the McDonald's on the lower level. Allow 3 hours.

Roosevelt Rd. and Lake Shore Dr. ⓒ **312/922-9410.** www.fieldmuseum.org. Admission $12 adults; $7 seniors, students with ID, and children 4–11; free for children 3 and under. Discounted admission Mon–Tues mid-Sept through Nov and Jan–Feb. Daily 9am–5pm. Closed Dec 25. Bus: 6, 10, 12, 130, or 146.

★ **John G. Shedd Aquarium** The Shedd is one of the world's largest indoor aquariums, and houses thousands of river, lake, and sea denizens in standard aquarium tanks and elaborate new habitats within its octagon-shaped marble building. The only problem with the Shedd is its steep admission price ($23 for adults). You can keep your costs down by buying the "Aquarium Only" admission, but you'll miss some of the most stunning exhibits. A GO Chicago Card or Chicago CityPass (see "Money-Saving Tourist Passes," at the beginning of the chapter) can also save you money if you visit enough of the other included attractions.

The first thing you'll see as you enter is the Caribbean Coral Reef. This 90,000-gallon circular tank occupies the Beaux Arts–style central rotunda, entertaining spectators who press up against the glass to ogle divers feeding nurse sharks, barracudas, stingrays, and a hawksbill sea turtle. A roving camera connected to video monitors on the tank's periphery gives visitors close-ups of the animals inside, but I'd recommend sticking around to catch one of the daily feedings, when a diver swims around the tank and (thanks to a microphone) talks about the species and their eating habits.

The exhibits surrounding the Caribbean coral reef re-create marine habitats around the world. The best is Amazon Rising: Seasons of the River, a rendering of the Amazon basin that showcases frogs and other animals as well as fish (although the sharp-toothed piranhas are pretty cool).

You'll pay extra to see the other Shedd highlights, but they're quite impressive, so I'd suggest shelling out for them if you plan to spend more than an hour here. The Oceanarium, with a wall of windows revealing the lake outside, replicates a Pacific Northwest coastal environment and creates the illusion of one uninterrupted expanse of sea. On a fixed performance schedule in a large pool flanked by an amphitheater, a crew of friendly trainers puts dolphins through their paces of leaping dives, breaches, and tail walking. FINE PRINT Check out the Oceanarium schedule as soon as you get to the Shedd; seating can fill up quickly, so you'll want to get here early. If you're visiting during a summer weekend, you may also want to buy your Oceanarium ticket in advance to make sure you can catch a show that day. Wild Reef—Sharks at Shedd is a series of 26 connected habitats that house a Philippine coral reef patrolled by sharks and other predators. The floor-to-ceiling windows bring the toothy swimmers up close and personal (they even swim over your head at certain spots).

If you want a quality sit-down meal in a restaurant with a spectacular view of Lake Michigan, check out Soundings. There's also a family-friendly cafeteria. Allow 2 to 3 hours.

1200 S. Lake Shore Dr. ⓒ **312/939-2438.** www.sheddaquarium.org. All-Access Pass (to all exhibits) $23 adults, $16 seniors and children 3–11, free for children 2 and under; admission to aquarium and Wild Reef $18 adults, $14 seniors and children; aquarium only $8 adults, $6 seniors and children. Free admission to aquarium only Mon–Tues Oct–Nov and Jan–Feb. Memorial Day to Labor Day daily 9am–6pm; early Sept to late May Mon–Fri 9am–5pm, Sat–Sun 9am–6pm. Bus: 6 or 146.

## 3 Neighborhoods Worth Exploring

To really get to know Chicago, break out of the downtown Loop and Michigan Avenue areas to explore the outlying neighborhoods. Walk the streets, browse the shops, grab a bite at a corner restaurant or a drink at a neighborhood tavern—you'll find a more down-to-earth view of Chicago than you will at the popular tourist destinations. I suggest several neighborhood-based itineraries in chapter 8.

### GOLD COAST

Some of Chicago's most desirable real estate and historic architecture are found along Lake Shore Drive, between Oak Street and North Avenue and along the adjacent side streets. Despite trendy little pockets of real estate popping up elsewhere, the moneyed class still prefers to live by the lake. This residential area has beautiful side streets for walking. On the neighborhood's western edge, the northern stretch of State Street just south of Division Street has, in recent years, developed into a thriving zone of restaurants, bars, and nightclubs.

The Charnley-Persky House (for more information on tours, see p. 122) is nearby, at 1365 N. Astor St., as is the Madlener House (4 W. Burton Place; see p. 134). If you're walking the neighborhood, don't miss ogling 1340 N. State Parkway—the original Playboy Mansion. Built in 1899, this very traditional-looking mansion was home to Playboy's Hugh Hefner during his Chicago heyday in the 1960s. The building has been converted into private condos, so you'll need your imagination to envision Hugh romping here with his bunnies. (Playboy Enterprises, now run by Hugh's daughter, Christie Hefner, is still headquartered in Chicago.)

## RIVER NORTH

Just to the west of the Mag Mile's zone of high life and sophistication is an old warehouse district called River North. This neighborhood is home to most chain restaurants that cater to kids, and the traditional tourist joints (Hard Rock Café, Rainforest Café, ESPN Zone). Over the past 15 to 20 years, the area has experienced a rebirth as one of the city's most vital commercial districts, and today it is filled with many of the city's hottest restaurants, nightspots, art galleries, and loft dwellings. Several large-scale residential loft-conversion projects have extended River North's cache to its western and southwestern fringes. Make sure to stop at the Merchandise Mart (www.themerchandisemart.com), the world's largest commercial building (it's second only to the Pentagon), built by Marshall Field as a wholesale emporium and completed in 1931. The public is welcome to explore the lobby and ground floor, which features Luxe Home, an eye-popping array of high-end home decorating and furnishing shops, including Christopher Peacock's kitchen design showroom. The building (you couldn't miss it if you tried) is located at the corner of Wells and Kinzie streets.

## OLD TOWN

West of LaSalle Street, principally on North Wells Street between Division Street and North Avenue, is the neighborhood of Old Town. On Wells Street, and a few blocks east and a few blocks west on North Avenue, you'll find a pleasant place to stroll during the day. This area was a hippie haven in the 1960s and 1970s, but in recent years its residential areas have been rapidly gentrified as Cabrini Green, the former housing project, has finally fallen to the wrecking ball. Old Town's biggest claim to fame, the legendary Second City

Comedy Club, has served up the lighter side of life to Chicagoans for more than 30 years. Along the way, make sure you stop at St. Michael's Church (1633 N. Cleveland Ave. between North Ave. and Eugenie St.; © **312/642-2498;** www.st-mikes.org), the anchor of the neighborhood. It's said that if you can hear the bells of St. Michael's, you know that you're in Old Town. Indeed, the clock tower of this monumental church presides over the neighborhood, casting a long shadow over the courtyard that leads to the entrance. Historically a German parish (as opposed to the Irish parishes found elsewhere in the city during the early 1900s), St. Michael's (named for the Archangel who drove Adam and Eve from paradise) is a massive Romanesque church that reveals a strong southern European influence. The latter is especially evident in the stained-glass windows, embellished with Catholic iconography, that were imported from Munich at the turn of the 20th century.

## LINCOLN PARK

Chicago's most popular residential neighborhood is fashionable Lincoln Park. The neighborhood is notable for visitors because it is bordered on the east by the huge park of the same name, which is home to two major museums and one of the nation's oldest zoos (established in 1868). The trapezoid formed by Clark Street, Armitage Avenue, Halsted Street, and Diversey Parkway also contains many of Chicago's most happening bars, restaurants, retail stores, music clubs, and off-Loop theaters—including the nationally acclaimed Steppenwolf Theatre Company. Any tour of the neighborhood must include stops at the Lincoln Park Zoo and the conservatory, as well as a stroll through the park of the same name. Another wonderful walking area is Armitage Street, filled with retail shops and neighborhood restaurants, and frequented by neighborhood residents and DePaul University students, from Halsted Street on the east to Racine Street on the west.

## LAKEVIEW & WRIGLEYVILLE

Wrigleyville is the name given to the neighborhood in the vicinity of Wrigley Field—home of the Chicago Cubs—at Sheffield Avenue and Addison Street. It's also become a fashionable residential neighborhood, and a slew of nightclubs and restaurants have popped up. Midway up the city's North Side is a one-time blue-collar, now mainstream middle-class and bohemian quarter called Lakeview. It has become one of the neighborhoods of choice for gays and lesbians, recent college graduates, and a growing number of residents priced out of Lincoln Park. The main thoroughfare is Belmont Avenue, between Broadway and Sheffield Avenue. Radiating from the intersection of Belmont Avenue and Clark Street is a string of shops catering to rebellious kids on tour from their homes in the 'burbs. (The Dunkin' Donuts on the corner is often referred to as "Punkin' Donuts" in their honor.) If you have preteens or young teens, they will be fascinated by the youth culture, the street life—and the shops.

Lakeview's principal commercial avenue is Southport Avenue. You'll find it a pleasant stroll. Start at the Music Box Theater (© 773/ 871-6604) at 3733 N. Southport Ave., north of Addison Street, and stroll south down this gentrifying retail row, with an interesting mix of quirky and artsy merchants and restaurateurs. (For more on the shops, see chapter 7, "Shopping".)

## UPTOWN & ANDERSONVILLE

Uptown, along the lake and about as far north as Foster Avenue, is home to a wave of recent immigrants, most notably Vietnamese and Chinese immigrants, who have transformed Argyle Street between Broadway and Sheridan Road into a teeming market for fresh meat, fish, and all kinds of exotic vegetables. Slightly to the north and west is the old Scandinavian neighborhood of Andersonville, whose main drag is Clark Street, between Foster and Bryn Mawr avenues. This is a family-friendly neighborhood, with the feel of a small Midwestern village, albeit one with an eclectic mix of Middle Eastern restaurants, a distinct cluster of woman-owned businesses, and a predominant gay and lesbian community. You'll find Ann Sather restaurant, the Swedish-American Museum, the Swedish Bakery, and Women and Children First, a not-to-be-missed independent bookstore.

## LINCOLN SQUARE

The anchor of this neighborhood, particularly in visitors' eyes, is the Old Town School of Folk Music's theater and education center, a beautiful restoration of a former library building, in this neighborhood west of Andersonville and slightly to the south, where Lincoln, Western, and Lawrence avenues intersect. Lincoln Square was the home to Chicago's once vast German-American community, and you'll find remnants of this in delicatessens and more. Today, the neighborhood is hopping with hot restaurants and chic shops as the surrounding leafy residential streets are experiencing an influx of middle-class families. The pedestrian mall that forms the heart of Lincoln Square makes for a great neighborhood stroll (and don't forget to stop at Café Selmarie—see chapter 3, "Cheap Eats").

## ROGERS PARK

Rogers Park, which begins at Devon Avenue, is on the northern fringes of the city, bordering suburban Evanston. Its western half has been a Jewish neighborhood for decades. The eastern half, dominated by Loyola University's lakefront campus, has become the most cosmopolitan enclave in the city: Asians, East Indians, Russian Jews, and German Americans live side-by-side with African Americans and the ethnically mixed student population drawn to the Catholic university. Much of Rogers Park has a neo-hippie ambience, but the western stretch of Devon Avenue is a Midwestern slice of Calcutta, settled by Indians who've transformed the street into a veritable restaurant row of tandoori chicken and curry-flavored dishes.

## WEST LOOP

West Loop, also known as the near west side, the neighborhood just across the Chicago River from the Loop, is the city's newest gentrification target, as old warehouses and once vacant lots are transformed into trendy condos. The stretch of Randolph Street just west of Hwy. 90/94 and the surrounding blocks are known as "restaurant row" for the many dining spots that cluster there. Nearby, on Halsted Street between Adams and Monroe streets, is Chicago's old "Greek Town," still the Greek culinary center of the city. Much of the old Italian neighborhood in this vicinity was the victim of urban renewal, but remnants of the old days still survive on Taylor Street; the same is true for a few old delis and shops on Maxwell Street, dating from the turn of the 20th century when a large Jewish community lived in the area.

## BUCKTOWN/WICKER PARK

Centered near the confluence of North, Damen, and Milwaukee avenues, where the Art Deco Northwest Tower is the tallest thing for miles, this resurgent area is said to be home to the third-largest concentration of artists in the country. Over the past century, the area has hosted waves of German, Polish, and, most recently, Spanish-speaking immigrants (not to mention writer Nelson Algren). In recent years, it has morphed into a bastion of hot new restaurants, alternative culture, and loft-dwelling yuppies surfing the gentrification wave that's washing over this still-somewhat-gritty neighborhood.

This is also a great walking neighborhood, with small funky shops specializing in jewelry, crafts, home furnishing and clothing, interesting local restaurants, and scenic residential architecture of walk-ups and brownstones on the side streets. Renegade Homemade is a great stop for crafts, and home goods hailing from every corner of the globe are within reach at Embelezar. You can find the latest underground music at Reckless Records, or customize your own T-shirt at T-Shirt Deli. A huge number of art galleries line the streets, such as AllRise Gallery (contemporary art) and the David Leonardis Gallery, which feature many genres. For live theater, there's Comedy Sportz Theater and its improv comedy, The Chicago Dramatists Theater, which is dedicated to developing new plays, and the Gorilla Tango Theater.

## SOUTH LOOP

The generically rechristened South Loop area was Chicago's original "Gold Coast" in the late 19th century, with Prairie Avenue (now a historic district) as its most exclusive address. But in the wake of the 1893 World's Columbian Exposition in Hyde Park, and continuing through the Prohibition era of the 1920s, the area was infamous for its Levee vice district, home to gambling and prostitution, some of the most corrupt politicians in Chicago history, and Al Capone's headquarters at the old Lexington Hotel. However, in recent years, its prospects have turned around. The South Loop—stretching from Harrison Street's historic Printers Row south to Cermak Road (where Chinatown begins), and from Lake Shore Drive west to the south branch of the Chicago River—is one of the fastest-growing residential neighborhoods in the city.

## PILSEN

Originally home to the nation's largest settlement of Bohemian-Americans, Pilsen (which derives its name from a city in Bohemia) was for decades the principal entry point in Chicago for immigrants of every ethnic stripe. Centered at Halsted and 18th streets just southwest of the Loop, it is now the second-largest Mexican-American community in the United States. One of the city's most vibrant and colorful neighborhoods, Pilsen has been happily invaded by the outdoor mural movement launched years earlier in Mexico, and it has a profusion of authentic taquerias and bakeries. The neighborhood's annual Day of the Dead celebration, which begins in September, is an elaborate festival that runs for 8 weeks. The artistic spirit that permeates the community isn't confined to Latin American art. In recent years a diverse group of artists, drawn partly by the availability of loft space in Pilsen, have nurtured a small but thriving artists' colony.

## BRIDGEPORT & CANARYVILLE

Bridgeport, whose main intersection is 35th and Halsted streets, has been the neighborhood of two Mayor Daleys, father and son (the son moved not too long ago to the new Central Station development in the South Loop area). After the old Comiskey Park was torn down, the Chicago White Sox stayed in Bridgeport, inaugurating their new stadium there. Nearby Canaryville, just south and west, is typical of the "back of the yard," blue-collar neighborhoods that once surrounded the Chicago Stockyards. Neither area offers much to the typical visitor; in fact, "outsiders" aren't all that welcome.

## HYDE PARK

Hyde Park's main attraction for families is the world-famous Museum of Science and Industry. Hyde Park is like an independent village within the confines of Chicago, right off Lake Michigan and roughly a 30-minute train ride from the Loop. The main drag is 57th Street, and the University of Chicago—with all its attendant shops and restaurants—is the neighborhood's principal tenant. The most successful racially integrated community in the city, Hyde Park is an oasis of furious intellectual activity and liberalism that, ironically, is hemmed in on all sides by neighborhoods suffering some of the highest crime rates in Chicago.

## 4 Parks & Gardens

### GRANT PARK

Modeled after the gardens at Versailles, Grant Park is Chicago's front yard, composed of giant lawns segmented by *allées* of trees, plantings, and paths, and pieced together by major roadways and a network of railroad tracks. Covering the greens is a variety of public recreational and cultural facilities (although these are few in number and nicely spread out, a legacy of mail-order magnate Aaron Montgomery Ward's *fin de siècle* campaign to limit municipal buildings in the park). Incredibly, the entire expanse was created from sandbars, landfill, and Chicago Fire debris; the original shoreline extended all the way to Michigan Avenue. Grant Park is the major venue for festivals in the city, but although it's beautiful, it has fewer attractions for families than Lincoln Park (see review below).

The immense Buckingham Fountain, accessible along Congress Parkway, is the baroque centerpiece of the park, composed of pink Georgia marble and patterned after—but twice the size of—the Latona Fountain at Versailles, with adjoining esplanades beautified by rose gardens in season. Throughout the late spring and summer, the fountain spurts columns of water up to 165 feet in the air, illuminated after dark by a whirl of colored lights, and building toward a grand finale before it shuts down for the night at 11pm. You'll find concession areas and restrooms here, as well.

Favorite annual events are the free outdoor blues festival (in June) and the jazz festival (Labor Day). Taste of Chicago (© **312/744-3315**), purportedly the largest food festival in the world (the city estimates its annual attendance at over 3.5 million), takes place every summer for 10 days around the July 4th holiday. Local restaurants serve up more ribs, pizza, hot dogs, and beer than you'd ever want to see, let alone eat. Scattered about the park are a number of sculptures and monuments, including a heroic sculpture of two Native Americans on horseback entitled *The Spearman and the Bowman* (at Congress Pkwy. and Michigan Ave.), which has become the park's trademark since it was installed in 1928, as well as likenesses of Copernicus, Columbus, and Lincoln *(The Seated Lincoln)*, the latter by the great American sculptor Augustus Saint-Gaudens, located on Congress Parkway between Michigan Avenue and Columbus Drive. On the western edge of the park, at Adams Street, is the Art Institute (p. 121), and at the southern tip of the Museum Campus are the Field Museum of Natural History (p. 140), the Adler Planetarium (p. 118), and the John G. Shedd Aquarium (p. 142).

331 E. Randolph St. © **312/742-7648.** Subway/El: Brown Line to the Loop. Bus: 3, 4, 6, 60, 146, or 151.

# MILLENNIUM PARK

At the north end of Grant Park along Michigan Avenue is the city's newest urban showpiece. The architectural highlight of the park is the Frank Gehry–designed Pritzker Music Pavilion, home of the free summer music concerts performed by the Grant Park Symphony Orchestra. Another popular attraction is the huge elliptical sculpture by British artist Anish Kapoor, his first public work in the U.S. Once you see the sculpture, officially titled *Cloud Gate,* you'll see why most Chicagoans affectionately call it "The Bean." For much more on the park, see p. 100.

Located on Michigan Avenue between Randolph and Monroe streets. Its eastern boundary is Columbus Drive, western boundary is Michigan Avenue, northern boundary is Randolph Street, and southern boundary is Monroe Street. Bus No. 151 Michigan Avenue or Subway/El: Red Line to Monroe or Lake.

# LINCOLN PARK

Straight and narrow Lincoln Park begins at North Avenue and follows the shoreline of Lake Michigan northward 6 miles to Ardmore Avenue (not far from the East Asian enclave radiating from Argyle Ave. and quaint Andersonville), making it the city's largest park. Within its elongated 1,200 acres are a world-class zoo, a half-dozen bathing beaches, a botanical conservatory, two excellent museums, a golf course, and the usual meadows, formal gardens, sporting fields, and tennis courts typical of urban parks. Attractions in the park include the Chicago History Museum (p. 124), Lincoln Park Zoo (p. 102), Lincoln Park Conservatory (p. 106), and Peggy Notebaert Nature Museum (p. 129).

The park's lakes, trails, and pathways make it ideal for biking, hiking, picnicking, and enjoying nature. Baseball, softball, and

## Go Fly a Kite in Grant Park!

If you're short on cash but loaded with free time in Chicago, here's a suggestion that might just make your day. Head over to a toy store (one centrally located store is Galt Toys, 900 N. Michigan Ave., 5th floor). Plunk down $10 for a funky green frog kite. Then take the No. 151 Michigan Avenue bus down to Grant Park, with its wide open spaces and proximity to the lakefront. This is Chicago, right? So you'll rarely experience a day that isn't windy enough to fly a kite.

soccer fields, and basketball and tennis courts are concentrated mainly around the South Field, Waveland, and Montrose sections. You'll find archery and a 9-hole golf course in the Waveland area; minigolf and a driving range are located near Diversey Harbor. Families can rent paddleboats and explore the South Pond from a little dock in front of Café Brauer, on the northwest side of lovely South Pond ($12 per half-hour for four-person paddleboats, $16 per half-hour for swan boats, which seat two and are shaped like—you guessed it—a giant white swan). You can also rent boats from the boathouse on North Pond. Boat rentals are available from May through September.

Families with small children won't want to miss the Farm-in-the-Zoo, on the southern end of South Pond. Five barns house cows, chickens, horses, goats, and other livestock. Kids can get a farmhand's-eye view of butter churning, milking, and other farm activities throughout the day.

The statue of the standing Abraham Lincoln (just north of the North Ave. and State St. intersection) in the park that bears his name is one of two in Chicago by Augustus Saint-Gaudens (*The Seated Lincoln* is in Grant Park). Saint-Gaudens also did the Bates Fountain near the conservatory. The statue marks the southern boundary of the park.

A one-time Chicago dining institution near the zoo, Café Brauer (www.cafebrauer.com) is a stunning facility. Operating a cafe and ice-cream parlor on the ground floor, and a ballroom called the Great Hall on the second floor that's flanked by two curving loggias, the return of the Brauer restores some of the elegant atmosphere that characterized the park around 1900, when this landmark building was erected. (If you visit on a weekend, chances are good that caterers will be setting up for a wedding in the Great Hall, but they'll usually let you in to sneak a peek.) Architect Dwight Perkins, who created this gem of a building, was one of the leaders of Chicago's Prairie School architecture movement, and Brauer is undeniably his masterwork. Best of all, though, is the picture-postcard view from the adjacent bridge spanning the pond of the John Hancock Center and neighboring skyscrapers beyond Lincoln Park's treetops.

If you're looking for an evening's entertainment, check out the Theater on the Lake, Fullerton Avenue, for open-air theater with a relaxed setting. For information, call © **312/742-7994.**

Bounded by Lake Shore Dr. from North to Bryn Mawr aves. © **312/742-7726.** The park's visitor center is in the Lincoln Park Cultural Center, 2045 N. Lincoln Park W.

Park open daily from dawn until dusk. Visitor center open year-round Mon–Thurs 9am–9pm; Fri 11am–7pm; Sat 8am–4pm; Sun 11am–5pm. Bus: 22, 145, 146, 147, 151, or 156.

## 5 Free & Dirt Cheap Tours

### GUIDED WALKING TOURS

It's a bit of a cliché to say that Chicago is a city of neighborhoods, but if you want to see what really makes Chicago special, that's where you have to go. And if you're a bit intimidated by public transportation and getting around a less tourist-friendly area of the city, an escorted tour is the perfect way to see places you'd otherwise miss.

★ **Chicago Architecture Foundation**   For first-time visitors, I highly recommend two tours for an excellent introduction to the dramatic architecture of the Loop. Historic Skyscrapers (10:30am on Wed; 10am–3pm on Thurs–Tues) covers buildings built between 1880 and 1940, including the Rookery and the Chicago Board of Trade; Modern Skyscrapers (1pm daily; additional tour at 5:30pm on Fri) includes modern masterpieces by Mies van der Rohe and postmodern works by contemporary architects. The 2-hour tours cost $15 each for adults and $12 each for seniors and students.

The CAF also offers more than 50 neighborhood tours, visiting the Gold Coast, River North, Grant Park, Old Town, the Jackson Boulevard Historic District, and even Lincoln Park Zoo. Most cost $10 and last a couple of hours.

Departing from the Chicago ArchiCenter, 224 S. Michigan Ave.; a few tours leave from the John Hancock Center, 875 N. Michigan Ave. ✆ **312/922-3432,** or 312/922-TOUR for recorded information. www.architecture.org. Tickets for most walking tours $10–$15. Subway/El: Brown, Green, Purple, or Orange line to Adams; or Red Line to Jackson.

**Chicago Neighborhood Tours**   Sponsored by the Department of Cultural Affairs, Chicago Neighborhood Tours are 4- to 5-hour narrated bus excursions to about a dozen diverse communities throughout the city. Every Saturday (not on major holidays and not during Jan generally, so call first) the tours visit different neighborhoods, from Chinatown and historic Bronzeville on the South Side to the ethnic enclaves of Devon Avenue and Uptown on the North Side. Neighborhood representatives serve as guides and greeters along the way as tour participants visit area landmarks, murals, museums, and shopping districts.

While these tours are definitely not cheap, they are worth a splurge. Tickets (including a light snack) are $30 for adults and $25 for seniors, students, and children 8 to 18 (free for under 8). Several specialty tours have recently been added to the mix, including Literary Chicago; the Great Chicago Fire; Roots of Blues, Gospel & Jazz; Threads of Ireland; Jewish Legacy; and an Ethnic Cemetery tour. These tours, which generally run 4 to 6 hours and include lunch, are more expensive ($40).

Embarking from the Chicago Cultural Center, 77 E. Randolph St. (℃) **312/742-1190;** www.chicagoneighborhoodtours.com. Tickets (including a light snack) are $30 for adults and $25 for seniors, students, and children 8 to 18. Bus: 3, 4, 20, 56, 145, 146, 147, 151, or 157. Subway/El: Brown, Green, Orange, or Purple line to Randolph; or Red Line to Washington/State.

**Chicago History Museum** A handful of walking tours are offered every summer of the Gold Coast, Old Town, and Lincoln Park neighborhoods. Led by museum docents, they average about four per month from June through August. Day and evening tours are available, and a few specialty walking tours usually are given as well.

Tours depart from the CHS museum at Clark Street and North Avenue, and light refreshments are served afterward. (℃) **312/642-4600;** www.chicagohistory.org. Tours are $10 per person, and registration is recommended but not required.

**Chicago Food Planet Tours** These guided, narrated food tours cover two Chicago neighborhoods: the near North (Old Town and Lincoln Park) and Bucktown/Wicker Park. While a bit pricey ($42), the tickets include multiple food tastings. The Near North tours include spots such as Bacino's Pizzeria, the Spice House (a spice and herb specialty shop, see p. 274), Ashkenaz Deli, and the Fudge Pot. In Bucktown/Wicker Park, you'll sample the offerings from a top-rated hot dog stand, a pastry and dessert stop, a pizzeria and brewery, and a cafe that creates and designs ice cream instantly on the spot.

For more information, call (℃) **800/979-3370;** www.chicagofood planet.com.

★ **Second City Tours** Like some humor with your history? Then check out Second City Comedy Club's walking tours of its Old Town neighborhood on Sundays and Wednesdays at 4pm from mid-July until October. A real deal at $15, the 2-hour tours can be booked by phone at (℃) **312/337-3992** or online at www.secondcity.com. Not only will your guide entertain and inform you about the architecture, history, and development of Old Town, but you'll also get the inside scoop about Second City, and the hang-outs and folklore of comedy alumni. Tours begin in the lobby of the Second City Theater.

## FREE SELF-GUIDED WALKING TOURS

**Chicago Greeter Walking Tours**    This program, run by the Chicago Office of Tourism, matches tourists with local Chicagoans, who act as volunteer guides. Visitors can request a specific neighborhood or theme (everything from Polish heritage sites to Chicago movie locations), and a greeter gives a free 2- to 4-hour tour. FINE PRINT Greeters won't escort groups of more than 6 people, and if you have a newborn baby, you're encouraged to wait until he or she is a little older. (Otherwise, children are more than welcome.) Specific requests for tours should be made at least a week in advance, but "InstaGreeters" are available on a first-come, first-served basis for 60-minute walking tours. Millennium Park also offers a greeter service, which originates from the Millennium Park Welcome Center (201 E. Randolph St.) and offers a free walking tour of the 25-acre park.

Now you can also bike alongside your Chicago Greeter, thanks to an expansion of this super-successful program. Yes, I am talking about free bicycles and bicycle-riding guides. Free! To get set up, you need to register at www.chicagogreeter.com, then scroll down a number of questionnaire-type points until you are asked to indicate which kind of tour you desire. And there, lo and behold, is a bicycle option for up to four visitors at a time, using bikes provided without charge by a prominent Chicago bicycle-rental firm. This is one of those deals that you just can't afford to pass up!

Chicago Cultural Center, 77 E. Randolph St. (at Michigan Ave.). © **312/744-8000.** www.chicagogreeter.com. Free admission. Fri–Sun 10am–4pm. Subway/El: Brown, Green, Orange, or Purple line to Randolph; or Red Line to Washington/State.

★ **El Tours**    For a distinctive downtown view at an unbeatable price—free!—hop aboard the Loop Tour Train, a special elevated train that runs on Saturday from May through September. Docents from the Chicago Architecture Foundation point out notable buildings along the way and explain how the El shaped the city. Riders must pick up tickets at the Chicago Cultural Center, 77 E. Randolph St., beginning at 10am on the day of the tour; tours leave at 11am, 11:40am, 12:20pm, and 1pm from the Randolph/Wabash El station. For more information, call © **312/744-2400,** or visit www.cityof chicago.org/exploringchicago.

**The Loop Sculpture Tour**   In the spirit of emphasizing free activities that are only-in-Chicago experiences, I can't fail to note the self-guided tour that lets you navigate through Grant Park and much of the Loop to view some 100 examples of Chicago's monumental public art. With the help of a very comprehensive free booklet, *The Chicago Public Art Guide* (free at the Chicago Cultural Center, 78 E. Washington St.), you'll get info on how to find the best examples of monumental public art.

One of the newer additions is the massive elliptical sculpture *Cloud Gate* (known as "The Bean," because it looks like a giant silver kidney bean) by British artist Anish Kapoor. The sculpture, in Millennium Park, was Kapoor's first public commission in the U.S. The single most famous sculpture is Pablo Picasso's *Untitled,* located in Daley Plaza and constructed out of Cor-Ten steel, the same gracefully rusting material used on the exterior of the Daley Center behind it. Perhaps because it was the buttoned-down Loop's first monumental modern sculpture, its installation in 1967 was met with hoots and heckles, but today "the Picasso" enjoys semiofficial status as the logo of modern Chicago. It is by far the city's most popular photo opportunity among visiting tourists. At noon on weekdays during warm-weather months, you'll likely find a dance troupe, musical group, or visual-arts exhibition there as part of the city's long-running "Under the Picasso" multicultural program. Call ⓒ **312/346-3278** for weekly updates of events.

## 6  Awesome Art & Architecture

### CHECKING OUT THE ARCHITECTURE

#### CHICAGO'S LOOP: AN ARRAY OF OUTSTANDING ARCHITECTURE

Chicago is home to hundreds of notable buildings, and the greatest concentration of outstanding landmark buildings is found in the Loop. While a Michigan Avenue Cliff neighborhood tour (the east side of the Loop, fronting south Michigan Ave.) is detailed in chapter 8, there is so much more architecture to see in the Loop that I am going to outline another tour of must-see buildings here.

First and foremost (and tallest) is Willis Tower (formerly Sears Tower), located at South Wacker Drive and Jackson Boulevard. Skip the overpriced ride to the top. For the record, the Willis Tower still holds the record in the category of "tallest skyscraper measured to the top of the antenna." There is a new feature called The Ledge, which are two glass boxes that extend 4.3 feet beyond the outer edge of the building, at 1,353 feet up. If you do want to spend the money for the ride to the 103rd floor ($15.95 for adults ages 12 and up), check out www.the-skydeck.com; © **312/875-9696.**

Your next stop should be the Civic Opera Building, which fronts the broad roadway of Wacker Drive (20 N. Wacker Dr.). Check out the Grand Foyer of the opera house, with its 40-foot-high ceiling and gold leaf–topped marble columns. Walking toward the river on Wacker Drive, you'll come to the green-hued facade of 333 W. Wacker Drive (at Lake St.). The glass reflects the Chicago River and was built in 1983. Across the river, you'll see the Merchandise Mart (Wells and Kinzie sts.). Moving into the heart of the Loop, walk to the Rookery Building (209 S. LaSalle St.), a relic of Old Chicago, completed in 1888. The rough granite apse and turrets show the influence of the heavy Romanesque style of H. H. Richardson. Check out the open interior court, designed by Frank Lloyd Wright. It rises the full height of the building's 11 stories, and was constructed from iron, copper, marble, glass, and terra cotta.

Next on the tour is the Chicago Board of Trade (141 W. Jackson Blvd.; © **312/435-3590;** www.cbot.com). This streamlined Art Deco building, one of the best examples of that style in the city, opened in 1930. It houses the raucous economic free-for-all that is the world's largest commodities exchange, where corn, wheat, and other futures contracts are traded. Along the landmark building's rear wall, a postmodern addition by Helmut Jahn offers a repetition of the pyramid-shaped roof. The statue of the Roman goddess Ceres on the top of the 45-floor structure strikes a quirky architectural note—she was left faceless because the designers figured nobody would get close enough to see her features. Due to security restrictions, the public is not permitted inside the building.

The Monadnock Block, located at 53 W. Jackson Blvd., actually consists of two buildings, built 2 years apart using two very different construction methods. **Monadnock I,** on the northern end, was built by Burnham and Root between 1889 and 1891, with deeply recessed windows at street level, encased by walls up to 8 feet thick. It was the last skyscraper in the United States to use this method of construction. **Monadnock II,** built by Holabird & Roche in 1893, is one of the country's first steel-framed buildings, but is noteworthy in that it maintains a continuity of style with Monadnock I.

The Marquette Building, located at 140 S. Dearborn St., was named for Jacques Marquette, a French Jesuit explorer who was one of the first Europeans to record the existence of the area now known as Chicago. This 1895 building was one of the country's first commercial skyscrapers. The marble lobby, which is worth seeing, commemorates the spirit of exploration with a series of explorer-themed relief sculptures and Tiffany windows. Next, it's hard to miss the Reliance Building, now the Hotel Burnham, 1 W. Washington St., kitty-corner from the State Street Macy's Department store. This prototype of the modern skyscraper was made possible by the development of high-speed elevators and steel framing. The terra-cotta and glass facade gives the 1895 building a modern appearance. Its window design—a large central pane of glass flanked by two smaller, double-hung windows for ventilation—eventually became known as the Chicago Window. It's now home to the Hotel Burnham (named for the building's famous architect, Daniel Burnham). Fans of architectural design should take the elevator to the splendid upper floors (those above the eighth floor are original).

Wrap up your Loop walking tour by checking out the historic theaters in the North Loop Theater District. The Versailles-inspired Cadillac Palace Theatre is a former movie palace that now hosts touring musicals, dance performances, and concerts. Another former movie palace, the spectacular B Ford Center for the Performing Arts Oriental Theatre, opened in 1926 and was restored in the 1980s to its original over-the-top Indian-inspired decor; it's worth seeing, no matter what's playing on the stage.

Marked by a nostalgic orange-lettered marquee, the landmark Chicago Theatre (© **312/443-1130**) was once the crown jewel of the movie theater empire of Balaban & Katz. It's the oldest Beaux Arts building in the city. The 3,800-seat hall opened in 1928 and was restored in 1986 as a showplace for Broadway musicals, concerts, and dramas.

FREE ★ **Chicago ArchiCenter**   Chicago's architecture is one of the city's main claims to fame, and a quick swing through this center, run by the well-regarded Chicago Architecture Foundation (conveniently located across the street from the Art Institute), will help you understand why. Exhibits include a scale model of downtown Chicago, profiles of the people and buildings that shaped the city's look, and a searchable database with pictures of and information on many of Chicago's best-known skyscrapers. "Architecture ambassadors" are on hand to provide information on tours run by the foundation (see "Guided Walking Tours," p. 153). Two galleries feature changing exhibits about ongoing Chicago design projects, so you can see first-hand how local architecture continues to evolve. There's also an excellent gift shop filled with architecture-focused books, decorative accessories, and gifts.

224 S. Michigan Ave. ✆ **312/922-3432,** ext. 241. www.architecture.org. Free admission. Exhibits Mon–Sat 9:30am–4pm. Shop and tour desk Mon–Sat 9am–6:30pm; Sun 9am–6pm. Bus: 3, 4, 145, 147, or 151. Subway/El: Brown, Green, Purple, or Orange line to Adams; or Red Line to Jackson.

## FREE ART

Art galleries provide some of Chicago's best free cultural resources. Not only do these mini-museums provide us with works of inspiration, but they are free for the browsing. Don't be shy about barging into a gallery or showroom with thousand-dollar pieces—shop owners are gracious and happy to welcome appreciators of art and objects, and while undoubtedly they'd rather you had millions to spend rather than tens, most are uncommonly welcoming.

The majority of fine-art dealers in the city are at River North, and particularly on the stretch of Wells Street that goes from Huron northwards, and west on the side streets. More recently, galleries have been opening in the converted loft buildings of the West Loop.

The Chicago Reader (**www.chicagoreader.com**) is the city's alternative weekly newspaper and a good source for all things art-related and free or cheap; Chicago Gallery News (**www.chicagogallerynews.com**) is the best source for the gallery scene and openings with free food.

**Alan Koppel Gallery**   This expansive gallery showcases modern and contemporary works of art as well as French and Italian furniture from the '20s through the '50s (in a separate area). Koppel also specializes in 20th-century photography, so if you're hankering for something by Diane Arbus, Man Ray, or Walker Evans, this is the place to look.

210 W. Chicago Ave. (at Wells St.). ✆ **312/640-0730.** www.alankoppel.com. Subway/El: Brown or Red line to Chicago.

**Aldo Castillo Gallery**   Aldo Castillo left his native Nicaragua in 1976, shortly after the Sandinistas began their revolution against the Somoza regime. He arrived in Chicago in 1985 and, 8 years later, appalled at the lack of attention given to Latin American art, opened his eponymous gallery in Lakeview, moving to his present River North location

## FREE Second Friday Gallery Crawls

In the Pilsen neighborhood, one of the most exciting art events takes place on the second Friday of every month. Along Halsted Street, galleries including Podmajersky Inc., Moka, Chicago Arts Department, and Listenbee Collection keep their doors open from 6 to 10pm. They offer free wine and snacks, and best of all, the chance to talk to Chicago's up-and-coming artists. Hey, the prices are so reasonable at these galleries that even the most frugal among us might walk away with a piece of art. 1919 S. Halsted St. ℭ **312/377-4444.** El: Orange Line to Halsted.

in 1993. Castillo continues to promote a range of work by emerging artists and established masters from Latin America, Spain, and Portugal.

233 W. Huron St. (btw. Franklin and Wells sts.). ℭ **312/337-2536.** www.artaldo.com. Subway/El: Brown or Red line to Chicago.

**Ann Nathan Gallery** Ann Nathan, who started out as a collector, shows exciting (and sometimes outrageous) pieces in clay, wood, and metal—along with paintings, photographs, and "functional art" (pieces that blur the line between furniture and sculpture). Nathan's space in the center of the River North district is one of the most beautiful in the city.

212 W. Superior St. (at Wells St.). ℭ **312/664-6622.** www.annnathangallery.com. Subway/El: Brown or Red line to Chicago.

**Carl Hammer Gallery** A former schoolteacher and one of the most venerated dealers in Chicago, Carl Hammer touts his wares as "contemporary art and selected historical masterworks by American and European self-taught artists"—but it's the "self-taught" part that warrants emphasis. Hammer helped pioneer the field known as "outsider art," which has since become a white-hot commodity in the international art world.

740 N. Wells St. (at Superior St.). ℭ **312/266-8512.** www.hammergallery.com. Subway/El: Brown or Red line to Chicago.

**Catherine Edelman Gallery** One of Chicago's leading galleries in contemporary photography, Catherine Edelman represents a wide range of photographers, including well-known names such as Sally

Mann. Across the street, **Stephen Daiter Gallery,** 311 W. Superior St. (☏ **312/787-3350**), also specializes in photography.

300 W. Superior St. (at Franklin St.). ☏ **312/266-2350.** www.edelmangallery.com. Subway/El: Brown or Red line to Chicago.

**Donald Young Gallery**  Internationally renowned on the contemporary art scene since the late 1970s, Donald Young returned to Chicago to much applause in 1999 after an 8-year residency in Seattle. His very dramatic West Loop gallery is a haven for critically acclaimed artists working in video, sculpture, photography, painting, and installation, including Anne Chu, Gary Hill, Martin Puryear, Bruce Nauman, Cristina Iglesias, Robert Mangold, and Charles Ray.

933 W. Washington St. (at Sangamon St.). ☏ **312/455-0100.** www.donaldyoung. com. Bus: 20 (Madison).

**Douglas Dawson Gallery**  Offering a unique perspective to the Chicago art scene, Douglas Dawson specializes in ancient and historic ethnographic art—everything from tribal textiles to furniture, although a principal focus is African ceramics. The gallery's spectacular loft space in the West Loop looks like a museum.

400 N. Morgan St. (at Kinzie St.). ☏ **312/226-7975.** www.douglasdawson.com. Bus: 65 (Grand).

**G.R. N'Namdi Gallery**  George N'Namdi founded his gallery, which specializes in African-American artists, 2 decades ago in the Detroit area. His son Jumaane operates this location (there's also another in New York). Artists they've helped bring to the attention of museums and art collectors include James Vanderzee, Al Loving, Edward Clark, and Robert Colescott.

110 N. Peoria St. (at Washington St.). ☏ **312/563-9240.** www.grnnamdi.com. Bus: 20 (Madison).

**Kavi Gupta Gallery**  Owner Kavi Gupta is widely credited with kicking off the West Loop art scene when he developed this property as a home for new galleries. Gupta specializes in contemporary art by national and international emerging artists, so you never quite know what you're going to see here. Also worth checking out in the same building are the **Carrie Secrist Gallery** (☏ **312/491-0917**) and **Thomas McCormick Gallery** (☏ **312/226-6800**).

835 W. Washington St. (at Green St.). ☏ **312/432-0708.** www.kavigupta.com. Bus: 20 (Madison).

**Marx-Saunders Gallery**   Chicago is home to two world-class galleries dealing in contemporary glass-art sculpture, conveniently located within steps of one another along Superior Street in River North. Marx-Saunders Gallery houses the city's largest showcase of glass art and features world-famous artists, past and present (William Morris, Mark Fowler, Therman Statom, and Hiroshi Yamano), as well as newcomers. Also worth a look for art-glass lovers is the nearby **Habatat Galleries Chicago,** 222 W. Superior St. (© **312/440-0288**).

230 W. Superior St. (btw. Franklin and Wells sts.). © **312/573-1400.** www.marxsaunders. com. Subway/El: Brown or Red line to Chicago.

**Maya Polsky Gallery**   Gallery owner Maya Polsky deals in international contemporary art and also represents some leading local artists, but she's best known for showcasing the contemporary and post-revolutionary art of Russia, including the work of such masters as Natalya Nesterova and Sergei Sherstiuk.

215 W. Superior St. (at Wells St.). © **312/440-0055.** www.mayapolskygallery.com. Subway/El: Brown or Red line to Chicago.

★ **Rhona Hoffman Gallery**   The New York–born Rhona Hoffman maintains a high profile on the international contemporary art scene. She launched her gallery in 1983 and, from the start, sought national and international artists, typically young and cutting-edge artists who weren't represented elsewhere in Chicago. Today she is the purveyor of such blue-chip players as Sol LeWitt and Jenny Holzer; she has also added young up-and-comers such as Dawoud Bey.

118 N. Peoria St. (btw. Randolph and Washington sts.). © **312/455-1990.** www. rhoffmangallery.com. Bus: 20 (Madison).

**Richard Gray Gallery**   Richard Gray—whose gallery opened in 1963—is widely considered the dean of art dealers in Chicago. (He's served as president of the Art Dealers Association of America and been a longtime board member of the Art Institute of Chicago.) The gallery specializes in paintings, sculpture, and drawings by leading artists from the major movements in 20th-century American and European art (he also has a second location in New York). Gray and his son, Paul, who now runs the Chicago gallery, have shown the work of such luminaries as Pablo Picasso, Jean Dubuffet, Willem de Kooning, Alexander Calder, Claes Oldenberg, Joan Miró, and Henri Matisse.

John Hancock Center, 875 N. Michigan Ave., Ste. 2503 (btw. Delaware and Chestnut sts.). © **312/642-8877.** www.richardgraygallery.com. Subway/El: Red Line to Chicago.

**Zolla/Lieberman Gallery** Bob Zolla and Roberta Lieberman kicked off the River North revival when they opened their gallery (considered the grande dame of the area) here in 1976. Today, Zolla/Lieberman, directed by Roberta's son William Lieberman, represents a wide range of artists, including sculptor Deborah Butterfield, installation artist Vernon Fisher, and painter Terence LaNoue.

325 W. Huron St. (at Orleans St.). ✆ **312/944-1990.** www.zollaliebermangallery.com. Subway/El: Brown Line to Chicago.

# 7 Free & Cheap Outdoors

## FREE CHICAGO'S BEACHES

Public beaches line Lake Michigan all the way up north into the suburbs and Wisconsin, and southeast through Indiana and into Michigan. The most well known is **Oak Street Beach;** its location at the northern tip of the Magnificent Mile creates some interesting sights as sun worshipers sporting swimsuits and carting coolers make their way down Michigan Avenue. The most popular is **North Avenue Beach,** about 6 blocks farther north, which has developed into a volleyball hot spot. With its landmark steamship-shaped beach house and Venice Beach–style gym, this is where the Lincoln Park singles come to play, check each other out, and fly by on bikes and in-line skates. Even though families might be outnumbered by singles, the atmosphere is open and easy, and you won't feel out of place in the least. The beach has a **Bike & Roll** shop (✆ 312/729-1000) for renting bicycles (open May 1–Sept 31), a chess pavilion, and **Castaways Bar & Grill** for sandwiches (✆ 773/281-1200; www.stefanirestaurants.com), which is open seasonally. It's also the place to be during the annual Air and Water Show, which takes place along the waterfront in August.

For more seclusion, try **Ohio Street Beach,** an intimate sliver of sand in tiny Olive Park, just north of Navy Pier, which, incredibly enough, remains largely ignored despite its central location. If you have a car, head up to **Montrose Beach,** a beautiful unsung treasure about midway between North Avenue Beach and Hollywood-Ardmore Beach (with plenty of free parking). Long popular with the city's Hispanic community, it has an expanse of beach mostly uninterrupted by piers or jetties, and a huge adjacent park with soccer fields and one big hill great for kite flying. Anglers can visit a small bait shop before heading for a nearby long pier designated for fishing, and teens can find a pickup game of volleyball here during the warmer months. **Hollywood-Ardmore Beach** (officially Kathy Osterman Beach), at the northern end of Lake Shore Drive, is a lovely crescent that's less congested and has steadily become more popular with gays who've moved up the lakefront from the Belmont Rocks, a longtime hangout.

If you've brought the family pooch along, you might want to take him for a dip at the **doggie beach** south of Addison Street, at about Hawthorne and Lake Shore Drive—although this minute spot aggravates some dog owners because it's situated in a harbor where the water is somewhat fouled by gas and oil from nearby boats. *Tip:* Try the south end of North Avenue Beach in early morning, before it opens to the public for the day. (Also consider that, in the off season, all beaches are fair game for dogs.)

Beaches officially open with a full retinue of lifeguards on duty beginning about June 20, but swimmers can wade into the chilly water from Memorial Day to Labor Day. Only the bravest souls venture into the water before July, when the temperature creeps up enough to make swimming an attractive proposition. Please take note that the entire lakefront is not beach, and don't do anything stupid such as diving off the rocks. Be extremely careful! The lake has drop-offs at points along the shore, and you can easily and quickly get into deeper water. Lake Michigan can develop large waves, too, so exercise the same caution you would at the ocean.

Oak Street, North Avenue, Loyola, Osterman, Montrose, South Shore, and Rainbow beaches are wheelchair- and stroller-friendly—they offer specially designed mats that create a path over the sand to the water. For questions about the 29 miles of beaches and parks along Lake Michigan, call the park district's lakefront region office at ℂ **312/742-5239.**

## BIKING

Biking is a great way to see the city, particularly the lakefront, along which a bike path extends for more than 18 miles. The stretch between Navy Pier and North Avenue Beach gets extremely crowded in the summer (you're jostling for space with in-line skaters, joggers, and dawdling pedestrians). If you're looking for more wide-open spaces, I recommend biking south from Navy Pier—once you're past the Museum Campus, traffic on the trail is light, and you can cruise all the way to Hyde Park. FINE PRINT If you want a more leisurely tour with good people-watching potential, head north (through the crowds) and be patient—once you pass Belmont Harbor, the traffic lets up somewhat. It's possible to ride all the way to Hollywood Beach, where the lakefront trail ends—a great workout.

To rent bikes, try **Bike Chicago,** which has locations at Navy Pier (✆ **312/595-9600**), North Avenue Beach (✆ **773/327-7206**), Millennium Park (✆ **888/BIKE-WAY** [245-3929]), the riverwalk (Wacker Dr. and Columbus St.—take the stairs down to the river; ✆ **312/595-9600**), and at the north end of the lakefront bike path at Foster Beach (✆ **773/275-2600**). Open from 8am to 8pm May through October (weather permitting), Bike Chicago stocks mountain and touring bikes, kids' bikes, kids' seats and trailers for any kids too young for a bike, strollers, and—most fun of all—quadcycles, which are four-wheeled contraptions equipped with a steering wheel and canopy that can accommodate four or five people. Rates for bikes start at $8 an hour ($6 for kids' bikes) and range up to about $34 a day (higher for high-end road bikes), with helmets, pads, and locks included. You can also rent bike seats for kids and wagons (the covered version that you pull behind your bike). If you'd like to cycle your way past some Chicago landmarks, guided tours are also available.

Both the park district (✆ **312/742-PLAY** [7529]) and the **Active Transportation Alliance** (✆ **312/427-3325;** www.activetrans.org) offer free maps that detail popular biking routes. The latter, which is the preeminent organization for cyclists in Chicago, also sells a much larger, more extensive map for $6.95 that shows routes within a seven-county area.

FINE PRINT Locking your bike anywhere you go is a no-brainer. More important, though, is never heading anywhere on the city's streets without first strapping on a helmet. Chicago Mayor Richard M. Daley is an avid cyclist himself and has tirelessly promoted the addition of designated bike lanes along many main thoroughfares. But, that said, most cabbies and drivers tend to ignore them. Bike with extreme caution on city streets (you can get a ticket for biking on the sidewalks), and stick to the lakefront path if you're not an expert rider.

## GOLF

Chicago has an impressive number of golf options within the city limits. The Chicago Park District offers six courses, three driving ranges, and three learning centers. Don't let a little cold weather stop you: As further evidence of the hardiness of Chicagoans, the golf courses are open year-round, even on Christmas Day! For tee times and information, call ℂ **312/245-0909.** Most recommended for kids is the **Diversey Driving Range,** 141 W. Diversey Pkwy. (ℂ **312/742-7929**), in Lincoln Park just north of Diversey Harbor; it's a fun way to get outside after dinner on a summer evening. This two-level range attracts all levels, from show-off scratch golfers to shanking beginners. The price is right ($9 for a bucket of balls), and the setting is pretty much perfect.

One of the most popular golf courses operated by the Chicago Park District is the 9-hole **Sydney Marovitz Course,** 3600 N. Lake Shore Dr., at Waveland Avenue. Many Chicagoans refer to it simply as "Waveland." Thanks to its picturesque lakefront location, it's always busy on weekends, so make a reservation well in advance (9 holes: $23.50 weekend, $20.50 weekday), and don't expect a quick round—this is where beginners come to practice. Another good bet, and one that's usually less crowded, is the 18-hole course in **Jackson Park** at 63rd Street and Stoney Island Avenue. These city-run courses are open from mid-April through November. For information on greens fees, locations, and hours, call the **Chicago Park District** golf office (ℂ **312/245-0909**), or go to www.cpdgolf.com.

In the northern suburbs, **Skokie Sports Park,** 3459 Oakton (ℂ **847/674-1500;** www.skokieparkdistrict.com), has an 18-hole around-the-world-themed miniature golf course, a 9-hole miniature golf course for the smallest tots, a two-tiered driving range, and junior golf lessons. The Traveler's Quest miniature golf course, geared toward older kids and adults, lets you putt around the Eiffel Tower and over the waterfall near Easter Island. Check out the African water hole (in which you putt into the hippo's mouth), the Japanese garden with lanterns and sizable hazards, and the Great Wall of China. The park is open April through October Sunday through Thursday from 8am to 10pm, Friday and Saturday until 11pm.

In nearby Lincolnwood, **Novelty Golf and Games,** 3550 W. Devon Ave. (ℂ **847/679-9434;** www.noveltygolf.com), has miniature golf, batting cages, a video arcade, and an ice-cream parlor. It's a 50-year-old operation that's open Saturday and Sunday from 11am to dusk from early March through late October, weather permitting.

## ICE SKATING

Whether you're executing graceful toe loops or merely stumbling across the rink, you can hit the ice in the heart of Chicago's Loop. The city's premier skating destination is the **McCormick Tribune Ice Rink** at Millennium Park, 55 N. Michigan Ave., at the intersection of Michigan Avenue and Monroe Street (© **312/742-5222;** www.millennium park.org). The location is unbeatable. You'll skate in the shadows of grand skyscrapers and within view of the lake. The rink is open daily from 9am to 9pm, November to March. Admission is free, and skate rentals are $10.

Year-round skating and ice-skating lessons are available at the only city-run indoor ice arena at **McFetridge Sports Complex** (known to many Chicago residents as California Park) located in the Lakeview neighborhood at 3845 N. California Ave., at Irving Park Road (© **773/478-2609**). Open skating sessions in the indoor rink are held Wednesday and Friday afternoons from 3:30 to 5pm, and Saturday and Sunday from 4:30 to 6pm. Skates can be rented for $3 a pair; the rink fee is $5 for ages 13 and up, $4 for ages 12 and under. The rink is huge and can be very crowded on weekends. You might want to take advantage of the free skating lessons, available on Monday from 5:15 to 5:55pm. There's also a relatively small rink at **Navy Pier,** 600 E. Grand Ave. (© **312/595-PIER** [7437]).

## IN-LINE SKATING

In-line skaters have been cruising Chicago's sidewalks, streets, and bike paths since the early 1990s. Numerous rental places have popped up, and several sporting-goods shops that sell in-line skates also rent them. The rentals generally include helmets and pads. **Bike Chicago,** with locations at Navy Pier (© **312/595-9600**), North Avenue Beach (© **773/327-7206**), Millennium Park (© **888/BIKE-WAY** [245-3929]), and more, charges $8 an hour or $30 a day (you can have the skates 8am–8pm).

The best route to skate, of course, is the lakefront trail that leads from Lincoln Park down to Oak Street Beach. Beware, though, that those same miles of trail are claimed by avid cyclists—and I've seen plenty of collisions between 'bladers and bikers. Approach Chicago lakefront traffic as carefully as you would a major expressway!

## SWIMMING

The Chicago Park District maintains about 30 indoor pools for lap swimming and general splashing around, but none are particularly convenient to downtown. If you are a resident, you should check out your local park (to find out where parks are located, see www.chicago parkdistrict.com). Some neighborhoods have incredible facilities that are safe and clean. For example, **Portage Park,** on Chicago's northwest side at 4100 Long Ave. (© **773/685-7235**), has a stunning outdoor Olympic-size pool, a diving board with three levels and its own dive pool, and a kids' pool with a water playhouse, waterfalls, and more. It's absolutely wonderful, and it's free. The neighborhood is populated by Hispanic and eastern European immigrants, and tons of kids jam the pool every summer weekend. Another great park for swimming is **Blackhawk Park,** at 2318 N. Lavergne Ave. in the Irving Park neighborhood (© **312/746-5014**). You'll find an outdoor spray pool and an indoor swimming pool. Pool hours vary according to age: Youth swim is at 3pm, teen swim at 5pm, and family swim at 7pm.

Still, my advice to visitors would be to skip the park district pools, because many are in off-the-beaten-track neighborhoods. As a visitor, your best bet for summer swimming is **Lake Michigan,** where beaches are open for swimmers Memorial Day through Labor Day from 9am to 9:30pm in areas watched over by lifeguards (no swimming off the rocks, please). It's a safe place to swim and a uniquely "Chicago" experience. Watch the news for beach closings, which happen occasionally, as the water is tested daily for bacteria. If you're a serious lap swimmer, you'll find company along the wall beginning at Ohio Street Beach, located slightly northwest of Navy Pier. The Chicago Triathlon Club marks a course here each summer with a buoy at both the ¼- and ½-mile marks. This popular swimming route follows the shoreline in a straight line. The water is fairly shallow. For more information, call the park district's beach and pool office (© **312/742-PLAY** [7529]).

The Chicago Park District manages 31 beaches along 24 miles of lakefront. Amenities vary, but most have a comfort station or a beach house and food vendors selling hot dogs, burgers, and soda. The two beaches I can recommend without hesitation are **Oak Street Beach** and **North Avenue Beach.** Both also feature a broader menu for dining: The Oak Street Beachstro (p. 76) serves gourmet salads, beef tenderloin, grilled salmon, and Key lime pie; the restaurant in the beach house at North Avenue Beach serves Jamaican jerk chicken and specialty ice cream.

For more information, call the park district's beach and pool office at ℃ **312/747-0832.**

## TENNIS

The best—and cheapest—tennis in the city is found at **Waveland Courts,** located on Lake Shore Drive at Addison. For about $5 per hour, you can play on these public courts. It's first-come, first-served, so get there early—the park is open from 6am to 11pm. Pay before you play at the trailer close to the Addison entrance. Tennis buffs report that the availability of courts is pretty good in the morning. League play takes place in the evenings, and it's difficult to get a court. Any non–tennis players in your family can play golf, which is also available here.

If it's lessons you're seeking, head for **McFetridge Sports Complex,** 3845 N. California Ave. (℃ **773/478-2609**). Students here report that the tennis pros are great, lessons are good, and the price is right. Court fees are $17/hour during the day, and $26/hour in the evening. You'll have no problem booking an indoor court in the summer, but in the winter, make sure to book ahead.

*Exploring on the cheap in Chicago doesn't mean giving up style—a concert at the Symphony Center can cost as little as $1. See p. 191.*

# ENTERTAINMENT & NIGHTLIFE

**G**ritty theater, late-night blues, house music, cutting-edge comedy, neighborhood bars, stellar opera—all these make up the smorgasbord that is Chicago after dark. Chicago's impressive entertainment scene has a uniquely laid-back, Midwestern vibe. To me, the most typical Chicago nightlife is to be found inside a neighborhood bar, where you'll find the natives hanging in a low-key atmosphere. Pick a neighborhood: You won't have to go far to find a tavern filled with locals, a jukebox, and a pool table.

You can go high-end and still feel the inviting atmosphere at the Chicago Symphony Orchestra and the Lyric Opera of Chicago (and

## The 411 on Chicago Nightlife

For up-to-date entertainment listings, check the local newspapers and magazines, particularly the At Play (Thurs) and On the Town (Fri) sections of the *Chicago Tribune* and the Weekend Plus (Fri) section of the *Chicago Sun-Times;* the weekly magazine *Time Out Chicago,* which has excellent comprehensive listings; and the *Chicago Reader* or *New City,* two free weekly tabloids with extensive listings. The *Tribune's* entertainment-oriented website, **www.metromix.com**; the *Reader's* website, **www.chicagoreader.com**; the local Citysearch website, **http://chicago.citysearch.com**; and **www.yelp.com** are also excellent sources of information, with lots of opinionated reviews.

you can score cheap tickets to both—I'll show you how). Broadway buffs can choose between big-league theaters such as Steppenwolf and The Goodman and the scrappy storefront companies around the city. The theater scene here was built by performers who valued gritty realism and a communal work ethic, and that down-to-earth energy is still very much present. Music and nightclub haunts are scattered throughout the city, but Chicago's thriving music scene is concentrated in Lincoln Park, Lakeview, and Wicker Park, where clubs are devoted to everything from jazz and blues to alternative rock and reggae.

While the city has its share of see-and-be-seen spots, Chicagoans in general are not obsessed with getting into the latest hot club; your ability to get behind the velvet rope is much higher (and the atmosphere much less high-pressure) than in some big cities.

And as for those see-and-be-seen spots, Chicago has dozens of über-hip lounges, some on rooftops with dazzling city views—another way that Chicagoans take advantage of our brief but gorgeous summers. In short, there's always something going on in the city and, unlike in Los Angeles or New York, you don't have to pay outrageous cover charges or be "chosen" to be a part of the scene. But keep in mind that the town isn't up all night: Bars close at 2am—some have a 4am license, but only some—so get an early start if you want a full night on the town in Chicago.

# 1 Cheap Opera (Chopera?)

**Chicago Opera Theater**   As the "other" opera company in town, Chicago Opera Theater doesn't get all the big names, but it does make opera accessible to a wider audience with an emphasis on American composers and performers who sing in English. It also helps that tickets are less expensive and more plentiful than those for the Lyric Opera. The opera has a wonderful educational outreach program that features one opera per season (a short one, usually!) that is performed by and for children. FINE PRINT Call well in advance for tickets to the next performance, as they always sell out. No matter what the bill, the talent and production values are top-notch.

Harris Theater for Music and Dance, 205 E. Randolph Dr. ℂ **312/704-8414.** www. chicagooperatheater.org. Tickets $30–$105 adults, children half-price. Subway/El: Red Line to Washington/State.

## Half-Price Theater Tickets

Why pay full price? **Hot Tix** (www.hottix.org) offers half-price tickets on the day of the show to more than 125 theaters throughout the Chicago area (on Fri, you can also purchase tickets for weekend performances). Tickets are sold Sunday through Thursday for the day of performance. Prices can range from $10 to $34.50, plus a $4.25 "convenience charge." You must buy the tickets in person at a Hot Tix outlet; the main Hot Tix box office is at 72 E. Randolph St., between Wabash and Michigan avenues. A second, smaller Hot Tix outlet is located in the heart of the city's shopping district, in the old pumping station at Michigan and Chicago avenues, which is now the **Chicago Water Works Visitor Center.** Its entrance is at 163 E. Pearson Street, across from the Water Tower Place mall. Hot Tix locations are open 10am to 6pm Tuesday through Saturday, and 11am to 4pm on Sunday. The Hot Tix website (www.hottix.org) lists what's on sale for that day, with frequent updates (the time of the updates is posted at the top of the website).

## Opera Underground

If you live in Chicago, you can join "Opera Underground", a club for young professionals. There is no charge to join and you can get a two-show package for $90 or a three-show package for $120. Tickets are for Wednesday evenings, and there is a pre-show reception at The Gage restaurant (24 S. Michigan Ave.) with free hors d'oeuvres and a cash bar from 6-7 p.m. Visit www.chicagooperatheater.org/tix/underground.html.

★ **Lyric Opera of Chicago**    A major American opera company, the Lyric attracts top-notch singers from all over the world. Naturally, this is not the first place you'd think of for a cheap night out, but if you're a student, the Lyric NExT program offers steeply discounted student tickets to the Opera's regular productions—as low as $20, when regular-priced seats are going for almost $200. For everyone else, try a matinee—performances are always less expensive than evening shows.

Just soaking in the ambience at the glamorous and opulent opera house is quite an experience. The handsome, 3,563-seat Art Deco Civic Opera House is the second-largest opera house in the country, built in 1929. Add to that the magnificence of the Lyric Opera Orchestra and chorus, the amazing sets and costumes, and the beautiful voices, and it's an experience you won't soon forget.

If you can't snag tickets or if you visit during the opera's off season in February and March, you can still check out the theater by taking a tour (✆ **312/827-5685**).

Civic Opera House, 20 N. Wacker Dr., at Madison St. ✆ **312/332-2244.** www.lyric opera.org. Tickets $45–$165. Subway/El: Brown Line to Washington.

## 2 The Theatah

**About Face Theatre**    About Face Theatre takes its mission seriously: to promote the creation of new works that examine gay and lesbian themes and experiences. While that often makes for a night of thought-provoking theater, the fare isn't always heavy with social-justice issues.

# RIVER NORTH & THE LOOP AFTER DARK

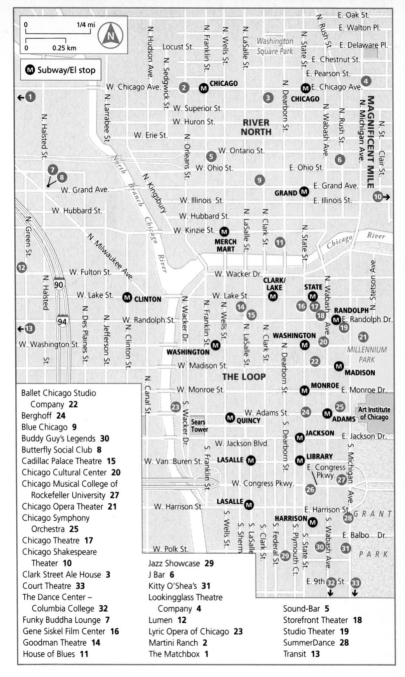

Ballet Chicago Studio
    Company **22**
Berghoff **24**
Blue Chicago **9**
Buddy Guy's Legends **30**
Butterfly Social Club **8**
Cadillac Palace Theatre **15**
Chicago Cultural Center **20**
Chicago Musical College of
    Rockefeller University **27**
Chicago Opera Theater **21**
Chicago Symphony
    Orchestra **25**
Chicago Theatre **17**
Chicago Shakespeare
    Theater **10**
Clark Street Ale House **3**
Court Theatre **33**
The Dance Center –
    Columbia College **32**
Funky Buddha Lounge **7**
Gene Siskel Film Center **16**
Goodman Theatre **14**
House of Blues **11**

Jazz Showcase **29**
J Bar **6**
Kitty O'Shea's **31**
Lookingglass Theatre
    Company **4**
Lumen **12**
Lyric Opera of Chicago **23**
Martini Ranch **2**
The Matchbox **1**

Sound-Bar **5**
Storefront Theater **18**
Studio Theater **19**
SummerDance **28**
Transit **13**

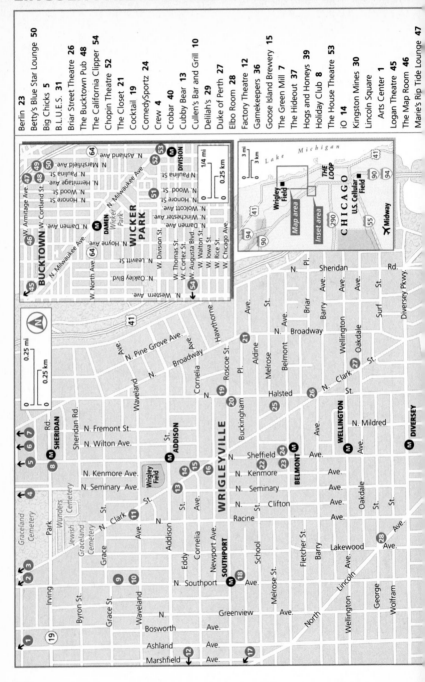

Berlin **23**
Betty's Blue Star Lounge **50**
Big Chicks **5**
B.L.U.E.S. **31**
Briar Street Theatre **26**
The Bucktown Pub **48**
The California Clipper **54**
Chopin Theatre **52**
The Closet **21**
Cocktail **19**
ComedySportz **24**
Crew **4**
Crobar **40**
Cubby Bear **13**
Cullen's Bar and Grill **10**
Delilah's **29**
Duke of Perth **27**
Elbo Room **28**
Factory Theatre **12**
Gamekeepers **36**
Goose Island Brewery **15**
The Green Mill **7**
The Hideout **37**
Hogs and Honeys **39**
Holiday Club **8**
The House Theatre **53**
iO **14**
Kingston Mines **30**
Lincoln Square
   Arts Center **1**
Logan Theatre **45**
The Map Room **46**
Marie's Rip Tide Lounge **47**

Music Box Theatre **9**
Old Town Ale House **43**
Old Town School
  of Folk Music **17**
Park West **34**
Pegasus Players **6**
Redmoon Theater **38**
Roscoe's Tavern **20**
Second City **42**
Sheffield's **22**
Smart Bar **11**
Smoke Daddy Rhythm and
  Bar-B-Que **51**
Southport Lanes &
  Billiards **18**
Spin **25**
Spoon **44**
Steppenwolf Theatre
  Company **41**
Theatre on the Lake **33**
Tilli's **35**
Too Much Light Makes the
  Baby Go Blind
  (The Neo-Futurarium) **3**
Trap Door Theatre **49**
Tuesday Funk: An Evening
  of Fiction, Essays and
  Poetry (Hopleaf Bar) **2**
Victory Gardens Theater **32**
The Wild Hare **16**

**M** Subway/El stop

One of the group's big hits was a very campy musical version of *Xena: Warrior Princess*. Performances are in the upstairs studio at Steppenwolf Theatre.

Office: 1222 W. Wilson Ave. ℭ **773/784-8565;** www.aboutfacetheatre.com. Tickets $20-$40.

**Blue Man Group**   Since 1997, the New York City performance phenomenon known as **Blue Man Group** has transformed the 625-seat Briar Street Theatre, beginning with the lobby, which is now a jumble of tubes and wires and things approximating computer innards. The show—which mixes percussion, performance art, mime, and rock 'n' roll—has become an immensely popular permanent fixture on the Chicago theater scene. The three strangely endearing performers, whose faces and heads are covered in latex and blue paint, know how to get the audience involved. Your first decision: Do you want the "splatter" or the "nonsplatter" seats? (The former necessitates the donning of a plastic sheet.) And here's your free-and-dirt-cheap tip: volunteer to usher and you can see the show for free. You just need to be at least 18, speak fluent English, and be capable of light lifting for clean-up. Four ushers are needed per performance, so call the box office. Show up an hour prior to show time, and wear black pants and white shirts; you get a seat, although it's not guaranteed where the seats will be. You just need to stay 15-30 mins after the show to help clean up.

3133 N. Halsted St. (at Briar St.). ℭ **773/348-4000.** Tickets $46–$56. Subway/El: Red or Brown line to Belmont.

**FREE** **Chicago Cultural Center**   Built in 1897, the Cultural Center's mandate has always been to provide the people of Chicago with access to the arts. The center puts on workshops and performances year-round, and concerts featuring Thai music or dance programs depicting the history and architecture of Chicago are just a few of the types of programs you might find. This is a great place to become familiar with many performing-arts genres active in Chicago, and with local artists like the Chicago Chamber Musicians, the Chicago Consortium of Community Music Schools, or the Chicago Cajun Aces. Best of all, it's free.

78 E. Washington St. ℭ **312/346-3278.** Free tickets. Subway: Red or Brown line to Randolph and State.

★ **Chicago Shakespeare Theater**   Winner of the 2008 Regional Theater Tony Award, this company does a great job of making Shakespeare accessible to all. They even reach out to families with offerings that include abbreviated versions of the Bard's work (the 2009 selection was a 75-min. abridgement of *Comedy of Errors*). This group's home on Navy Pier is a visually stunning, state-of-the-art jewel. The centerpiece of the glass-box complex, which rises seven stories, is a 525-seat court-yard-style theater patterned loosely after the Swan Theater in Stratford-upon-Avon. The complex also houses a 180-seat studio theater, an English-style pub, and lobbies with commanding views of Lake Michigan and the Chicago skyline. The Jentes Family Auditorium is the venue for kid-friendly shows, while the main theater presents three plays a year—almost always by the Bard—with founder and artistic director Barbara Gaines usually directing one of the shows.

800 E. Grand Ave. ✆ **312/642-2273.** www.chicagoshakes.com. Tickets $40–$68. Discounted parking in attached garage. Subway/El: Red Line to Grand, then bus 29 to Navy Pier.

**Chicago Theatre**   This 1920s music palace has been reborn as an all-purpose entertainment venue, hosting everything from pop acts (Mariah Carey, Norah Jones) and magicians to stand-up comedy (Lewis Black).

175 N. State St. (at Lake St.). ✆ **312/443-1130.** Subway/El: Red Line to Lake/State; Brown or Orange line to Clark/Lake.

**Chopin Theatre**   Located in Wicker Park, this independent arts center was founded in 1990, featuring its own productions, plus film showings, music, dance, and social events. The charming, kitschy theater was built in 1918 as a vaudeville theater and has a main stage, cabaret studio, art gallery, lounge, and cafe. You'll find unique Polish theater productions and other Eastern European artists performing here (the owners are Eastern European). Truly a notable independent theater, and not to be missed by the free and cheap traveler, thanks to a very laid-back ticket pricing structure (one recent show was $12, "more if you've got it, less if you're broke").

1543 W. Division St. ✆ **773/278-1500.** www.chopintheatre.com. Tickets $12–$25. Subway/El: Blue Line to Division.

★ **Court Theatre**   One of Chicago's outstanding cultural institutions, this intimate theater is tucked away on the University of Chicago campus. A professional theater company based here produces five plays per season, focusing on classic works. There's not a bad seat in the house, which is a black box–style theater with a semi-circle stage. Quality actors, free parking at the parking ramp next door,

## Chicago Indie Theater on the Cheap (and Sometimes Free!)

Virtually every show that goes up in Chicago, big or small, has a preview, industry, or pay-what-you-can performance (sometimes they have all three) where tickets are much cheaper than the usual price. Check www.theatreinchicago.com or the website of the theater or the company putting on the performance to find out when these are.

The League Of Chicago Theatres (www.chicagoplays.com) also has a great program that runs throughout all of October called the Free Night Of Theatre initiative, where they release a certain number of free tickets from a different company every night.

Chicago even has an organization of volunteer theatre ushers called The Saints (www.thesaints.org) that supplies trained volunteer ushers to theatres upon request—a great way to see a show for free.

and inexpensive tickets ranging from $24 to $32 make this a win. If you want to make it dirt cheap, rush tickets are available one hour before the show, for any seat in the house. $5 for U of C students, $10 for all other students, half-price for non-students. Recent performances have included Ma Rainey's *Black Bottom* and *The Year of Magical Thinking*.

5535 N. Ellis Ave. (btw. 55th and 56th sts.) ℅ **773/753-4472.** www.courttheatre.org. Subway/El: Red Line to 55th St./Garfield; walk across the street to the no. 55 bus, exit at Ellis Ave.

**Factory Theater** This irreverent young troupe offers the quintessential low-budget Chicago theater experience. The group specializes in original works written by the ensemble, many of which aim at a young, nontheatrical crowd (you're encouraged to bring your own beer and drink it during the late-night shows). The company's biggest hit was the raunchy trailer-park potboiler *White Trash Wedding and a Funeral,* and other recent productions (such as the Renaissance-Fair-inspired *RenFair: A Fistful of Ducats*) continue the irreverent fun. But the Factory also makes room for serious dramatic works written by members of its ensemble.

3504 N. Elston Ave. ℅ **312/409-3247;** www.thefactorytheater.com. Tickets $15-$20. Subway/El: Red Line to Addison, then bus 152 (Addison St.).

**Goodman Theatre**  If you're here around the holidays, you might be able to score tickets to the Goodman's annual production of *A Christmas Carol,* a Chicago holiday tradition. The show runs from mid-November to the end of December and sells out, but through the "Tix at Six" program (which offers half-price, day-of-show tickets, many of which are excellent seats that have been returned by subscribers), you might get lucky. FINE PRINT Tix at Six tickets go on sale at the box office at 6pm for evening performances and at noon for matinees.

170 N. Dearborn St. ℂ **312/443-3800.** www.goodman-theatre.org. Tickets $30–$50 main stage, $10–$30 studio. Subway/El: Red Line to Washington/State or Lake/State; Brown or Orange line to Clark/Lake.

**The House Theatre**  If you're looking for the up-and-coming stars of Chicago theater, keep your eyes on the House. This group of young actors takes on big themes (Harry Houdini and his obsession with death; the space-age tales of Ray Bradbury) and turns them into non-stop spectacles of drama, music, and comedy. Despite the usual budget constraints, the sets and special effects are impressive—as are the troupe's energy, imagination, and humor. Come see them while their tickets remain ultra-affordable.

1543 W. Division St. ℂ **773/251-2195;** www.thehousetheatre.com. Tickets $17-$22. Subway/El: Red Line to Belmont, then bus 77 (Belmont Ave.)

**Lincoln Square Arts Center**  With staged readings, plays, and music and dance performances by different performing arts companies, like Alcyone Theater and Babes with Blades, this theater aims to tackle social, political, and spiritual issues. And, close to our hearts, they want to present shows that are not only thought-provoking, but affordable. You can also take part in writing and theatrical workshops here. Readings take place on Mondays at 7:30pm and cost $5.

4754 N. Leavitt. ℂ **773/275-7930.** http://lincolnsquareartscenter.com. Subway/El: Brown Line to Western.

**Lookingglass Theatre Company**  A rising star on the Chicago theatrical scene, Lookingglass produces original shows and unusual literary adaptations in a highly physical and visually imaginative style. Its location in the Water Tower Pumping Station—just off Michigan Avenue and within walking distance of many downtown hotels—makes it especially visitor-friendly. Recent offerings included *Metamorphoses,* a sublime and humorous modern recasting of Ovid's myths that became a hit in New York, and *Lookingglass Alice,* an acrobatic retelling of *Alice in Wonderland.* Ensemble member Mary Zimmerman—who directed *Metamorphoses*—has built a national reputation for her creative interpretations of literature, so if she's directing a show while you're in town, don't miss it. Lookingglass shows emphasize visual effects as much as they do acting, whether it's having performers wade through a giant shallow pool or take to the sky on a trapeze.

821 N. Michigan Ave. (at Chicago Ave.). ℂ **312/337-0665.** www.lookingglasstheatre. org. Tickets $25–$55. Subway/El: Red Line to Chicago.

**Pegusus Players**  Performing in a rented college auditorium in the gritty North Side neighborhood of Uptown, Pegasus Players specializes in the kind of intellectually demanding fare that bigger mainstream theaters are afraid to risk. The group prides itself on picking shows that highlight social issues, such as *Heat Wave,* a dramatization of the tragic summer of 1995, when extreme weather led to the death of more than 700 Chicagoans, most of them elderly and poor.

1145 W. Wilson Ave., O'Rourke Performing Arts Center, Truman College. ℂ **773/ 878-9761;** www.pegasusplayers.org. Tickets $15-$25. Subway/El: Red Line to Wilson.

**Redmoon Theater**  Redmoon Theater might well be the most intriguing and visionary theater company in Chicago. Founded in 1990, the company produces "spectacle theater" involving masks, objects, and an international range of puppetry styles in indoor and outdoor venues around town. Utterly hypnotic, highly acrobatic and visceral, and using minimal narration, Redmoon's adaptations of Melville's Moby Dick, Mary Shelley's Frankenstein, Victor Hugo's The Hunchback of Notre Dame, and Rachel's Love, an original work based on Jewish folktales, were revelations that earned the company an ardent and burgeoning following. Every September, Redmoon presents an annual "spectacle," transforming a public park into a site for performance art, larger-than-life puppet shows, and dramatic visual effects.

Office at 1438 W. Kinzie St. ℂ **312/850-8440;** www.redmoon.org. Tickets $20-$30.

★ **Steppenwolf Theatre Company**  Focusing on original, edgy drama, this veteran company has launched the careers of many well-respected actors, including Joan Allen, John Malkovich, and Gary Sinise. A number of the original works and classic revivals staged at the company's state-of-the-art complex go on to Broadway. Steppenwolf often has $20 seats available beginning at 11am on the day of a performance; call or stop by the Audience Services office at the theater.

1650 N. Halsted St. (at North Ave.). © **312/335-1650.** www.steppenwolf.org. Tickets $20–$55. El: Red Line to North/Clybourn.

**Storefront Theater**   Every kind of lively art, from theater, dance, performance art, chamber opera, puppetry, and cabaret to staged readings, finds a home here. Located in the Gallery 37 Center for the Arts, in the heart of the Loop's revitalized theater district, this state-of-the-art black box theater provides a forum for Chicago's best artists to show off their accomplishments.

66 E. Randolph St. © **312/742-8497**. www.dcatheater.org. Tickets $9-$18; some productions each year are free. Subway/El: Brown Line to Randolph.

**Studio Theater**   When you pop in to the Chicago Cultural Center, you might find yourself seeing a show here, at an intimate stage. The theater is used as an incubator space, giving Chicago's best off-Loop theater companies the opportunity to share their work with downtown audiences. The Department of Cultural Affairs provides the space for free to encourage the growth of new creative talent. Ticket prices are kept low or admission is free for select events to allow everyone the chance to enjoy some of Chicago's best theater.

77 E. Randolph St. © **312/744-6630.** Subway/El: Brown, Green, Orange, or Purple line to Randolph; or Red Line to Washington/State. Bus: 3, 4, 20, 56, 60, 127, 131, 145, 146, 147, 151, or 157.

**Theatre on the Lake**   What a great way to see two of the city's signature strengths: a sublime skyline view from the water's edge, and an evening of off-Loop Chicago theater. The Prairie School-style building, built in 1920 as a sanitarium for babies and children suffering from tuberculosis, has hosted theatrical productions along the lake for half a century, but in recent years, the park district has hit upon a perfect programming gimmick. Each week a different independent theater company gets to strut its stuff, usually restaging a play they performed earlier in the year. Performances run from June into August on Wednesday to Sunday evenings, and some shows do sell out, so it pays to reserve in advance. At intermission, you can walk out the back door and look south to the city lights. If it's a cool night, bring a sweater, because the screened-in theater is open to the night air (allowing the noise of traffic on Lake Shore Dr. to intrude somewhat).

And a warning for those hot summer nights: The building is not air-conditioned.

Fullerton Ave. and Lake Shore Dr. ℂ **312/742-7994.** Tickets $18. Bus: 151 (Sheridan).

★ **Too Much Light Makes the Baby Go Blind** The longest-running show in town offers thirty "plays" (sketches ranging in tone from humorous to touching) in 60 minutes—a bargain at any price. Seats are first-come, first-served, so arrive at least an hour before the curtain goes up. The shows run Friday and Saturday at 11:30pm and Sunday at 7pm.

At the Neo-Futurarium, 5153 N. Ashland Ave. ℂ **773-275-5255.** www.neofuturists. org. Tickets are $9 plus the roll of a single-sided die (in other words, $10–$15). Bring $15 cash and you're in good shape (cash only). El: Red Line to Berwyn.

FREE ★ **Tuesday Funk: An Evening of Fiction, Essays and Poetry** This free reading series takes place at Hopleaf Bar, in the Andersonville neighborhood, at 7pm on the first Tuesday of the month. Seriously good stories from stars on the Chicago literary scene, accompanied by some seriously good Belgian beer, mussels, and frites.

Hopleaf Bar, 5148 N. Clark St. (at Foster Ave.) ℂ **773/334-9851.** http://tuesdayfunk. blogspot.com. Subway/El: Red Line to Berwyn. Bus: 22 to Foster.

**Trap Door Theatre** Trap Door is emblematic of the streetwise, no-holds-barred brand of off-Loop theater. A risk-taking, emotionally high-voltage company that has somehow stayed afloat (despite performing in a converted garage hidden behind a Bucktown restaurant), Trap Door concentrates on plays with a social or political bent. Many tend to be original works or decidedly noncommercial, provocative pieces by rarely produced cerebral artists, many of them European. (A few years ago, the show AmeriKafka, inspired by writer Franz Kafka and his visit to a performance by a Yiddish theater troupe, even featured a brief X-rated puppet show.) Prepare to be challenged: Theater doesn't get any more up close and personal than this.

1655 W. Cortland St. ℂ **773/384-0494;** www.trapdoortheatre.com. Tickets $15-$20. Subway/El: Blue Line to Division.

★ **Victory Gardens Theater** Victory Gardens is one of the few pioneers of off-Loop theater that has survived from the 1970s. It's hard to go wrong with a show here. The company was rewarded for its unswerving commitment to developing playwrights with a Tony Award for regional theater in 2001—a real coup for a relatively small

## Become a Saint

You can usher to see the show for free at Victory Gardens and many other Chicago venues by joining The Saints (www.saintschicago.org). The Saints is a 2,000-member organization of volunteers for the performing arts that serve over 80 of the Chicago and suburban theater, dance, and music organizations. Most Chicago venues are ushered by Saints volunteers. Join for a $65 annual fee, and choose the shows you want to usher online. You must be 16 to join.

theater. The plays tend to be accessible stories about real people and real situations—nothing too experimental. Even though most shows don't feature nationally known actors, the casts are always first-rate. Even better, if you're a student, rush tickets are available 30 minutes before the show for half price.

Victory Gardens stages shows at its main stage inside the former Biograph movie theater (known in Chicago lore as the place where the FBI gunned down bank robber John Dillinger in 1934). Smaller independent companies play on four smaller stages at the Victory Gardens Greenhouse Theater, 2257 N. Lincoln Ave., a few blocks south.

2433 N. Lincoln Ave. (1 block north of Fullerton Ave.). ✆ **773/871-3000.** www.victory gardens.org. Tickets $30–$45. Subway/El: Red or Brown line to Fullerton.

## 3 Dance

**Ballet Chicago Studio Company** Under artistic director Daniel Duell, a former New York City Ballet dancer, the group is notable for its specialty: the ballets of Balanchine. The ballet performs one full-length story ballet a year, usually in April or May. Most performances take place at the Athaneum Theatre, 2936 N. Southport Ave., and tickets go on sale 1 month before the performances through Ticketmaster (✆ **312/902-1500**). For a current performance schedule, check the company's website.

17 N. State St. ✆ **312/251-8838.** www.balletchicago.org. Tickets $12–$25. Subway/El: Orange, Brown, Purple Express, Green, or Pink line to Adams/Wabash; Blue or Red line to Monroe.

## Ravinia Festival

Ravinia (② **847/266-5100** or 312/RAVINIA (728-4642); www.ravinia. org), summer home of the Chicago Symphony Orchestra in suburban Highland Park, is a Chicago summer tradition. Tickets are as low as $10 (the average price is $25) for lawn tickets. Located in Highland Park, at Green Bay and Lake-Cook roads, the festival strives to be budget-friendly by maintaining low ticket prices and inviting patrons to pack their own picnics and sit on the lawn. There's even a series of Kraft Kids Concerts that reach out to the next generation of music lovers on various Saturdays and Sundays.

Adults will want to join Chicago natives by chilling on the lawn while catching a pop act, dance performance, operatic aria, or blues concert. Tickets are available for the lawn and the covered pavilion, where you get a reserved seat and a view of the stage. The lawn is the real joy of Ravinia: sitting under the stars and a canopy of leafy branches while listening to music and indulging in an elaborate picnic (it's a local tradition to try to outdo everyone else by bringing candelabras and fine china). I've been here for everything from Beethoven symphonies to folksy singer-songwriters, and the setting has been magical every time.

**Chicago Human Rhythm Project**  This group performs an annual tap-dance festival that was created in 1990 and brings together tap and percussive dancers from all over the world. It's an impressive sight (and sound). Dancers spend a month in Chicago, taking a series of workshops and outreach programs. It all culminates in a stirring week of performances in July and August at locations throughout the city and suburbs.

② **773/281-1825.** www.chicagotap.com. Tickets about $20.

**The Dance Center—Columbia College Chicago**  Columbia College, a liberal-arts institution specializing in the arts and media, has been growing by leaps and bounds in recent years. Its Dance Center—the hub of Chicago's modern dance milieu—features an intimate "black box" 275-seat performance space with stadium seating and marvelous sightlines. The Dance Center hosts at least a dozen performances a year by both international and national touring groups and home-grown choreographers.

1306 S. Michigan Ave. ✆ **312/344-8300.** www.colum.edu/dance_center. Tickets $15–$25. Bus: 151. Subway/El: Red Line to Roosevelt.

★ **Dance Chicago**    Dance Chicago is a highly engaging festival that spans about 2 months and showcases the talents of up-and-coming contemporary-dance companies and choreographers. It usually takes place from October to December. In recent years the programs have included jazz, hip-hop, tap, ballroom, tango, salsa, swing, and more. There are usually special performances for kids, too. Venues change from year to year; in 2009, performances were being held in north suburban Skokie and on the north side of the city. Check the website for the latest.

✆ **773/989-0698.** www.dancechicago.com. Tickets $15–$25.

★ **Hubbard Street Dance Chicago**    Dance lovers recommend that if you're going to see just one dance performance while you're in town, make it Hubbard Street, Chicago's best-known dance troupe whose mix of jazz, modern, ballet, and theater dance has won many devoted local fans. Sometimes whimsical, sometimes romantic, the crowd-pleasing 22-member ensemble incorporates a range of dance traditions, from Kevin O'Day to Twyla Tharp, who has choreographed pieces exclusively for Hubbard Street. Although the troupe spends most of the year touring, it has regular 2- to 3-week Chicago engagements in the fall and spring. In the summer the dancers often perform at Ravinia Festival (p. 186).

Office: 1147 W. Jackson Blvd. ✆ **312/850-9744.** www.hubbardstreetdance.com. Tickets $20–$75.

**River North Dance Company**    Chicago can be a brutal testing ground for start-up dance companies, who have to struggle to find performance space and grab publicity. But the odds didn't buckle the well-oiled knees of the River North Dance Company. This terrifically talented jazz dance ensemble performs programs of short, Broadway-style numbers by established and emerging choreographers. FINE PRINT You never know where the company will pop up next, so call for information on upcoming shows.

Office: 1016 N. Dearborn St. ✆ **312/944-2888.** www.rivernorthchicago.com. Tickets $25–$30.

★ **FREE** **SummerDance**   It's free! It's fun! The hugely popular annual Chicago SummerDance Festival usually runs from late June through August in the Spirit of Music Garden in Grant Park. Presented by the Chicago Department of Cultural Affairs, the festival features 1-hour dance lessons to taped music (you can learn everything from ballroom dancing to country line dancing), followed by dancing to live orchestras, every Thursday, Friday, and Saturday evening from 6 to 9:30pm, and Sunday afternoons beginning at 4pm, weather permitting. The festival also presents folk dance from Scandinavia, Israel, Ireland, Scotland, Wales, and other regions at various venues throughout the city.

Grant Park, 601 S. Michigan Ave. (btw. Harrison and Balbo, across from Columbia College). For complete information on what's scheduled, call the Chicago Department of Cultural Affairs at ℂ **312/744-6630.** Free admission. Subway/El: Red Line to Jackson.

## 4  Comedy Clubs

Chicago has always nurtured young comics, and while you're here, you definitely must explore Chicago's comic side. From the storied Second City company to iO, and scrappier, up-and-coming troupes, Chicago is a training ground for the nation's best comedians.

**ComedySportz**   Most improv-comedy shows aren't exactly family-friendly, but ComedySportz does away with the bar-like atmosphere and R-rated topics to deliver shows that are funny for the whole family. Chicago's only all-ages professional improv troupe sets two groups of five comedians against each other to compete for audience applause. "It isn't *about* sports—it *is* a sport," is the tagline here. Catch the ComedySportz4Kids show on Saturdays at 2pm (kids 10 and under welcome; tickets $8). Kids can participate in the show, or just watch—either way, it's a blast. For everyone else, there are three free shows on Wednesday nights, and $10 student rush tickets are available every night 30 minutes before the curtain rises.

929 W. Belmont Ave. ℂ **773/549-8080.** www.comedysportzchicago.com. Tickets $21. Subway/El: Blue Line to Belmont.

★ **iO** Formerly ImprovOlympic, iO engages the audience as the talented cast solicits suggestions and creates original performances. Once a theme is decided, a series of skits, monologues, and songs are built around it. Unscripted nightly performances have included a variety of themes, from free-form pieces to shows loosely based on concepts such as *Star Trek* or dating. Like all improv, it's a gamble: It could be a big laugh, or the amateur performers could go down in flames. Successful alums include Mike Myers, the late Chris Farley, Tim Meadows, Andy Dick, and Conan O'Brien's former *Late Night* sidekick, Andy Richter. The shows at 8pm on Wednesday are free, as are certain student performances (check the website's calendar for current free shows)—otherwise, tickets range from the very reasonable price of $5 to $14.

3541 N. Clark St. (at Addison St.). ℂ **773/880-0199**. http://ioimprov.com. Tickets $5–$14. Subway/El: Red Line to Addison.

### Grant Park Movie Festival

Each summer, more than 170 current and classic movies are shown in neighborhood parks throughout the city, from June through September. One of the central locations is Butler Field in Grant Park, where you can spend Tuesday nights watching classic movies for free. Movies start at around 8pm (depending on when the sun sets). Rain won't stop the screenings, unless lightning, strong winds, and other severe conditions are present. Grab a picnic basket, fill it with snacks and drinks (but no alcohol, which is prohibited in the seating areas) and a blanket and enjoy the show. A nearby sandwich shop is **Pastoral**, where generous sandwiches will run you only $7. Pastoral is located at 53 E. Lake St. (ℂ **312/658-1250**). Butler Field (Michigan Ave. and Monroe St.; ℂ **312/744-3315**; www.explore chicago.org).

**Second City**  For more than 40 years, Second City has been the top comedy club in Chicago and the most famous of its kind in the country. Photos of famous graduates line the lobby walls, including Elaine May, John Belushi, and former *Saturday Night Live* cast members Tina Fey, Horatio Sanz, and Rachel Dratch. Today's Second City is a veritable factory of improv, with shows on two stages (the storied main stage and the smaller Second City ETC) and a hugely popular training school. To sample the Second City experience, catch the free post-show improv session (it gets going around 10:30pm); no ticket is necessary if you skip the main show (except Fri).The main-stage ensembles change frequently, and the shows can swing wildly back and forth on the hilarity meter. In recent years, the club has adopted the long-form improvisational program pioneered by iO (see above), which has brought much better reviews. Check the theater reviews in the *Reader,* a free local weekly, for an opinion on the current show.

1616 N. Wells St. (in the Pipers Alley complex at North Ave.). © **877/778-4707** or 312/337-3992. www.secondcity.com. Tickets about $20. Subway/El: Brown Line to Sedgwick.

## 5 Retro & Indie Movie Theaters

★ **Gene Siskel Film Center** Named after the late *Chicago Tribune* film critic, this theater for serious film buffs is part of the School of the Art Institute of Chicago. If you're a student, tickets are a real bargain at $7 ($10 general admission). The theater offers an array of foreign, art, and experimental films, as well as lectures and discussions with filmmakers.

164 N. State St. © **312/846-2600.** www.siskelfilmcenter.org. El: Red Line to Washington; or Brown Line to Randolph.

**Logan Theatre** One of the few remaining second-run movie theaters in the city. You can check out a pretty recent film for $4 here. There's a definite vintage feel to the place, which has four small screens, each boasting decent digital surround sound. The place is a little shabby, but retains a nice neighborhood feel. It's easily accessible by public transportation.

2646 N. Milwaukee Ave. © **773/252-0627.** El: Blue Line to Logan Square.

★ **Music Box Theatre** This atmospheric movie house, designed to re-create the open-air feeling of an Italian courtyard, opened in 1929. The now-restored theater screens cult, independent, classic, and foreign films. Tickets are $9.25, with a $1 first-show-of-the-day discount Monday through Thursday.

3733 W. Southport Ave. © **773/871-6604.** www.musicboxtheatre.com. Tickets $9. Subway/El: Brown Line to Southport.

# 6 Concert Venues

★ **Blue Chicago**    Blue Chicago pays homage to female blues belters with a strong lineup of the best women vocalists around. The 1940s-style brick-walled room, decorated with original artwork of Chicago blues vignettes, is open Monday through Saturday, with music beginning at 9pm. Admission allows you to club-hop between this venue and a second location, open Tuesday through Sunday, down the street at 536 N. Clark St.

534 N. Clark St. (at the Blue Chicago store). ✆ **312/642-6261.** www.bluechicago. com. Tickets $8 Sun–Thurs, $10 Fri–Sat. Free for children 12 and under. Subway/El: Red or Brown Line to Chicago.

**B.L.U.E.S.**    Live music plays 365 days a year in a dark, narrow club that seats patrons up close to the performers.

2519 N. Halsted St. (at Wrightwood Ave.). ✆ **773/528-1012.** www.chicagobluesbar. com. $5–$8 cover. El: Brown Line to Diversey.

★ **Buddy Guy's Legends**    If Chicago is the body and soul of blues music, then this club—owned and operated by rock-'n'-roll Hall-of-Famer Buddy Guy—is its heart. The club's renowned guitar collection features instruments played by the likes of Eric Clapton and John Lee Hooker.

754 S. Wabash Ave. (btw. Balbo and 8th sts.). ✆ **312/427-0333.** www.buddyguys. com. Usually under $10 cover. El: Red Line to Harrison/State.

**FREE** Chicago Musical College of Rockefeller University    Hear outstanding students and amazing young artists for free at this downtown location, with solo and ensemble performances by guest artists, faculty, and students.

430 S. Michigan Ave., at Congress. ✆ **312/341-3780.** Evening performances begin at 7:30pm, and daytime concerts start at 1pm. All classical music performances are free; opera performances are $10. Subway/El: Red Line to Harrison.

★ **Chicago Symphony Orchestra**    The CSO is among the best symphonies in the world—a legacy of the late maestro Sir Georg Solti, who captured a record-breaking 31 Grammy Awards for his CSO recordings. In addition to classical music, the "Symphony Center Presents" series has included some of the top jazz, world beat, Latin, and cabaret artists in the world in recent years. Although they're in high demand, good seats often become available on concert day. Gallery seats at the top of the hall are the least expensive. Student tickets are just $10 when you buy them online at the CSO website. Call Symphony Center or stop by the box office to check availability.

But the real free and dirt cheap bargain is the **Civic Orchestra of Chicago,** the training orchestra of the Chicago Symphony since 1919. They are amazing, and also highly regarded by music fans. The Civic Orchestra presents six free programs a year at Orchestra Hall. Tickets are $1 (basically, you're paying a handling fee). Tickets are general admission, so you can sit anywhere you like.

Orchestra Hall, in Symphony Center, 220 S. Michigan Ave. ⓒ **312/294-3000.** www. cso.org. Tickets $25–$110; box seats $185. Subway/El: Red Line to Jackson.

**House of Blues**   The largest outpost in the growing House of Blues chain, this 55,000-square-foot complex, extravagantly decorated with 600 pieces from owner Isaac Tigrett's collection of Mississippi Delta folk art, isn't really a blues club as much as a showcase for rock, R&B, zydeco, reggae, and everything else. Prices depend on the act, but tickets for up-and-comers can be as cheap as $8. Gospel as well as blues originated in Chicago, and the House of Blues's popular Sunday gospel brunch, offering a Southern-style buffet, brings a different Chicago gospel choir to the stage each week; this is a splurge at $38 per person, but it is all you can eat (plus champagne mimosas). If you decide to indulge, get tickets in advance, as the two weekly "services" (10am and noon) often sell out.

329 N. Dearborn St. (at Kinzie St.). ⓒ **312/923-2000** for general information, 312/923-2020 for concert information. www.hob.com. Ticket prices vary depending on the act. Subway/El: Red Line to Grand.

★ **Jazz Showcase**   Spanning more than 50 years and several locations, founder Joe Segal has become synonymous with jazz in Chicago. There are two shows a night (three on Sun), and reservations are recommended when a big-name headliner is featured. Such well-regarded musicians as McCoy Tyner, Clark Terry, Maynard Ferguson, and Ahmad Jamal have made appearances in recent years. Shows are at 8 and 10pm and admission ranges from $20 to $25. FINE PRINT If you have a student ID, admission can be as low as $5. The Segals make an effort to cultivate new generations of jazz lovers: Each Sunday, the club offers a 4pm matinee show that admits kids under 12 for free and has a nonsmoking policy (they also give discounts to students at this show).

The Segals' latest outpost is the new **Joe's Be-bop Cafe and Jazz Emporium** at Navy Pier, 600 E. Grand Ave. (© **312/595-5299**), a Southern-style barbecue restaurant with live music nightly.

806 S. Plymouth Court (in the historic Dearborn Station building, just south of Polk St.). © **312/360-0234.** www.jazzshowcase.com. Tickets $20–$25. Subway/El: Red Line to Harrison.

**Kingston Mines**   This veteran roadhouse attracts hard-core fans and celebs with two stages' worth of down-home blues. Performances last until 4am on Saturdays.

2548 N. Halsted St. (at Wrightwood Ave.). © **773/477-4646.** www.kingstonmines. com. $12 cover Sat–Wed. El: Brown Line to Diversey.

★ **Old Town School of Folk Music**   Country, folk, bluegrass, Latin, Celtic—the Old Town School of Folk Music covers a spectrum of indigenous musical forms. A full schedule of classes, concerts, and special events are geared to everyone from children ages 6 months (their famous "Wiggleworms" classes) to seniors. The school is best known as a training center offering a slate of music classes, but it also hosts everyone from the legendary Pete Seeger to bluegrass phenom Alison Krauss. The school's home, in a former 1930s library, is the world's largest facility dedicated to the preservation and presentation of traditional and contemporary folk music.

To check out Old Town School for dirt cheap, stop in on the first Friday of every month. Bring an instrument, a couple of songs, dancing shoes, and friends. The cafe is open, and as a centerpiece event, the school features a concert performance by a member of its excellent faculty or staff. Doors open at 5pm and there is a $5 donation.

4544 N. Lincoln Ave. (btw. Wilson and Montrose aves.). © **773/728-6000.** www.old townschool.org. Tickets $10–$25. Subway/El: Blue Line to Western.

## 7 Bars & Clubs with Live Music

FINE PRINT The club and music scene is always changing, often outdating recommendations before the ink can dry on a page. It's best to check online or call to make sure a bar or club is still playing the music you're looking for on the night you intend to go.

★ **The California Clipper**   This lovingly restored 1940s tavern, with a gorgeous Art Deco bar and red walls, is worth a trip out to

Humboldt Park on the weekends for its live rockabilly and "country swing." Music starts at 10pm, Friday and Saturday nights.

1002 N. California Ave. ✆ 773/384-2547. www.californiaclipper.com. No cover. El: Blue Line to California, then take a cab.

**Cubby Bear** Cubs fans and the surrounding neighborhood's young professionals head to this tri-level landmark to vent before and/or after games. Pool tables, darts, and TV screens offer diversions. At night, the club is one of Chicago's premier rock venues.

1059 W. Addison St. (across from Wrigley Field). ✆ **773/327-1662.** www.cubbybear. com. Concert tickets under $10. Cover about $7, depending on the act. El: Red Line to Addison.

★ **Cullen's Bar and Grill** This Irish watering hole attracts a diverse crowd, from singles to families, and features a large selection of beer and great food, including tasty grilled shrimp and huge Caesar salads. After you've downed a pint or two, stick around for the live Celtic music or take in a movie at the old-time Music Box Theatre next door (p. 190).

3741 N. Southport Ave. ✆ **773/975-0600.** No cover. El: Brown Line to Southport.

**Elbo Room** The eclectic acts at this small live music venue range from hip-hop to Goth to rockabilly. The crowds are equally diverse.

2871 N. Lincoln Ave. (at George St.). ✆ **773/549-5549.** www.elboroomchicago.com. $3 and up cover; no cover in the upstairs lounge. El: Brown Line to Diversey.

★ **The Green Mill** Known for offering great jazz in a historical setting, this former speak-easy was established in 1907 and frequented by infamous mobster Al Capone. Today, you can hear Latin jazz, big band jazz, jazz piano, and more. Sunday nights, it hosts the famous Uptown Poetry Slam with Marc Smith.

4802 N. Broadway (at Lawrence Ave.). ✆ **773/878-5552.** Free to $8 cover. El: Red Line to Lawrence.

★ **The Hideout** Head to this friendly tavern for the best lineup of folk and "alt country" bands in the city. The location epitomizes the term "out of the way," but it's worth the trip (about a $10 cab ride from the Magnificent Mile).

1354 W. Wabansia Ave. (btw. Elston Ave. and Throop St.). ✆ **773/227-4433.** www. hideoutchicago.com. Usually $5–$10 cover. El: Blue Line to Damen.

**The Wild Hare**   Dreadlocks and Red Stripe beer abound at Chicago's premier reggae club, which has hosted such notables as the Wailers and Yellowman.

3530 N. Clark St. (at Addison St.). © **773/327-4273.** No cover until 9:30pm Mon–Tues; otherwise $8–$12. El: Red Line to Addison.

# 8 Dance Clubs

**Crobar**   Young, hip patrons wag their tails to electro, techno, and progressive beats at one of Chicago's largest dance halls. You can check out specials like $1 drinks on Recession Buster Fridays through their website—otherwise, you can end up spending too much at a big nightclub like this.

1543 N. Kingsbury St. (south of North Ave.). © **312/337-5001.** www.crobar.com. No cover to $20 cover, depending on the night. El: Red Line to North/Clybourn.

★ **Funky Buddha Lounge**   A bit off the beaten path, west of the River North gallery district, this club blends in with its industrial surroundings—even the whimsical Buddha sculpture on the heavy steel front door is a rusted husk. Inside is a different scene altogether: low red lighting, seductive dens with black-leather and faux leopard-skin sofas, lots of candles, and antique light fixtures salvaged from an old church. The DJs are among the best in the city, flooding the nice-size dance floor with everything from hip-hop, bhangra, and funk to African, soul, and underground house. The crowd is just as eclectic as the music—everything from yuppies and after-dinner hipsters to die-hard clubhoppers and barely legal wannabes. Hugely popular Thursday nights pack in the young, mostly white club kids; Friday and Saturday feature a cool, eclectic crowd decked out in funky gear. The bus runs to this area, but take a cab at night. FINE PRINT Get in free before 11pm with that night's password, which you can get from their website and by adding the club as a friend on Facebook.

728 W. Grand Ave. © **312/666-1695.** www.funkybuddha.com. Cover $10–$30. Free before 11pm with that night's password. Bus: 65 (Grand Ave.).

**Hogs & Honeys**   Dance on the bar, ride the mechanical bull, and kick back to the sounds of Kid Rock on the sound system at this *Coyote Ugly*–inspired honky-tonk.

901 W. Weed St. © **312/804-1459.** www.hogsandhoneys.com. $5 cover; $3 for a ride on the mechanical bull. Subway/El: Red Line to North/Clybourn.

**Lumen** The gimmick at this newer spot, which occupies a former meat-packing facility in the West Loop, is light, particularly the overhead LED display, which changes color throughout the night. The 5,000-square-foot space features concrete, stainless steel, and bamboo in its design, along with the aforementioned light spectacle, which is coordinated with its powerful sound system. There's no VIP list, which gives it an everyman kind of feel, and means minimal line-waiting out front.

839 W. Fulton Market, at Halsted St. ℂ **312/733-2222.** No cover charge on Fri; on Sat, no cover charge until 10:30pm. Subway/El: Green Line to Clinton.

★ FREE **Smart Bar** One of the coolest clubs in Chicago is tucked away in the dimly lit basement of Metro, one of Chicago's best live rock venues. DJs here do some serious spinning; every night features a different style of music. Lots of free nights during the week; a recent schedule showed free shows Wednesday and Thursday nights and text-message specials that get you in free before 11pm on the weekend.

3730 N. Clark St. ℂ **773/549-0203.** www.smartbarchicago.com. Cover $5–$15. El: Red Line to Addison.

**Sound-Bar** DJs are the draw at this multilevel, high-tech dance club, which prides itself on booking top nightlife names. The young, club-savvy crowd comes for electronic dance, trance, and house music. If you want a primer on Chicago house music, this is a good place to start.

226 W. Ontario St. (at Franklin St.). ℂ **312/787-4480.** Cover $10–$20. Check the website for free cover deals on weekends with an RSVP. El: Red Line to Grand.

**Transit** Carved out of a warehouse space beneath the elevated train tracks just west of the hip Randolph Street restaurant row, Transit is an excellent no-nonsense dance club that doesn't trick itself out with a wacky theme. Its 10,000 square feet feature a sleek, boldly colored geometric interior with modern, minimalist furniture. The bone-rattling, state-of-the-art sound system and DJs—spinning progressive dance, remixed hip-hop, and R&B—don't disappoint the die-hard dance fans. Come wearing your best club attire.

1431 W. Lake St. ℂ **312/491-8600.** www.transitnightclubchicago.com. Cover free until midnight on Fri and Sat, $10 after midnight. Subway/El: Green Line to Ashland.

# 9 Bars

**Berghoff**   This local institution attracts an older, pinstripe-wearing crowd, and holds Chicago liquor license no. 1, issued at the end of Prohibition. It features a good selection of German beers, 20-foot ceilings, a checked linoleum floor, and sepia photos of old Chicago. German and Austrian food, plus some standard American items, are on the menu. Don't hesitate—go for the schnitzel.

17 W. Adams St. (at State St.). ✆ **312/427-3170.** www.berghoff.com. El: Red or Blue line to Jackson/State or Monroe/State.

**Betty's Blue Star Lounge**   Wicker Park scene makers have turned Betty's, an unpretentious, low-key neighborhood tavern just south of Wicker Park in Ukrainian Village, into a trendy late-night destination. Part local watering hole, part biker bar, it's your typical pool-table-and-darts joint earlier in the evening, but Thursday through Saturday the bar transforms into a jam-packed venue for local bands and DJs. The action is in the back room, equipped with a stellar sound system and lots of mirrors.

1600 W. Grand Ave. ✆ **312/243-8778.** www.bettysbluestarlounge.com. Bus: 65 (Grand Ave.).

**The Bucktown Pub**   The owners' collection of groovy 1960s and '70s rock-'n'-roll posters and cartoon art is phenomenal. However, most Bucktown patrons are more interested in nursing their pints of imported and domestic microbrews than in gawking at the walls. Other Wicker Park/Bucktown bars try to come off as low-key; this is the real thing, where attitude is firmly discouraged at the door. The psychedelic- and glam-rock-filled jukebox keeps toes tapping, and competition on the skittle-bowling machine can get quite fierce. Credit cards not accepted.

1658 W. Cortland St. (at Hermitage Ave.). ✆ **773/394-9898.** www.bucktownpub. com. Subway/El: Blue Line to Damen.

**Butterfly Social Club**   At last, a nightclub that Al Gore can appreciate. This environmentally friendly lounge features treehouse-like nooks, organic juices in drinks, and is smoke-free (fittingly, it opened on Earth Day in 2007). It uses solar power for some of its electrical needs, and incorporates recycled and natural materials into its design,

# Chicago Sporting Moments

With da Bears, da Bulls, and da Black Hawks, not to mention two iconic baseball teams, there's no question that Chicago is a sports town—but it's not a cheap one. Fortunately, there are a number of affordable options for other pro and college teams who call the city home.

- The **Chicago Wolves** won the 2008 American League hockey championship, and are (oddly) an affiliate of the NHL's Atlanta Thrashers. The team (usually home to several past and future NHLers) plays out of Rosemont's Allstate Arena (6920 N. Mannheim Rd., ✆ **847/724-GOAL**; www.chicagowolves.com), where tickets are $13-$30.

- Basketball fans should check out the **DePaul Blue Demons** (✆ **773/325-SLAM**; www.depaulbluedemons.com), the college team well-known for it's basketball program, who are part of the NCAA Division 1. Several of their players have graduated to the NBA in recent years. Also worth seeing is the improving WNBA's **Chicago Sky** (✆ **312/828-9550**; www.wnba.com/sky). Both teams play out of the Allstate Arena; tickets for the Blue Demons range from $20-$35; Sky tickets start at $15.

- The city's college football team is the **Northwestern Wildcats** (✆ **847/491-CATS**; www.nusports.cstv.com), who play out of Ryan Field in nearby Evanston. Games attract upwards of 30,000 lively fans, while tickets cost $25-$50.

- Chicago's Major League Soccer team, the **Chicago Fire,** plays at its own 20,000-seat stadium in suburban Bridgeview (about 12 miles southwest of downtown). The season runs from late May through October (✆ **888/MLS-FIRE;** http://chicago.fire.mlsnet.com). Games have a family feel, with plenty of activities for kids and affordable ticket prices ($15-$60).

such as "trees" made from mud, sand, clay, and straw. DJs spin upbeat world music that thumps through speakers made of recycled wood. 722 W. Grand Ave. (btw. Union Ave. and Halsted St.). ✆ **312/666-1695.** www.funkybuddha.com. Bus: 65 (Grand Ave.).

**Delilah's** Ironically situated smack dab in the middle of yuppie Lincoln Park, this friendly punk-rock bar stocks the best selection of whiskeys in town (over 135 varieties from around the globe). DJs and a jukebox supply the tunes.

2771 N. Lincoln Ave. ✆ **773/472-2771.** www.delilahschicago.com. El: Brown Line to Diversey.

★ **Duke of Perth** This congenial Scottish pub attracts a young crowd with its $9.25 all-you-can-eat fish-and-chips special on Wednesdays and Fridays, its selection of single-malt scotch, and an outdoor beer garden that's inviting on summer nights.

2913 N. Clark St. (at Wellington Ave.). ✆ **773/477-1741.** www.dukeofperth.com. El: Brown Line to Diversey.

**Gamekeepers** This sports bar appeals to a young crowd intent on watching the game on three big-screen TVs and 36 monitors. Check their website for food specials like 50¢ taco Mondays, $2 burger Tuesdays, and 10¢ jumbo wing Thursdays.

345 W. Armitage Ave. (at Lincoln Ave.). ✆ **773/549-0400.** www.gamekeepers chicago.com. El: Brown Line to Armitage.

**Holiday Club** Home to Chicago's most diverse jukebox, plus Golden Tee golf and video poker, this laid-back joint attracts a good-looking young crowd and shakes out gallons of martinis and manhattans every night. Comfort food like meatloaf ($8.50) and sloppy joes ($8.50) served with a choice of potato or salad hit the spot after a drink or two.

4000 N. Sheridan Rd. ✆ **773/486-0686.** www.holidayclubchicago.com. El: Red Line to Sheridan.

**J Bar** The gathering place for stylish locals in their 20s and 30s, this lounge is just off the lobby of the James Hotel. Low-slung leather couches and high-concept drinks (the house martini blends blue raspberry vodka and elderflower cordial) give this the vibe of an upscale urban club. FINE PRINT Check out weeknight specials such as SuperFun Wednesdays for $2 mini burgers, $6 cocktails, and good hip-hop DJs.

610 N. Rush St. (at Wabash Ave.) ✆ **312/660-7200.** www.jameshotels.com. El: Red Line to Grand.

**Kitty O'Shea's** The brogues at this hotel bar are as authentic as the Guinness on tap. You'll find live Irish entertainment, a jukebox stacked with favorite Gaelic tunes, and an older crowd enjoying the excellent Irish pub food.

In the Chicago Hilton and Towers, 720 S. Michigan Ave. (btw. Balbo and 8th sts.). ℂ **312/922-4400.** El: Red Line to Harrison.

★ **The Map Room**  Nearly 200 beers are offered (20 or so are on tap) at this tavern, frequented by an artistic and eclectic crowd of 30-somethings from the neighborhood. In the morning, this is a coffee bar; in the late afternoon, the drinks start flowing. Sunday night at 8pm is movie night.

1949 N. Hoyne Ave. (at Armitage Ave.). ℂ **773/252-7636.** www.maproom.com. El: Blue Line to Damen.

**Marie's Rip Tide Lounge**  The retro cool of this late-night dive bar on the after-dark circuit makes Marie's a hoot. It seems like everything here (from the decor to the jukebox music to the $4 beers) hasn't been updated since the '60s, though charming owners Shirley and Marie do decorate for the holidays—don't miss their Christmas and Valentine's Day decor.

1745 W. Armitage Ave. (at Hermitage Ave.). ℂ **773/278-7317.** El: Blue Line to Damen.

**Martini Ranch**  Looking for a late-night libation? Martini Ranch serves 40 different versions of its namesake cocktail until 4am during the week, attracting bar and nightlife insiders—and a fair share of insomniacs. The Western theme is subtle (paintings of Roy Rogers and other cowpoke art) and the seating is minimal (come early to snag one of the four red booths), but fans swear by the chocolate martini, and the pop-rock soundtrack keeps the energy level high. If the crowded bar scene is too much, chill out at the pool table in the back room, or settle down at one of the tables in the heated beer garden.

311 W. Chicago Ave. (at Orleans St.). ℂ **312/335-9500.** www.martiniranchchicago. net. Subway/El: Red or Brown line to Chicago.

★ **The Matchbox**  This tiny corner bar (3 ft. wide at its narrowest; 10 ft. at its widest) claims to be "Chicago's most intimate bar." It's not for the claustrophobic, but it is the perfect spot for a late-night martini ($8).

770 N. Milwaukee Ave. (at Ogden Ave.). ℂ **312/666-9292.** El: Blue Line to Chicago.

**Old Town Ale House**  This legendary saloon has played host to many a Second City comedian, including John Belushi, who commanded the pinball machines here during his Second City days. A bit dingy, but full of local flavor.

219 W. North Ave. (at Wells St.). ☎ **312/944-7020.** www.oldtownalehouse.net. El: Brown Line to Sedgwick.

**Sheffield's**   Play pool, golf, or board games at this welcoming neighborhood bar. In the winter, cozy up to the fireplace; in the summer, the outdoor beer garden is one of the city's best. Choose from 100 beers, including the tongue-in-cheek "bad beer" (think cheap domestic) of the month.

3258 N. Sheffield Ave. (at Belmont Ave.). ☎ **773/281-4989.** www.sheffieldschicago. com. El: Red or Brown line to Belmont.

★ **Smoke Daddy Rhythm and Bar-B-Que**   A great bar with live music 7 nights a week (mostly gritty, Chicago-style blues and jazz, played by small combos, due to the bar's intimate size). Arrive early if you want to sample the excellent slow-cooked barbecue, which arrives in retro plastic baskets. FINE PRINT There's no cover charge if you're eating dinner; if you come just for music and drinks, you'll pay the charge.

1804 W. Division St. ☎ **773/772-6656.** www.thesmokedaddy.com. No cover with dinner; cover varies, and only applies if you don't order dinner. El: Blue Line to Damen.

★ **Southport Lanes & Billiards**   This is one of only 10 remaining hand-set bowling alleys in the country. Match that novelty factor with above-average bar food, including a turkey Reuben ($9.95), chili nachos ($6.95), and quesadillas ($5.95), and you've got a winner. You'll find about 17 beers on tap for about $4 each, and wine is about $8 a glass. FINE PRINT If you don't want to spring for bowling, on Monday night, there's free ping-pong. Bowling costs $15/lane after 6pm Monday through Thursday, $20/lane Friday and Saturday, $10/ lane after 6pm Sunday, and shoes are $3.

3325 N. Southport Ave. ☎ **773/472-5896.** www.sparetimechicago.com. El: Brown Line to Southport.

**Spoon**   The closest Old Town has to a trendy nightspot, this bar and restaurant pulls in an attractive, professional crowd on weekend evenings. The modern, loftlike space would be right at home in the River North neighborhood, but it's a novelty in tradition-bound Old Town. Although Spoon attracts loud groups of singles on weekends, weeknights are a little less frenzied, and locals are able to sip their Mucho Mango martinis in peace.

1240 N. Wells St. (at Division St.). ℂ **312/642-5522.** www.spoonchicago.com. Subway/El: Red Line to Clark/Division.

**Tilli's** A favorite gathering spot for good-looking 20- and 30-somethings, Tilli's is an upscale version of the neighborhood bar. In nice weather, the entire front opens to the street; when it's chilly, try to snag a table near the brick fireplace in the main dining room. You can snack on appetizers or order dinner, but the main attraction is the front room, where everyone people-watches around the bar. On Sundays and Wednesdays, you'll get a half-priced bottle of wine with two entrees. Drinks specials each night usually run about $5.

1952 N. Halsted St. (at Armitage St.). ℂ **773/325-0044.** www.tillischicago.com. Subway/El: Brown Line to Armitage.

## 10 Brewpubs

**Clark Street Ale House** A handsome, convivial tavern and a popular after-work spot for white- and blue-collar types alike, Clark Street Ale House features a large open space filled with high tables and a long cherrywood bar along one wall. Better than the atmosphere are the 95 varieties of beer, a large majority of them from American microbreweries. The bar also offers a wide selection of scotches and cognacs.

742 N. Clark St. ℂ **312/642-9253.** Subway/El: Red or Brown line to Chicago.

★ **Goose Island Brewery** The best-known brewpub in town has its own brews on tap (sample three for $5). The enclosed patio is especially family-friendly and provides a beautiful setting for casual dining. There's a kids' menu (the baked mac and cheese is popular) if you couldn't snag a babysitter for the night. Don't miss the freshly baked pretzels with a choice of Dusseldorf mustard, cheese spread, or marinara sauce.

3535 N. Clark St. (at Sheffield Ave.). ℂ **773/832-9040.** www.gooseisland.com. El: Red Line to Addison.

## 11 Gay & Lesbian Bars & Clubs

**Berlin** One of the more enduring dance floors in Chicago, Berlin is primarily gay during the week but draws dance hounds of all stripes on weekends and for special theme nights (disco the last Wed of every month, Prince music the last Sun of the month). It has a reputation for outrageousness and creativity, making it prime ground for people-watching. The space isn't much—basically a square room with a bar on one side—but the no-frills dance floor is packed late into the evening. FINE PRINT The cover charge applies only on Friday and Saturday after midnight, about an hour earlier than most people show up.

954 W. Belmont Ave. (at Sheffield Ave.). ℂ **773/348-4975.** www.berlinchicago.com. Cover $3–$5. Subway/El: Red or Brown line to Belmont.

★ **Big Chicks** One of the more eclectic bars in the city, Big Chicks is a magnet for the artsy, goateed set (perhaps a bit weary of the bars on Halsted St.), some lesbians, a smattering of straights, and random locals from the surrounding rough-hewn neighborhood (the bar's motto is "Never a Cover, Never an Attitude"). They come for owner Michelle Fire's superb art collection, the midnight shots, and the free buffet on Sunday afternoon. There is also dancing on weekends. The same owner also runs the restaurant next door, **Tweet,** 5020 N. Sheridan Rd. (ℂ **773/728-5576**), which offers a menu of mostly organic American comfort food; it has become a popular gay-friendly weekend brunch spot.

5024 N. Sheridan Rd. (btw. Argyle St. and Foster Ave.). ℂ **773/728-5511.** www.big chicks.com. Subway/El: Red Line to Berwyn.

**The Closet** The Closet is an unpretentious neighborhood spot with a loud and constant loop of music videos (and sports, when the game matters) that draws mostly lesbian regulars, although gay men and straights show up, too. The space is not much bigger than a closet, which makes it easy to get up close and personal with other partiers. There's also a small dance floor that's usually packed on weekends. Open until 4am every night, 5am on Saturday. Drink specials include dirt cheap pints of Miller Lite ($2.50) every day.

3325 N. Broadway (at Buckingham St.). ℂ **773/477-8533.** www.theclosetchicago. com. No cover. Subway/El: Red or Brown line to Belmont.

**Cocktail** This corner spot, less frenzied than its neighbors, is more of a friendly hangout than a cruising scene; it's easy to converse and watch the passing parade from big picture windows. This is one of the few places on the street where both men and women congregate.

3359 N. Halsted St. (at Roscoe St.). ℭ **773/477-1420.** www.cocktailbarchicago.com. Subway/El: Red or Brown line to Belmont.

**Crew** Crew is a gay-friendly sports bar, where local softball leagues stop by for a drink after the game. Up to eight pro games play on multiple TVs, and there's a full menu of sandwiches, salads, and shareable appetizer plates. Located in the residential neighborhood of Uptown, a few miles north of the main Halsted Street strip, Crew attracts a crowd that's more interested in hanging out than hooking up.

4804 N. Broadway (at Lawrence St.). ℭ **773/784-CREW** (2739). www.worldsgreatest bar.com. Subway/El: Red Line to Lawrence.

★ **Roscoe's Tavern** The picture windows facing Halsted make Roscoe's, a gay neighborhood bar in business since 1987, an especially welcoming place. It has a large antiques-filled front bar, an outdoor patio, a pool table, and a large dance floor. The 20- and 30-something crowd is friendly and laid-back—except on weekends when the dance floor is hopping. The cafe serves sandwiches and salads.

3356 N. Halsted St. (at Roscoe St.). ℭ **773/281-3355.** www.roscoes.com. Cover after 10pm Sat $4. Subway/El: Red or Brown line to Belmont.

**Spin** This dance club attracts one of Halsted Street's most eclectic crowds, a mix of pretty boys, nerds, tough guys, and the occasional drag queen. The video bar in front houses pool tables and plays a steady stream of dance-friendly music videos. The club thumps with house music. Spin keeps regulars coming back with daily theme parties, featuring everything from Friday-night shower contests to cheap drinks.

800 W. Belmont Ave. (at Halsted St.). ℭ **773/327-7711.** www.spin-nightclub.com. Cover $5 Sat. Subway/El: Red or Brown line to Belmont.

*Chicago's abundant parks and green spaces are a free gift widely used by residents of Chicago.*

# FREE & DIRT CHEAP LIVING

hicago certainly is an expensive place to live. Our cost of living is about 60% higher than the United States average, which means that Des Moines looks pretty good in comparison. But stacked up against New York City, Chicago's cost of living is a whopping 50% lower, and it's 20% lower than Los Angeles (according to www.bankrate.com's cost of living calculator, in 2009). So buck up, Chicagoans: It could be worse—much, much worse. We've still got the amazing cultural advantages of a big city, the entertainment, the shopping, the architecture, the buzz, and if you follow the tips in this chapter, you might even have some money left over after experiencing it all.

Life in the city isn't always easy, but it's full of adventures and discoveries, and this chapter will show you where to look to get a break when you're just starting out.

## 1  Free & Cheap Classes & Talks

### LECTURES & SEMINARS

One of the best things about living in a city is access to free and dirt cheap readings, lectures, and seminars.

★ **Chicago Council on Global Affairs**   With your $60 annual membership ($35 for students), you'll get to hang out at some of the most happening politically and globally oriented events in the city (not to mention mixing with up-and-coming young professionals during cocktail hour). Tickets for individual events are a little pricier at close to $30 for some events, but are often significantly cheaper if you're a student. From Daryl Hannah (the environmentalist and actor) to *New York Times* writer Thomas Friedman, this group hosts an impressive array of speakers who address the hot topics of the day. FINE PRINT Events may also require a small fee for members.

332 S. Michigan Ave. ℂ **312/726-3860.** www.thechicagocouncil.org. Event locations vary; see website for details. Subway/El: Orange, Brown, Purple Express, Pink, or Green line to Adams/Wabash; or Blue or Red line to Monroe.

**Discovery Centre**   Widely known in Chicago, this learning center offers a full range of classes for reasonable prices (a one-time wine tasting course is $39; a month-long belly dancing class, $89; a 5-week introductory photography class, $89). Classes meet all over the Chicago area.

Office: 2940 N. Lincoln Ave. ℂ **773/348-8120.** www.discoverycenter.cc. Subway/El: Red Line to Belmont.

**Fermilab**   Seriously, Fermilab? Yes, Fermilab, the world's leading particle physics lab. The public lecture series, held on occasional Friday evenings, features scientists presenting their work to a lay audience. Most lectures are about physics, but some are about biology, paleontology, climatology, and more. Tickets are $5, and it's worth calling ahead, because lectures sometimes sell out. There is also an art series and a film series. To get acquainted, start out with the Fermilab public tours. And Ask a Scientist is a short talk given on the first

# THE LOOP, RIVER NORTH & MAGNIFICENT MILE

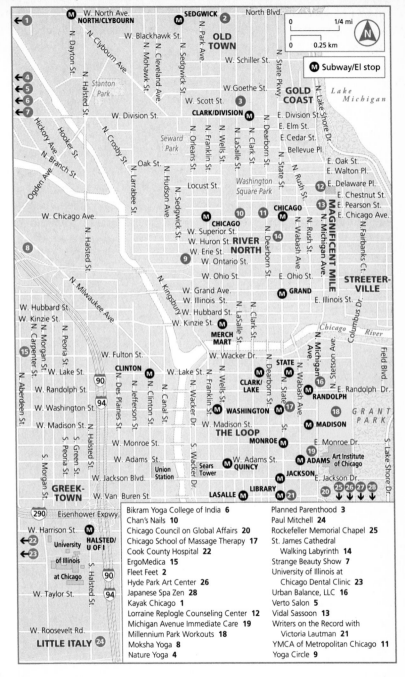

Bikram Yoga College of India **6**
Chan's Nails **10**
Chicago Council on Global Affairs **20**
Chicago School of Massage Therapy **17**
Cook County Hospital **22**
ErgoMedica **15**
Fleet Feet **2**
Hyde Park Art Center **26**
Japanese Spa Zen **28**
Kayak Chicago **1**
Lorraine Replogle Counseling Center **12**
Michigan Avenue Immediate Care **19**
Millennium Park Workouts **18**
Moksha Yoga **8**
Nature Yoga **4**

Planned Parenthood **3**
Paul Mitchell **24**
Rockefeller Memorial Chapel **25**
St. James Cathedral
　Walking Labyrinth **14**
Strange Beauty Show **7**
University of Illinois at
　Chicago Dental Clinic **23**
Urban Balance, LLC **16**
Verto Salon **5**
Vidal Sassoon **13**
Writers on the Record with
　Victoria Lautman **21**
YMCA of Metropolitan Chicago **11**
Yoga Circle **9**

Sunday of every month, followed by a behind-the-scenes tour. Registration is required. Check the calendar of tours and special events for dates and more information.

In west suburban Batavia, about 45 miles west of Chicago. ✆ **630/840-5588.** www.fnal.gov. Open daily 8am–6pm. (A map of Fermilab's public areas is available on their website.) From the city, travel west on I-290 (Eisenhower) to I-88. Exit I-88 at Farnsworth, and go right (north). Farnsworth becomes Kirk Rd. Follow Kirk Rd. to Pine St. Turn right at Pine St., Fermilab's main entrance.

★ **FREE** Hyde Park Art Center    The **Hyde Park Art Center**'s mission is to stimulate and sustain the visual arts in Chicago. As one of the oldest alternative art spaces in the city, the HPAC has an exemplary record of exhibiting a wide range of work by emerging artists through its **Exhibitions Program.** Free events might include panel discussions, gallery talks, poetry readings, music performances, open house events, and a series of short pieces by guest writers that expand upon the approaches and ideas presented in each exhibition and engage a broad audience. "Cocktails and Clay" is a longstanding favorite of Chicagoans in the know. FINE PRINT On the second Friday of the month from 8pm to midnight, you pay a $15 cover (drinks $4), but you can play with clay (the art center's artists and teachers will show you how to do handbuilding and coils), explore the exhibitions, dance, and make new friends.

5020 S. Cornell Ave. ✆ **773/324-5520.** www.hydeparkart.org. Free admission. Subway/El: Metra Electric to 51st/53rd St., exit at 51st St., walk half a block east and turn left (north) on Cornell.

**FREE** Indian Boundary Park and Cultural Center    Tucked away in the West Ridge neighborhood, this center offers a lovely public zoo area, plus a children's spray pool and sandbox, and tennis courts. For those seeking cheap classes, there is a beautiful auditorium with a stage that's used for programs, theater productions, concerts, and recitals. You'll find painting, piano, dance, and voice lessons for both children and adults here (for a very reasonable $35-$50 for 12 weeks), some of which take place on a scenic back porch. Indian Boundary is a residency site in the Civic Orchestra of Chicago's program, so check the website for a regular schedule of free concert performances throughout the year.

2500 W. Lunt Ave. (near the interseciton of Touhy and Western avenues). ✆ **773/764-3338.** www.chicagoparkdistrict.com. Free admission except for some special events and programs.

★ **FREE** Rockefeller Memorial Chapel    Gothic grandeur reigns in the soaring stone exterior and stained glass interior of the **Rockefeller Memorial Chapel,** the spiritual and ceremonial center of the **University of Chicago.** The chapel serves as a venue for concerts, theater, exhibits, lectures, and interfaith worship, and boasts the newly restored Laura Spelman Rockefeller carillon and E. M. Skinner pipe organ. Events range from worship services and religious education classes to community outreach, performances by world-renowned musicians, and lectures by some of the world's leading minds. Tours of the tower are offered daily at 5:30pm, and the organ can be heard on Sundays at the worship service and at many of the evening recitals scheduled. FINE PRINT Some events are ticketed, and most of those are free, and daily entrance to the chapel is free.

5850 W. Woodlawn Ave. ✆ **773/702-2100.** http://rockefeller.uchicago.edu. Subway/El: X28 Stony Island Express to Stony Island & 59th St.; walk west to Woodlawn.

★ **FREE** Writers on the Record with Victoria Lautman    This free series of interviews with famed authors is a collaboration between 98.7 WFMT radio (Chicago's classic music station) and the Chicago Public Library at the Harold Washington Library Center. Now in its sixth season, Ms. Lautman has interviewed many of the best writers of our time, from Richard Russo to Augusten Burroughs and Anne Lamott. Live interviews take place at 6pm weekdays (days are announced on the WFMT's website). Interviews are broadcast at noon, on the first Sunday following the taping.

The Chicago Public Library at the Harold Washington Library Center, Cindy Pritzker Auditorium. 400 S. State St. ✆ **312/747-4050.** www.wfmt.com. Subway/El: Orange, Brown, Purple Express, or Pink line to Library; Blue or Red line to Jackson.

# 2 Cheap(er) Health & Wellness

It's a sad fact that health insurance has become something of a luxury these days, and many of us live hoping not to get sick, or injured. There's no need to go without care completely, as a variety of clinics and community organizations offer sliding-scale fees, so you can get treatment for everything from a simple cold to a chronic illness.

## ACUPUNCTURE

**Lincoln Square Acupuncture**    Sliding-scale fees from $20 to $50 make the acupuncture services here very affordable (i.e. if you can

# LINCOLN PARK & WRIGLEYVILLE

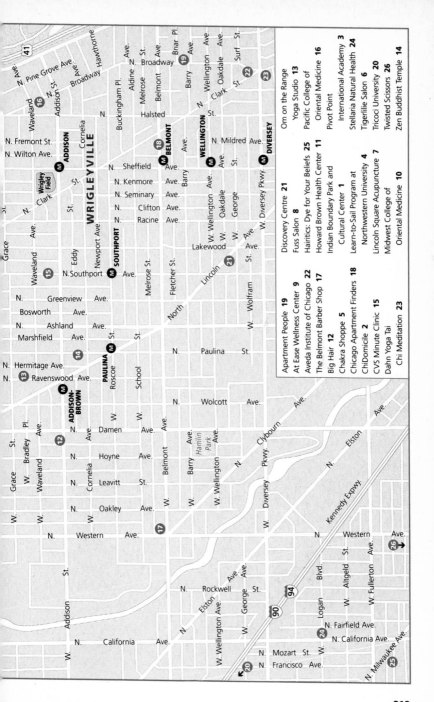

Apartment People **19**
At Ease Wellness Center **9**
Aveda Institute of Chicago **22**
The Belmont Barber Shop **17**
Big Hair **12**
Chakra Shoppe **5**
Chicago Apartment Finders **18**
ChiDomicile **2**
CVS Minute Clinic **15**
Dahn Yoga Tai
Chi Meditation **23**

Discovery Centre **21**
Fuss Salon **8**
Hairitics: Dye for Your Beliefs **25**
Howard Brown Health Center **11**
Indian Boundary Park and
Cultural Center **1**
Learn-to-Sail Program at
Northwestern University **4**
Lincoln Square Acupuncture **7**
Midwest College of
Oriental Medicine **10**

Om on the Range
Yoga Studio **13**
Pacific College of
Oriental Medicine **16**
Pivot Point
International Academy **3**
Stellaria Natural Health **24**
Tigerlilie Salon **6**
Tricoci University **20**
Twisted Scissors **26**
Zen Buddhist Temple **14**

pay $35 a week, pay that; if for some reason you can only pay $20 for 1 week, then pay $20). FINE PRINT Services are given in a community setting, which is common in China, but might take a bit of getting accustomed to for Westerners.

4720A N. Lincoln Ave. ℂ **773/878-3888.** www.squarenergy.com. Subway/El: Brown Line to Western.

FREE **Midwest College of Oriental Medicine** Taking a holistic approach to illnesses, especially those of the chronic sort, has gained a lot of ground in recent years, and acupuncture is among the most well known of options. At this college, the best deal is the free acupuncture treatments (new patients are welcomed on Mondays and Wednesdays; call for information). Natural herbs and a nutritionist are also on staff and happy to help.

4334 N. Hazel St., Ste. 206 (btw. Cullom Ave. and Junior Terrace). ℂ **773/975-1295.** www.acupuncture.edu/midwest. Subway/El: Red Line to Wilson.

**Pacific College of Oriental Medicine** Services here are $30 (about $15 for students), a real steal. They include acupuncture, cupping, Chinese massage, shiatsu, Swedish massage, and Thai massage. People use their services to relieve chronic pain, sports injuries, weight loss, snoring, colds, and flu.

3646 N. Broadway. ℂ **773/477-1900.** www.pacificcollege.edu. Subway/El: Red Line to Addison.

## COUNSELING

**Lorraine Replogle Counseling Center** Part of Fourth Presbyterian Church's community outreach, this center is open to people of all faiths. The center offers individual and couples counseling, crisis intervention, short-term support groups, educational seminars, and premarital seminars and counseling. The center is open by appointment from 9am to 8pm, Monday through Friday. Fees are determined primarily by your resources.

126 E. Chestnut St. ℂ **312/787-8425.** www.fourthchurch.org. Subway/El: Red Line to Chicago, then bus no. 151 to Chestnut.

**Urban Balance, LLC** Located in the Loop, the counselors here provide therapy and counseling and are available by appointment, even on evenings and weekends. They specialize in dealing with typical urban stresses, relationship issues, and addiction. They work with individuals, families, and groups, and offer a sliding fee scale based on income.

180 N. Michigan Ave., Ste. 905 (at Lake St.). ℂ **312/726-7170.** www.urbanbalance. org. Subway/El: Red Line to Lake; or Orange, Brown, Purple Express, Green, or Pink line to Randolph/Wabash.

## DENTAL CARE

**The Chicago Dental Society**    The website of this organization is a good resource If you're seeking a dentist, and includes an updated list of dentists offering free and sliding scale services. See www.cds.org.

**University of Illinois at Chicago Dental Clinic at The College of Dentistry**    This clinic offers general and specialized dental care for children and adults. They accept public aid, and charge set fees for those not on public aid. FINE PRINT They have an appointment-only policy, so make sure to call ($153 for your first screening, due on the day of your visit). There is also an urgent care program, which again is offered on an appointment-only basis. Services are administered by dental students.

801 S. Paulina St. ℂ **312/996-7555.** http://dentistry.uic.edu. Mon–Fri 8am–4pm. Subway/El: Pink Line to Polk; Blue Line to Cermak.

## HEALTH CARE

**Access Community Health Network**    The Chicago area's largest private primary health care provider to the underserved and those living in low-income neighborhoods, this group runs 50 clinics in the area. They provide everything from dental care to OB-GYN and general medical services, and offer a sliding fee scale based on income.

For locations, call ℂ **866/88-ACCESS** (882-2237). www.accesscommunityhealth.net.

**Cook County Hospital**    Founded in 1855 with the mission of providing quality health care to Chicagoans regardless of their ability to pay, the John H. Stroger Hospital of Cook County is a 480-bed, state-of-the-art facility. It boasts one of the most respected emergency rooms in Chicago, and you will not be turned away for lack of health insurance. The HIV clinic is known for its excellence. Once inside, you will find amazing doctors, but the wait to see one is reputed to be long and arduous.

1901 W. Harrison St. (at Wolcott Ave.). ℂ **312/864-6000.** www.cchil.org. Subway/El: Blue Line to Cermak.

**CVS Minute Clinic**   With convenient locations around the city (Southport and Addison is a good choice on the north side), CVS Pharmacy's Minute Clinic is a good choice if you feel yourself coming down with a sinus infection or sore throat that threatens to be something worse than the common cold. This no-appointment-necessary clinic could be just the ticket to recovery—simply walk in, sign up to see the nurse practitioner, wait, have your visit, and get any prescription you might need sent to any pharmacy you like. They take insurance, but if you don't have insurance, you'll find the prices very reasonable (for something routine like a sinus infection, you should be in and out with your prescription for under $100—less than urgent care centers).

3637 N. Southport Ave. ⓒ **866/389-2727.** www.minuteclinic.com. Mon–Fri 8am–8pm; Sat–Sun 10am–4pm. Subway/El: Brown Line to Southport.

**ErgoMedica**   Efficient, professional, speedy health care is offered in a loftlike, modern setting. They take walk-ins, and it will cost you less than at a regular physician's office, but make sure to ask about costs before taking your appointment, just to be sure. If you have Blue Cross Blue Shield health insurance, it's accepted here (no other insurance types are accepted).

311 N. Aberdeen St. (btw. Jackson Blvd. and Van Buren St.). ⓒ **312/733-0909.** Bus: No. 20 to Madison and Aberdeen.

**Howard Brown Health Center**   One of the nation's largest lesbian, gay, transgender, and bisexual health care organizations, Howard Brown serves more than 28,000 adults and youths yearly. This reputable clinic offers primary care and a reasonable sliding scale discount, based on your income.

4025 N. Sheridan Rd. ⓒ **773/388-1600.** www.howardbrown.org. Subway/El: Red Line to Sheridan.

**Michigan Avenue Immediate Care**   Used by many students at the Loop's Columbia University and School of the Art Institute campuses, this clinic is great if you're on vacation or new to the city and find yourself sick. Fresh fruit, granola, and free Wi-Fi make the wait bearable. During the height of the flu season you'll have a wait, but never fear: This clinic is great with common ailments. They accept insurance and extend 35% off to self-pay patients.

104 S. Michigan Ave. (btw. Adams and Monroe sts.), Ste. 905. ⓒ **312/201-1234.** www.michiganavenueimmediatecare.org. Bus: 151 to Madison/Monroe.

**Planned Parenthood (Near North Side)**    Reproductive health services for both men and women can be found at the Chicago branch of this national organization. Emergency contraception, HIV testing, and routine gynecological exams are just a few of the organization's offerings. Drop-ins are taken first-come, first-served, but it's best to make an appointment. A second centrally located clinic is found in the Loop at 18 S. Michigan Ave. (btw. Madison and Monroe sts.; ✆ **312/592-6700**).

1200 N. LaSalle St. (btw. Division and Goethe). ✆ **312/266-1033.** www.ppgg.org. Bus: 151 to Stockton/LaSalle.

## 3  Cheap Housing Resources

Housing prices are down across the country compared to a couple of years ago, even in Chicago. A glut of condominiums is pushing down prices for both buyers and renters. Now, condos that were intended for sale are being rented, a potential boon for apartment-hunters.

### MIXED-INCOME DEVELOPMENTS

Developers and the city offer low-rise, mixed-income buildings in neighborhoods throughout the city, where affordable housing can be had if you have the patience to endure the long waiting lists. For example, a new development may be required to offer a certain percentage of its units to middle or lower-income residents.

Below are two places where you might be able to find a lead on such vacancies, presuming your income is low enough.

**Chicago Housing Authority**    The largest owner of rental properties in the city, the CHA provides 50,000 Chicagoans with homes. In addition to offering apartments, the CHA oversees the administration of housing vouchers that allow low-income families to rent in the private market.

60 E. Van Buren St. ✆ **312/742-8500.** www.thecha.org. Subway/El: Red Line to Jackson.

**Metropolitan Planning Council**    This group is dedicated to shaping Chicago by developing, promoting, and implementing solutions for growth. Their website is a good source for updates on local housing developments.

140 S. Dearborn St. ✆ **312/922-5616.** www.metroplanning.org. Subway/El: Red Line to Monroe.

## NO-FEE RENTALS

Gearing up to put a deposit on an apartment can be daunting, what with first and last month's rent and a deposit the usual protocol. To add to that, having to set down a broker's fee—typically a month's rent or a 10% to 15% surcharge—is an extra punch to the gut. To avoid one, go straight to the source, and speak directly with the landlord if you know what building you're interested in. If you don't, a few websites can help you sift through the offerings.

**Apartment People** This is a big agency that represents loads of buildings, meaning that you will get a ton of listings, but you might have to wade through some less-than-stellar ones on your way to the apartment of your dreams.

3121 N. Broadway (btw. Barry and Briar). ✆ **773/248-8800.** www.apartmentpeople. com. Subway/El: Purple Express, Brown, or Red line to Belmont.

**Chicago Apartment Finders** In the Lakeview neighborhood, this agency will help you find an apartment for free. Three Chicago offices are ready to help you with whatever neighborhood, price range, and amenities you desire.

906 W. Belmont (btw. Wilton Ave. and Clark St.). ✆ **773/883-8800.** www.chicago apartmentfinders.com. Subway/El: Purple Express, Brown, or Red line to Belmont.

**ChiDomicile** This agency specializes in independently owned properties on the Near North and North Side, including Lincoln Square, Andersonville, Edgewater, Rogers Park, and Evanston.

On the corner of Ashland & Balmoral. ✆ **773-256-8704.** www.chidomicile.com. Subway/El: Red Line to Lawrence.

**Craigslist** The Chicago list remains a top source for apartment searching, as you can often bypass the brokers and go directly to the owners themselves.

www.craigslist.com.

## 4 Cheap Beauty & Bodywork

**At Ease Wellness Center** Offering massage, chiropractic, and physical therapy, this spot is perfect for working out that kink in your neck. Flexible payment programs are offered if you don't have insurance.

4403 N. Broadway. ✆ **773/561-7966.** Subway/El: Red Line to Wilson.

**Chakra Shoppe**   Specializing in the health and energy of your body, this fabulous shop offers everything from aura spray to free meditation (once a month). Walk out feeling that your mind and body connection is rejuvenated.

5034 N. Lincoln Ave. ✆ **773/271-3054.** www.chakrashoppe.com. Subway/El: Brown Line to Western.

★ **Chicago School of Massage Therapy**   Affordable relaxation therapy that won't stress your wallet: The student clinic offers one amazing deal—a full 55-minute massage for $40 (and sometimes less). Students have completed 50 hours of coursework and a proficiency exam, so you will be in semi-expert hands. If you book online, they offer a $5 discount.

17 N. State St. ✆ **312/753-7990.** www.cortiva.com. Subway/El: Red Line to Washington.

**Japanese Spa Zen**   A huge range of services, from Brazilian waxes (for men and women), to Japanese herbal medicine baths ($35) and Swedish, Thai, and Japanese massage (among others) makes this spa a great deal if you are near Hyde Park. Most massage is available in 30-minute increments for $35. Haircuts are also a good deal, starting at $25 for women and $20 for men.

1380 E. 53rd St. ✆ **773/955-5353.** Subway/El: Green Line to 51st.

**Stellaria Natural Health**   Massages, acupuncture, and herbal medicine are the specialties of this holistic health center. You can also partake in yoga, tai chi, and belly dancing lessons.

2755 W. Logan Blvd. ✆ **773/486-3797.** Subway/El: Blue Line to California.

## SALON STYLING

Chicago's top-notch salons offer plenty of discounted cuts and coloring services with their stylists-in-training, so if you're willing to spare a few hours as a hair model and have an open mind, you could come away with a first-rate 'do at just a fraction of what it would normally cost.

★ **Aveda Institute of Chicago**   Training aestheticians and stylists for jobs at Aveda spas and salons is the number-one job here, and you can benefit from reasonably priced hair and skin care services as the students learn, plus hair removal and makeup services. A haircut with style and finish for men and women is $14—imagine that, the same price for men *and* women! FINE PRINT On Fridays and Saturdays, the price goes up to $16. Full highlights are $60 to $70, and facials start at $30.

2828 N. Clark St. (btw. Diversey and Broadway). ✆ **773/883-1560.** www.avedainstitute chicago.com. Subway/El: Purple Express and Brown Line to Diversey.

★ **The Belmont Barber Shop**   The epitome of a modern barbershop, this place has a pool table and beer available while you wait. Haircuts ($15) are no-frills but quality. Your two other options are a hot lather straight razor shave ($30) and both, $45. Pretty straightforward, right? Quality cut, shave, good music, good conversation, beer if you like it—what more can you ask? Call at least a couple of hours ahead of time for an appointment, and a couple of days in advance during the holidays. FINE PRINT Cash only.

2328 W. Belmont Ave. (btw. Clybourn and Oakley aves.). ✆ **773/296-0894.** www. belmontbarbershop.com. Subway/El: Brown Line to Paulina.

**Big Hair**   Women's haircuts for $20 ($25 with shampoo) are the main attraction at this funky Roscoe Village salon. Walk-ins are welcome. Fresh, professional hairstyles in a no-attitude atmosphere, and for a price that can't be beat. Color will run you about $55. FINE PRINT Cash only.

2012 W. Roscoe St. (btw. Damen and Seeley aves.). ✆ **773/348-0440.** www.bighair chicago.com. Subway/El: Brown Line to Addison.

**Chan's Nails**   Nail services tend to be pricier in Chicago than in other major cities, making the $30 manicure/pedicure here a real steal. Walk-ins are welcome. Service is quick and cheap.

112 W. Chicago Ave. ✆ **312/280-8310.** El: Red Line to Chicago.

**Fuss Salon**   Small but comfortable, you'll be fussed over at this popular salon. You can walk in, although it's best to make an appointment. Moderately priced services (women's haircuts for $50, mens for $25) in an intimate atmosphere mean you can't go wrong.

1528 W. Montrose Ave. ✆ **773/293-4640.** Subway/El: Brown Line to Montrose.

**Hairitics: Dye for Your Beliefs**   Go for the name alone! Cuts, color, waxing—they do it all here. No pretensions here, the vibe is cool and mellow, there's an eclectic mix of music playing and art on the walls, and a women's cut will set you back only about $35. Walk-ins and credit cards are accepted.

2340 N. Milwaukee Ave. (btw. Belden and Medill aves.). ✆ **773/772-9355.** Subway/ El: Blue Line to California.

**Paul Mitchell** *The* school as long as you have time on your hands (at least 2½ hours), you can get a rocking hairstyle here for the bargain basement price range of $12 to $17. Bring a book and relax (and, if you are pressed for time, make sure to book for a weekday and not a Saturday). Instructors flit around the salon, making sure that the aspiring stylists are doing every step correctly (another reason why cuts take time here). Credit cards and walk-ins accepted.

1225 S. Halsted St. (btw. 12th Place and O'Brien St.). ℂ **312/733-9285.** www.pmts chicago.com. Bus: No. 18 to Halsted and Rochford.

★ **Pivot Point International Academy** The atmosphere here is clearly one of a school, and if you keep reminding yourself that this is a student salon and spa, and the stylists and aestheticians are here to learn, you can have a great, relaxing experience. Facials are a popular option, and cost a mere $30 for an hour-long service. A haircut is only $11, a shampoo and blow dry $8, and full highlights start at $50. *Note:* The school's main campus is now located in north suburban Evanston, and is very accessible by El.

1560 Sherman Ave., north suburban Evanston (btw. Grove St. and Orrington Ave.). ℂ **847/905-5300.** http://pivot-point.com. Subway/El: Purple Evanston Express to Davis St.

**Strange Beauty Show** Slightly higher in price, but still well within the "reasonable" range, you'll pay $45 to $50 for a women's haircut here, and $95 to $100 for full highlights. This place offers an upbeat atmosphere that will have you walk out smiling and fantastic cuts and styling that are well worth it if you have a little bit of money to spend.

1118 N. Ashland Ave. (btw. Thomas St. and Haddon Ave.). ℂ **773/252-9522.** www. strangebeautyshow.com. El: Blue Line to Division.

**Tigerlilie Salon** With cuts starting at $25 and color at $70, this funky salon is definitely a value. Modern glamour mixes with funky vintage here, and the cuts are truly above average—and the color is even better. If you want a funky new 'do that puts a modern spin on a classic style of the past, this is the salon for you.

4755 N. Lincoln Ave. ℂ **773/506-7870.** wwww.tigerlilie.com. El: Brown Line to Western.

**Tricoci University** One of Chicago's many training centers for Mario Tricoci Salons, this location is a bit off the beaten track (on the northwest side, in the Norwood Park neighborhood), but at $13 to $17 for a cut, it's worth the trek. (If you drive, make sure to get there early so you can park near the salon). Full highlights are a mere $45. Don't forget about spa services—manicures can be had for $8.

5321 N. Harlem Ave. ✆ **773/467-1900.** www.tricociuniversity.com. El: Blue Line to Harlem.

**Twisted Scissors** Creative, alternative, and laid back, a cut here will cost you about $35. The place has a biker-chick vibe, but if that's not you, don't let it scare you away. Free wine or beer, coffee, and tea are on offer. You can pay for services and products with a credit card, but tips are cash only. Call ahead for an appointment—this place is super popular.

2001 N. Point St. (btw. Armitage Ave. and Francis Place). ✆ **773/227-1077.** El: Blue Line to California.

**Verto Salon** This hip, trendy salon with a modern decor won't break the bank at $45 and up for hairstyles, and $130 for full highlights. Walk-ins are accepted, but it's best to make an appointment.

1412 W. Division St. ✆ **773/904-8282.** www.vertosalon.com. El: Blue Line to Division.

★ **Vidal Sassoon** This Water Tower salon offers classes for visiting hairdressers, and if you can make a 3-hour time commitment, you can get a fab haircut for free. Sign up to be a model in other training programs and you can score a top-notch haircut for $25. The world-renowned salon asks potential models to be open to cut and/or color. You'll be supervised by a Sassoon instructor, but be prepared to hang out for up to 3 hours for a cut and 5 hours for color. Call to see what the salon's needs are.

835 N. Michigan Ave. (Water Tower Place Mall), 3rd Floor. ✆ **312/751-2216.** www.sassoon.com. Subway/El: Red Line to Chicago. Bus: 151 Michigan Ave. to Chestnut.

## 5 Free & Cheap Sports & Recreation

### BIKE, RUN, WALK . . . GET MOVING!

**Active Transportation Alliance** This pro-cycling group runs the annual Boulevard Lakefront Tour (mid-Sept) and Bike the Drive (Lake Shore Drive, that is, which takes place in mid-May). Their website offers support for cyclists, including tips and tricks to help those who want to bike to work.

9 W. Hubbard St. ℭ **312/427-3325.** www. activetrans.org. Subway/El: Red Line to Grand.

CARA The top choice for serious runners in Chicago, and one of the largest running organizations in the Midwest, the Chicago Area Runners Association sponsors training programs for all distances—their training program for the Chicago Marathon is especially popular. Not only that, but as you pace yourself through multiple miles, you might find yourself making new friends . . . and perhaps even budding romances. An annual membership is $44 and gets you a wide range of discounts and benefits.

549 W. Randolph St. ℭ **312/666-9836.** www.cararuns.org. Subway/El: Green Line to Clinton.

Chicago Cycling Club For a mere $20 membership fee, you can take part in weekly rides through Chicago neighborhoods.

## Old-School Bowling on the Cheap

A cheap alternative to the city's big bowling alleys, Lincoln Square Lanes is a 12-lane old-style bowling alley located above a hardware store in Lincoln Square. During prime time on Fridays and Saturdays, lanes are $40/hour (which means, bring a big group). After 11pm, it's $3 a game. Add with $3 bottles of beer, and you're set. You'll have to score by hand. (It's not that hard! A spare equals 10 plus your next ball; a strike is 10 plus your next two balls. There you have it.) Wood paneling and a mural depicting Abraham Lincoln add to this place's 1970s charm (4874 N. Lincoln Ave., at Ainslie St.; ℭ **773/ 561-8191;** El: Brown Line to Western).

If you want to socialize and ride, then choose a Sunday trip, which is a leisurely ride of 15 to 35 miles, often with a planned snack or meal stop. Saturdays are for midrange tours of 35 to 50 miles, at a more brisk pace, and roadies' events are 50 to 100 miles in length at a fast pace (road bikes recommended). Special rides include camping trips and rides to Ravinia.

ℭ **773/509-8093.** www.chicagocyclingclub.org.

Chicago Friars Ski and Bike Club If you like activity year-round, then you'll love the Chicago Friars. All levels are welcome, and for a $30 membership, you can also attend their social events, such as pub crawls, "meet and eats," Ravinia outings, picnics, and ball games.

Camping, biking, and canoeing trips, pumpkin-carving contests, and campfires are offered in the non-skiing season.

www.chicagofriars.com.

★ FREE **Fleet Feet Running Groups**   This premier Chicago running store has running groups that gather twice a week at their three retail locations. The fun runs last anywhere from 3 to 8 miles, running through Lincoln Park, the lakefront, and the path along the Chicago River. Even more amazing are the historic runs—you can get your workout and learn a few things about Jackson Park and the 1893 Worlds Fair, Rosehill Cemetery, and the Chicago Fire. Best of all? The groups are free and open to the public. FINE PRINT Make sure to RSVP online or by calling, and show up ready to run.

Two locations: Old Town, 1620 N. Wells St. ℂ **312/587-3338.** Subway/El: Brown Line to Sedgwick. Lincoln Square, 4555 N. Lincoln Ave. ℂ **773/271-3338.** Subway/El: Brown Line to Western. www.fleetfeetchicago.com.

★ FREE **Millennium Park Workouts**   Imagine 300 people doing tai chi on the lawn surrounding Pritzker Pavillion: This amazing sight is not a hallucination, it's the Millennium Park Workouts. Every Saturday morning, Fitness Council, Lakeshore Athletic Club, and McDonald's sponsor free yoga, Pilates, dance fitness, and tai chi workout classes at Millennium Park on the lawn of the Pritzker Pavilion, from 8 to 11am. These classes are run by the professional instructors of the Lakeshore Athletic Club (at Illinois Center). Check out the Millennium Park website or follow the park on Facebook for specific information, as classes and times change constantly.

www.millenniumpark.org.

**YMCA of Metropolitan Chicago**   If you want a straightforward gym membership, with no frills, and for a low, low price (and who doesn't want all of the above?), check into the YMCA. Rates average about $47 for a monthly individual membership (and, if you're smart, and of course you are, you'll sign up when there are special offers that waive the initiation fee, which generally costs about 1 month's fee). If you're a member of a YMCA in another city, you're allowed 15 visits per year to other YMCAs, so you'll be able to work out here while you're in town. Swimming pools, fitness rooms with elliptical trainers, rowing machines, treadmills, free weights, weight machines, and more should keep everyone happy. What you won't find: an Internet cafe, fancy juice bar, and women wearing tons of makeup to work out. Classes, from boxing to spinning, are free. Financial assistance is available for those who qualify. Most Ys are open for extensive hours, from around 5:30am to 11pm, so there's no excuse for not finding time to work out. Twenty locations throughout the city; check the website for the Y nearest you.

801 N. Dearborn St. ✆ **312/932-1200.** www.ymcachgo.org.

## CHICAGO PARK DISTRICT

Chicago boasts an incredible park district that offers the cheapest sports and recreation classes around. With everything from archery to tai chi, ice hockey to indoor tennis, bargains are to be found among the 500-plus programs offered year-round. You can find a plethora of free activities, cheap classes, easy fitness opportunities, and more at www.chicagoparkdistrict.org (✆ **312/742-PLAY** [7529]).

## M-M-M-MEDITATION

A little peace of mind is priceless, and in the city, there are a number of places to help you achieve it.

**FREE** St. James Cathedral Walking Labyrinth  Located on the upper level of the plaza between this beautiful Episcopal church and 65 E. Huron, this outdoor labyrinth is open to the public 24 hours a day. The concept is to walk slowly through the labyrinth until you reach a meditative state, which centers mind and heart.

65 E. Huron St. ✆ **312/787-7360.** www.saintjamescathedral.org. Subway/El: Red Line to Chicago.

Zen Buddhist Temple  Public meditation sessions are held at 9:30am and 4pm on Sundays (there's a $5 suggested donation). If you find yourself interested in pursuing meditation further, there are classes and retreats here, too. The place is a bit funky looking (it originally served as a Masonic Temple), but it's been restored inside.

1710 W. Cornelia Ave. (btw. Hermitage and Lincoln aves.). ✆ **773/528-8685.** www. zenbuddhisttemple.org. Subway/El: Brown Line to Paulina.

## SWIMMING POOLS

The Chicago Park District runs an incredible number of swimming pools—77 to be exact—some indoors (26 of them), some outdoors (51 of them). The Park District offers aquatic exercise classes, lap swim, open swim, and swimming lessons. To sign up, call ☏ **312/742-PLAY** (7529), or check out the offerings on www.chicagoparkdistrict.com.

One of my favorites is the Portage Park Pool at 4100 N. Long Ave. (☏ **773/685-7285**), where the open public swim is free. The Olympic-size pool features a large deck for sunning, misting sprays, and an interactive water play area with slide. The park also contains a smaller heated pool. The 37-acre park is much more than a pretty picture—it's the site for hundreds of valuable sports, early childhood recreation, and cultural programs, as well as fantastic family special events. Another good public swimming pool is located in Smith Park, 2526 W. Grand Ave. (☏ **312/742-7534**).

**YMCA of Metropolitan Chicago**    Swim teams, swim lessons, and water exercise are offered through a YMCA membership, which gets you access to member pools. One of the cheapest options might be getting your swim time in during "Community Swim." At the Lakeview branch, for example, you can receive three free passes to the facilities, as long as you present a valid state ID or driver's license. After your passes are used, it's time to sign up for membership.

801 N. Dearborn St. ☏ **312/932-1200.** www.ymcachgo.org.

## WATERSPORTS

It's one thing to enjoy the amazing views of Lake Michigan any time you turn east, but getting out on the water is much more challenging, as sports like sailing aren't known for being dirt cheap. Here are some of the better and least expensive options:

★ **Kayak Chicago**    A not-to-be-forgotten introduction to Chicago is a kayak tour of the Chicago River. Granted, it's a splurge, with a 3-hour paddle setting you back $50. But as a special treat, kayaking the river is an experience you won't forget, whether you sign on for a fireworks paddle, architectural/history paddle, sunset paddle, or lake paddle. Come prepared to get a little wet and be out in the sun.

1501 N. Magnolia Ave. (at LeMoyne). ☏ **630/336-7245.** www.kayakchicago.com. Wed–Sun 10am–7pm Memorial Day to October. Subway/El: Red Line to North/Clybourn.

**Learn-to-Sail Program at Northwestern University**    Sailing lessons are not cheap. But one of the cheaper ways to learn in an excellent program is Northwestern University's sailing program. (The University is located on the shore of Lake Michigan in north suburban Evanston.) For $299, you'll get eight lessons, plus a 1-month membership to Northwestern's sailing center. Sure, $299 is not even close to free or dirt cheap, but compare this price to many Chicago sailing schools that charge somewhere in the range of $100 for a single lesson.

Northwestern University Fitness and Recreation Department, 2311 Campus Dr., Evanston. ✆ **847/491-4142.** www.fitrec.northwestern.edu. Subway/El: Purple Express to Davis.

## YOGA & TAI CHI

Taking time to de-stress and improve your health? Sounds like a winning combination. Yoga and tai chi promote both, with yoga the more aerobic option and tai chi focusing on gentle, flowing movements.

**Bikram Yoga College of India**   For the bargain-basement price of $29 for unlimited classes for your first month, this is a low-risk way to check out Bikram yoga. Bikram will get you sweating, give you an amazing workout, and leave you feeling like you're walking on air the next day (but while you're sweating it out in a 100°F/38°C or hotter room, you might be questioning your decision!). And, you've only invested $29 if you decide Bikram isn't for you.

1344 N. Milwaukee Ave. ✆ **773/395-9150.** www.105f.com. El: Blue Line to Division.

**Dahn Yoga Tai Chi Meditation**   The focus of Dahn yoga and tai chi is on balancing your energy, doing meditative movements, and getting in tune with your brain vibrations. Dahn yoga is comprised of stretching, breathing, and meditation, while tai chi uses slow and graceful movements to release stress and recharge your body with fresh energy. Individual classes are $20, with discounts for introductory classes and packages available on the website.

2732 N. Clark St. ✆ **773-755-9566.** www.dahnyoga.com. Subway/El: Red Line to Fullerton.

**Moksha Yoga**   A free community class on Sunday is the way to get started at this studio, which offers a variety of styles, including vinyasa and ashtanga (a 10-class package is $110). A great expanse of windows looks out over the city, adding to the inspirational effect.

700 N. Carpenter St. ✆ **312/942-9642.** www.mokshayoga.com. El: Blue Line to Chicago; Blue O'Hare Line to Grand.

**Nature Yoga**   Classes at this storefront studio will leave you feeling completely blissed out, especially if you manage to attend one of their donation classes ($5 suggested). There is a donation class daily from 4 to 5:15pm, and on Saturdays at that time, there's a community class (30 students maximum allowed), which is free. Regular classes cost $15 per 75- to 90-minute session. Hatha blend, pranayama (science of breath), and partner yoga are among the wide range of classes on offer.

2021 W. Division St. ℂ **773/227-5720.** El: Blue Line to Division.

**Om on the Range Yoga Studio**    If you are into sweating it out with Bikram yoga, then you'll surely get your money's worth with the $20 this studio charges for 1 week of unlimited classes for new students only. FINE PRINT  Once you've run through your $20 week, make sure you're ready to feel the heat before you cough up the big bucks for a month of classes ($150 for a month of unlimited classes). Normal and unpretentious, with large classes comprised of everyone from beginners to veteran yogis, this studio welcomes all. Bring lots of water!

3759 N. Ravenswood Ave. ℂ **773/525-9642.** www.omontherange.net. El: Brown Line to Addison.

★ **Yoga Circle**    An excellent studio tucked away on the second floor of a building near the Ohio Street off-ramp of the Kennedy Expressway, Yoga Circle has been around for a long time, and its instructors are expert at teaching the Iyengar style of yoga. In fact, Yoga Circle's instructors are recognized as some of the best in the city, and classes reach across all age groups. An 8-week introductory course will run you $100, plus a $25 one-time registration fee.

401 W. Ontario St. (btw. Kingsbury and Orleans sts.). ℂ **312/915-0750.** www.yoga circle.com. Subway/El: Brown Line to Chicago.

*Bargain hunters will thrive at Chicago's many vintage and discount stores.*

# SHOPPING

**W**hen you're looking to score on the shopping front, finding what you want at a bargain-basement price can feel like a needle-in-a-haystack hunt. Hopefully that will change, once you've read this chapter. Chicago has plentiful options for shopping, whether you're looking for hip clothing, shoes that not only look great but that you can actually wear to hoof it around the city, goofy gifts, or souvenirs. Let's just say that you'd be crazy to pay full price on Michigan Avenue when similar merchandise abounds off the beaten track for much, much less.

If you're a bargain hunter (and you know you are), then you'll love Chicago's incredibly diverse shopping scene. Every style, era, and financial status is represented here—not in big, homogenous shopping malls, but in hundreds of boutiques and secondhand stores scattered throughout the city. Whether you're looking for a pair of hot new jeans or a bottle of vino, fresh baguette, and a chunk of cheddar, Chicago's got it.

Chicago is also loaded with thrift stores and secondhand clothing emporiums, a prime source of cool couture for local hipsters (though prices on hip quasi-vintage clothing can be steep). Damen, Division, Milwaukee, and Lincoln are streets that are some of the best spots for super scores. Surprisingly (and this might change as the economy improves), department stores should not be automatically ruled out as an option. With discounts as deep as 75% on sale merchandise, it can pay to peruse the sale racks at some of the big stores on Michigan Avenue, especially during sale season (in Jan for winter merchandise, and July for summer merchandise, for example). For everyday discounts on all kinds of merchandise, there is a strip of stores on State Street that will fulfill your bargain-hunting fantasies, from Loehmann's to Filene's, TJ Maxx, Marshall's, and even Old Navy. (Outside of the city, for those willing to drive for a deal, you'll find outlet malls in west suburban Aurora, north suburban Gurnee, and in Michigan City, Indiana.)

Pick a shopping neighborhood, give yourself a spending budget, and you're sure to end up with at least a few affordable take-home treasures.

## 1 Dirt Cheap Shopping Zones

Chicago has many shopping areas, but the following places are where you'll find the best deals.

### STATE STREET & THE LOOP

Shopping in the Loop is mostly concentrated along State Street, from Randolph Street south to Congress Parkway (although there are stores sprinkled elsewhere, they're mostly places that cater to office workers: drugstores, sandwich shops, and chain clothing stores). State Street was Chicago's first great shopping district—by World War I,

# THE LOOP, RIVER NORTH & MAGNIFICENT MILE

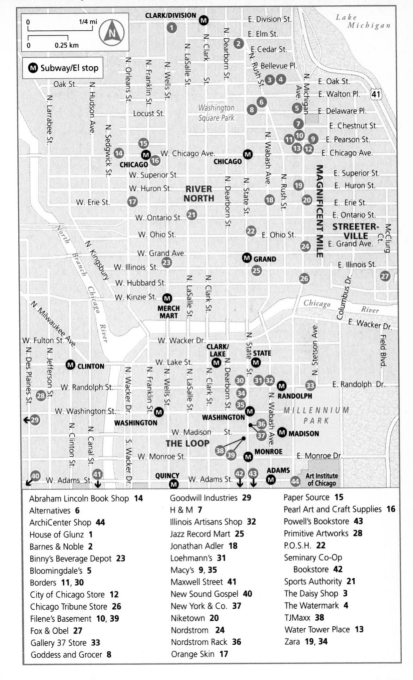

| | | |
|---|---|---|
| Abraham Lincoln Book Shop **14** | Goodwill Industries **29** | Paper Source **15** |
| Alternatives **6** | H & M **7** | Pearl Art and Craft Supplies **16** |
| ArchiCenter Shop **44** | Illinois Artisans Shop **32** | Powell's Bookstore **43** |
| House of Glunz **1** | Jazz Record Mart **25** | Primitive Artworks **28** |
| Barnes & Noble **2** | Jonathan Adler **18** | P.O.S.H. **22** |
| Binny's Beverage Depot **23** | Loehmann's **31** | Seminary Co-Op |
| Bloomingdale's **5** | Macy's **9, 35** |   Bookstore **42** |
| Borders **11, 30** | Maxwell Street **41** | Sports Authority **21** |
| City of Chicago Store **12** | New Sound Gospel **40** | The Daisy Shop **3** |
| Chicago Tribune Store **26** | New York & Co. **37** | The Watermark **4** |
| Filene's Basement **10, 39** | Niketown **20** | TJMaxx **38** |
| Fox & Obel **27** | Nordstrom **24** | Water Tower Place **13** |
| Gallery 37 Store **33** | Nordstrom Rack **36** | Zara **19, 34** |
| Goddess and Grocer **8** | Orange Skin **17** | |

## Jewelers' Row

It's not quite as impressive as the Big Apple's diamond district, but Chicago's own "Jewelers' Row" is certainly worth a detour for rock hunters seeking a deal (the area is known for its discounted loose diamonds). Half a dozen high rises along the Wabash Avenue El tracks in the heart of the Loop service the wholesale trade, but the one at 5 S. Wabash Ave. opens its doors to customers off the street. There's a mall-like retail space on the ground floor crammed with tiny booths manned by smooth-talking reps hawking their wares. You can grab a map here for a self-guided tour of the rest of the building's tenants. It's quite an experience because many of the booths are closet-size cubbyholes with hunched-over geezers who look as if they've been eyeballing solitaire and marquise cuts since the Roosevelt administration—Teddy, that is.

seven of the largest and most lavish department stores in the world were competing for shoppers' loyalties along this half-mile stretch. The area has been eclipsed by Michigan Avenue, and State Street is now lined with discount stores and fast-food outlets. However, one grand old department store makes it worth a visit: **Macy's at State Street** (formerly Marshall Field's), 111 N. State St., at Randolph Street (© **312/781-1000**). A city landmark and one of the largest department stores in the world, it occupies an entire city block and features the largest Tiffany glass mosaic dome in the U.S. If you're in Chicago between Thanksgiving and New Year's, Macy's has maintained a long-time Marshall Field's tradition: lavishly decorated holiday windows and lunch under the Great Tree in the store's restaurant, the Walnut Room.

Along State Street near Macy's, you'll find discount retailers including TJ Maxx, Filene's Basement, Nordstrom Rack, plus Old Navy and Chicago's hometown chain, Sears. The other stores along State Street are not particularly distinctive—the place still has a no-frills aura compared to Michigan Avenue—but it stays busy thanks to the thousands of office workers who stroll around during their lunch hour or after work. On weekends, the street is considerably more subdued.

# RIVER NORTH

Since the 1960s, when the Chicago Imagists (painters Ed Paschke, Jim Nutt, and Roger Brown among them) attracted international attention with their shows at the Hyde Park Art Center, the city has been a fertile breeding ground for emerging artists and innovative art dealers. Today, the primary gallery district is concentrated in the River North neighborhood, where century-old, redbrick warehouses have been converted into lofty exhibition spaces. More recently, a new generation of gallery owners has set up shop in the rapidly gentrifying West Loop neighborhood, where you'll tend to find more cutting-edge work. The River North gallery district is an easy walk from many hotels; the West Loop may seem a little farther afield, but it's only a short cab ride from downtown (you can also take the bus, but I'd recommend a taxi at night). This district is fabulous for window-shopping and exploring to see what's new on the art scene. What River North is not fabulous for is buying, since free and dirt cheap galleries are found in other neighborhoods, including Wicker Park, Pilsen, and Andersonville, for example.

The River North gallery season officially gets underway on the first Friday after Labor Day in September. Besides fall, another great time to visit the district is from mid-July through August, when the Chicago Art Dealers Association presents **Vision,** an annual lineup of programs tailored to the public. Early September also offers the annual ★ **Around the Coyote** festival in Wicker Park/Bucktown (call ✆ **773/342-6777** for information), when scores of artists open their studios to the public (the name refers to the now-departed Coyote Gallery, which used to stand at the corner of Damen and North aves.).

The *Chicago Reader,* a free weekly newspaper available at many stores, taverns, and cafes on the North Side, publishes a very comprehensive listing of current gallery exhibitions, as does the quarterly *Chicago Gallery News* (www.chicagogallerynews.com), which is available free at the city's three visitor information centers. Another good resource is the Chicago Art Dealers Association (✆ **312/649-0065;** www.chicagoartdealers.org); the group's website has descriptions of all member galleries. For descriptions of the city's top galleries, see "Art Galleries" under "Bargain Shopping from A to Z," later in this chapter.

Along with its status as Chicago's primary art-gallery district, River North—the area west of the Magnificent Mile and north of the Chicago River—has attracted many interesting home-design shops concentrated on Wells Street from Kinzie Street to Chicago Avenue. My favorites include **Manifesto,** 755 N. Wells St., at Chicago Avenue (✆ **312/664-0733**), which offers custom-designed furniture, as well as imports from Italy and elsewhere in Europe; **Mig & Tig,** 540 N. Wells St., at Ohio Street (✆ **312/644-8277**), a charming furniture and decorative-accessories shop; and ★ **Lightology,** 215 W. Chicago Ave., at Wells Street (✆ **312/944-1000**), a massive lighting store that carries a mind-boggling array of funky lamps, chandeliers, and glowing orbs from more than 400 manufacturers (even if you have no intention of flying home with a stack of lamps in your luggage, it's fun to browse).

Looming above the Chicago River at the southern end of River North is the ★ **Merchandise Mart,** the world's largest commercial building. The massive complex was built in 1930 by Marshall Field & Company and was bought in 1945 by Joseph P. Kennedy (JFK's dad); the Kennedy family ran the Mart until the late 1990s. Now the building houses mostly interior-design showrooms, which are open only to professional designers. One exception is Luxe Home, a collection of kitchen and bath showrooms on the first floor, all of which are open to the public (and worth a look for interior-design junkies). Public tours of the whole complex are offered once a week, usually on Fridays ($12 adults; ✆ **312/527-7762** for dates and reservations).

## ARMITAGE AVENUE

Hovering between the North Side neighborhoods of Old Town and Lincoln Park, Armitage Avenue has emerged as a shopping destination in its own right, thanks to an influx of wealthy young professionals who have settled into historic town homes on the neighboring tree-lined streets. The main shopping district is concentrated between Halsted Street and Racine Avenue; I'd suggest starting at the Armitage El stop (Brown Line), working your way east to Halsted Street, and then wandering a few blocks north to Webster Street. As you stroll around, you'll get a good sense of the area's strong community spirit, with neighbors greeting each other and catching up on the street corners.

The shops and boutiques here are geared toward a sophisticated, well-heeled shopper and make for great browsing. (Most are suited for female shoppers—sorry, guys). You'll find trendy clothing boutiques, including that of local-gal-made-good **Cynthia Rowley** (808 W. Armitage Ave.; ✆ **773/528-6160**); jaw-droppingly beautiful home-decor stores; beauty emporiums; and one of my favorite impossible-to-classify gift shops, **Art Effect** (p. 252). Tiny **Multiple Choices,** 840 W. Armitage Ave. (✆ **773/477-4520**), is full of colorful ceramics and creative gifts (including Big Ten college board games such as "Wisconsinopoly"). The upscale pet accessories shop **Barker & Meowsky,** 1003 W. Armitage Ave. (✆ **773/868-0200**), has everything you need to spoil furry family members, including catnip cigars, doggy "sushi," and designer-inspired outfits.

Despite the area's upscale feel, you can snag bargains at some top-notch discount and consignment shops, including **Lori's Designer Shoes, McShane's Exchange, Fox's,** and **The Second Child** (see "Vintage Fashion/Resale Shops" under "Bargain Shopping from A to Z," below).

> ## A Rare Oak Street Bargain
>
> Oak Street, just west of Michigan Avenue, is not the place to come shopping for bargains—with one exception—Bravco, 43 E. Oak St. (✆ **312/943-4305**). This crowded, narrow drugstore seems out of place among the hip boutiques, but it's a popular spot among Chicago hairstylists and makeup artists. You'll find an excellent selection of professional hair and beauty products (including Aveda, Sebastian, and Bumble and Bumble) here for much less than they cost at salons. Even if you haven't heard of some of the brands, trust me, if Bravco carries them, they're hot.

## LINCOLN PARK & LAKEVIEW

A few major north-south thoroughfares—Lincoln Avenue, Clark Street, and Broadway—are the main shopping streets in both Lincoln Park (south of Diversey Pkwy.) and Lakeview (north of Diversey). Most of the shops cater to young singles who live in the surrounding apartment buildings; you'll find plenty of minimart groceries, some clothing and shoe boutiques, and the occasional used-book store, but not much that's worth a special trip.

Radiating from the intersection of Belmont Avenue and Clark Street is a string of shops catering to rebellious kids on tour from their homes in the 'burbs (the Dunkin' Donuts on the corner is often referred to as "Punkin' Donuts" in their honor). One constant in the ever-changing youth culture has been the **Alley,** 3228 N. Clark St., at Belmont Avenue (© **773/883-1800**), an "alternative shopping complex" selling everything from plaster gargoyles to racks of leather jackets. It has separate shops specializing in condoms, cigars, and bondage wear. **Tragically Hip,** a storefront women's boutique, 931 W. Belmont Ave. (© **773/549-1500**), next to the Belmont El train stop, has outlasted many other similar purveyors of cutting-edge women's apparel.

You can get plugged into what the kids are reading at **Chicago Comics,** 3244 N. Clark St. (© **773/528-1983**), considered one of the best comics shops in the country. Besides the usual superhero titles, you'll find lots of European and Japanese comics, along with underground books and 'zines.

## SOUTHPORT AVENUE

West of Lakeview, a few blocks from Wrigley Field, this residential area was considered up-and-coming about 10 years ago; now it's definitely arrived. The mix of restaurants, cool (but not *too* cool) clothing boutiques, and cafes appeals to the upscale urban families who have flocked to the area (watch out for strollers hogging the sidewalk). It's worth a look if you want to hang out in a neighborhood that's a little more laid-back than the Gold Coast or Wicker Park. Start at the Southport El stop on the Brown Line, and work your way north to Grace Street (round-trip, the walk will take you about half-an-hour—but allow more if you're doing some serious shopping or want to stop for lunch). Along the way you'll pass the historic ★ **Music Box Theater** at 3733 N. Southport Ave. (© **773/871-6604**), north of Addison Street, which shows independent films from around the world. Nearby, at consignment store **Leahey & LaDue,** 3753 N. Southport Ave. (©**773/929-4685**), you'll score deals on "gently used" designers brands—even more so if you are lucky enough to hit their twice-yearly 50%-off sale, in January and July. Great music on the sound systems, colorful displays, and interesting and trendy jewelry (starting at about $20) to accessorize your new outfit make this a fun place to shop. Just south of here, you can pop into ★ **Click Shoes & More,** 3729 Southport Ave. (© **773/244-9141**), for a great selection of footwear that makes you feel like you just stepped into your dream closet with every pair of shoes you'd love to own. Custom-made messenger bags are another attraction here (choose your own fabric), for about $40. A great sale area and terrific, cutting-edge styles at great prices make this a win.

## WICKER PARK/BUCKTOWN

The go-go gentrification of the Wicker Park/Bucktown area has been followed by not only a rash of restaurants and bars but also retailers with an artsy bent that reflect the neighborhood's bohemian spirit. Mixed in with old neighborhood businesses, such as discount furniture stores and religious-icon purveyors, are a proliferation of antique-furniture shops, too-cool-for-school clothing boutiques, and eclectic galleries and gift emporiums. Despite the hefty price tags in many of these shops, the neighborhood still feels gritty—so come here if you want to feel like you've gotten a real urban fix.

Start at the Damen El stop on the Blue Line, and walk north along Damen to Armitage Avenue to scope out the trendiest shops. If you've got time, some stores are also scattered along Milwaukee Avenue south of North Avenue.

If you are a fan of the handmade items featured on Etsy.com, then you're going to love ★ **Habit,** 1951 W. Division St. (© **773/342-0093**), which sells only items from small designers, many of them local. This is a particularly good place to look for a dress or jewelry (around $20–$30 per piece). Attention, guys: The store carries menswear from indie designers, too. **Una Mae's Freak Boutique,** 1528 N. Milwaukee (© **773/276-7002**), has loads of vintage clothing in good condition. The store looks like a cute boutique with eclectic and homey touches, but without the boutique prices. Vintage is definitely the way to go for bargains here (dresses as little as $11), but don't miss the modern, hipster clothing either. **Pitaya,** 1463 N.

### Taking a Break in Wicker Park

When you're ready to rest your weary self, settle down at a local coffeehouse and soak in Wicker Park's artsy vibe. **Earwax Café,** 1564 N. Milwaukee Ave. (© **773/772-4019**), attracts the jaded and pierced set with a no-frills, slightly edgy atmosphere. **Filter,** across the street at 1585 N. Milwaukee Ave. (© **773/227-4850**), is a little more welcoming; comfy couches fill the main dining room, which features paintings by local artists. Both cafes are near the bustling intersection of North, Milwaukee, and Damen avenues—the heart of Wicker Park—and draw a steady stream of locals. It's here you'll realize that Wicker Park is really just a small town—with cooler hair and funkier shoes.

## Just the Facts: Hours, Taxes & Shipping

Store hours are generally Monday through Saturday from 10am to 6pm and Sunday from noon to 5pm. Most department stores stay open later, as do shops around Michigan Avenue, the most heavily visited area (by tourists). Sales tax in Chicago is a whopping 10.25% (the highest in the country, at press time), which is added on at the register for all goods and services purchased. If you live out of state and buy an expensive item, you might want to have the store ship it home for you. You'll have to pay for shipping, but you'll escape paying the sales tax. Most of the city's shops can wrap your purchase and ship it anywhere in the world. If they can't, you can send it yourself, through UPS (© 800/742–5877), FedEx (© 800/463–3339), or the U.S. Postal Service.

Milwaukee (© 773/276-4000), is a small, independent boutique offering cute, flirty, affordable pieces and funky make-up. Trendy but decent quality for the price (about $25 for a top or $35 for a dress) is the name of the game here. Tucked away on a residential street is ★ **Beta Boutique,** 2016 W. Concord Place (at Damen Ave.) (© 773/276-0905), which is known for its "stacked racks" events offering 40% to 90% off designer prices (racks are arranged by price – $10, $20, and so on). Stylish, trendy clothing at killer prices: What more can you ask?

## WEST DIVISION STREET

Once home to just a few pioneering restaurants, Division Street is quickly being transformed from a desolate urban landscape to a hot shopping destination. It's a work in progress (you'll still find some boarded-up buildings among the cool boutiques), but for now this is what Wicker Park used to be: a place where rents are still cheap enough for eager young entrepreneurs. Start at the Division El stop on the Blue Line, and head west along Division; most stores are concentrated between Milwaukee Avenue and Damen Avenue (a round-trip walk will take about half-an-hour). Along the way, you'll stroll past eclectic clothing and shoe boutiques, bath-and-beauty shops, and home-decor stores such as **Porte Rouge,** 1911 W. Division St. (© 773/269-2800), which is filled with French antiques and housewares (they'll even offer you a complimentary cup of tea). The mix of people living here—from working-class Latino families to self-consciously edgy young singles—makes the local cafes great for people-watching.

## 2 Bargain Shopping from A to Z

### ART

★ **Around the Coyote Gallery**   A nonprofit gallery that sponsors an annual art festival of the same name, this gallery is a standout among standout galleries in Wicker Park. Both prominent and emerging artists are shown here, and one of its strengths is its international diversity. Not to be missed. 19351/2 W. North Ave. ✆ **773/342-6777.** www.aroundthecoyote.org. Subway/El: Blue Line to Grand.

**Chicago Center for the Print**   A good place for the dirt cheap shopper to find vintage European posters as well as contemporary prints. You can even have your new purchase framed on-site. This is a warm, welcoming environment that is highly conducive to browsing. 1509 W. Fullerton Ave. ✆ **773/477-1585.** www.prints-posters.com. Subway/El: Red Line to Fullerton.

**Contemporary Art Workshop**   Another low-on-the-snootiness-scale gallery, this space has long been recognized as one of the oldest artist-run alternative gallery spaces in the nation. You never know what you'll find here, since exhibitions range from sculpture to oil painting and more. 542 W. Grant Place. ✆ **773/472-4004.** www.contemporary artworkshop.org. Subway/El: Red Line to Fullerton.

**Gallery 37 Store**   Paintings, sculptures, and furniture here are all produced by high school students who are studying with professional artists through a city-run program. Not only are the pieces inexpensive, but you'll be supporting the city's future artists in their work. 86 E. Randolph St. ✆ **312/744-7274.** http://egov.cityofchicago.org/gallery37center. Subway/El: Brown Line to Randolph.

**Glass Art Designs**   Glass fusing is the name of the game at this distinctive gallery, where you can even take a basic-level glass-fusing class and produce your very own creation. 1807 W. Sunnyside Ave. ✆ **773/297-5975.** www.glassartdesign.com. Subway/El: Brown Line to Montrose.

**Granville Gallery**   Although the main business here is framing, you can stop by this retro-looking gallery to check out the artwork. Oil paintings, posters, rubbings from Thai temples, shadow boxes—you name it, and you can peruse it here. They've been in business for 60 years, so these people know their stuff. 6200 N. Broadway. ℂ 773/764-1919. www.granvillegallerychicagoframing.com. Subway/El: Red Line to Granville.

**Illinois Artisans Shop**   Showcasing the best crafts produced by artists in the state-sponsored Illinois Artisans Program, this is a good source for unique, reasonably priced gifts and souvenirs including pottery, textiles, paintings, and mementos. 100 W. Randolph St. ℂ 312/814-5321. www.museum.state.il.us/ismsites/chicago. Subway/El: Red Line to Lake.

**Jonathan Adler**   Known for his needlepoint throw pillows, you can get ideas for all of those "homemade" touches you need to make a house a very hip home (and if you want to buy, try an inexpensive contemporary home-furnishings retailer such as CB2). 676 N. Wabash St. ℂ 312/274-9920. www.jonathanadler.com. Subway/El: Red Line to Grand.

★ **Las Manos Gallery**   Showing works ranging from paintings to mixed media, this unpretentious gallery is owned by principal artist Michelle Peterson-Albandoz. A choice group of high-quality artists shows here. 5220 N. Clark St. ℂ 773/728-8910. www.lasmanos gallery.org. Subway/El: Red Line to Berwyn.

★ **Primitive Art Works**   Winding your way through this 31,000-square-foot store, you'll feel as if you've taken an exotic worldwide journey. Packed with furniture, rugs, jewelry, and beads from various cultures, this store might yield a giant Buddha head acquired from a Korean temple that was being destroyed on one day; on another, you might discover an exquisite embroidered rug from Turkmenistan. 130 N. Jefferson St. ℂ 312/575-9600. www.beprimitive. com. Subway/El: Brown Line to Chicago.

## ART & CRAFT SUPPLIES

**Pearl Art and Craft Supplies**   Graphic designers, artists, and arts and crafts aficionados flock to Pearl for every art supply known on earth. If you need to pick up supplies for a rainy-day project, you'll love Pearl. 255 W. Chicago Ave. (at Franklin St.). ℂ 312/915-0200. www.pearlpaint.com. Subway/El: Brown Line to Chicago.

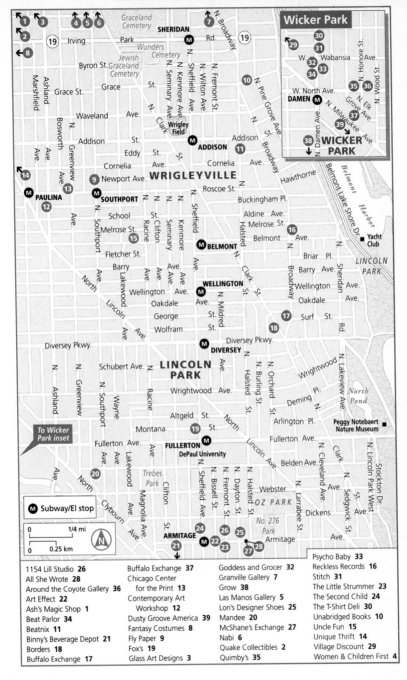

Wicker Park

Graceland Cemetery

SHERIDAN

Wrigley Field

ADDISON

WRIGLEYVILLE

PAULINA

SOUTHPORT

BELMONT

WELLINGTON

DIVERSEY

LINCOLN PARK

FULLERTON
DePaul University

To Wicker Park inset

M Subway/El stop

0        1/4 mi
0        0.25 km

ARMITAGE

WICKER PARK

DAMEN

Yacht Club

LINCOLN PARK

Peggy Notebaert Nature Museum

Trebes Park

OZ PARK

No. 276 Park

## BOOKS

**Abraham Lincoln Book Shop**　This bookstore boasts one of the country's most outstanding collections of Lincolniana, from rare and antique books about the 16th president to collectible signatures, letters, and other documents illuminating the lives of other U.S. presidents and historical figures. The shop carries new historical and academic works, too. 357 W. Chicago Ave. (btw. Orleans and Sedgwick sts.). ✆ **312/944-3085.** www.alincolnbookshop.com. Subway/El: Brown Line to Chicago.

**Barnes & Noble**　This two-level Gold Coast store comes complete with a cafe in case you get the munchies while perusing the miles of books. There's another store in Lincoln Park, at 659 W. Diversey Ave., 1 block west of Clark Street (✆ **773/871-9004**), and one at 1441 W. Webster Ave., at Clybourn Avenue (✆ **773/871-3610**). 1130 N. State St. (at Elm St.). ✆ **312/280-8155.** www.barnesandnoble.com. Subway/El: Red Line to Clark/Division.

**Borders**　This place is like a mini–department store, with books, magazines, CDs, and computer software spread over four floors, and a cafe with a view overlooking State Street. The Loop location is found at 150 N. State St., at Randolph Street (✆ **312/606-0750**). There's another location in Lincoln Park at 2817 N. Clark St., at Diversey Avenue (✆ **773/935-3909**). 830 N. Michigan Ave. (at Pearson St.). ✆ **312/573-0564.** www.borders.com. Subway/El: Red Line to Randolph.

**Powell's Bookstore**　Used books, especially from scholarly and small Chicago presses, dog-eared paperbacks, and hardcover classics fill the shelves at this booklover's haven. There are also outlets in Lakeview at 2850 N. Lincoln Ave. (✆ **773/248-1444**), and Hyde Park at 1501 E. 57th St. (✆ **773/955-7780**). 828 S. Wabash Ave. (btw. 8th and 9th sts.). ✆ **312/341-0748.** www.powellschicago.com. Subway/El: Red Line to Harrison.

**Seminary Co-Op Bookstore**　A classic campus bookstore located near the University of Chicago, this shop has extensive philosophy and theology sections and is one of the premier academic bookstores in the country. 5757 S. University Ave. (btw. 57th and 58th sts.). ✆ **773/752-4381.** www.semcoop.com. Bus: 69 (Jeffrey Express).

**Unabridged Books**    This quintessential neighborhood bookseller in the area known as Boys Town has strong sections in gay and lesbian literature, travel, film, and sci-fi. 3251 N. Broadway (btw. Belmont Ave. and Addison St.). © **773/883-9119.** www.unabridgedbookstore. com. Subway/El: Red Line to Addison.

★ **Women & Children First**    This feminist and children's bookstore holds the best selection in the city of titles for, by, and about women. But the shop is far from a male-free zone; the owners promote great independent fiction—by authors of both genders—making this a good place to discover books that have been overlooked by the bestseller lists. There's a section devoted to lesbian and gay books, and the store has a busy schedule of author appearances. 5233 N. Clark St. (btw. Foster and Bryn Mawr aves.). © **773/769-9299.** www.womenand childrenfirst.com. Subway/El: Red Line to Berwyn.

## CLOTHES

★ **McShane's Exchange**    This consignment shop has a selection that's a few steps above that at the standard thrift store, and for designer bargains, it can't be beat. The store expands back through a series of cramped rooms, with clothes organized by color, making it easy to scope out the perfect black dress. The longer a piece stays in stock, the lower the price drops—and I've done plenty of double takes at the price tags here: Calvin Klein coats, Prada sweaters, and Armani jackets all going for well under $100. If that's not tempting enough, you'll also find barely used shoes and purses. McShane's has another location with a similar selection at 1141 W. Webster St. (© **773/ 525-0211**). 815 W. Armitage Ave. (at Halsted St.). © **773/525-0282.** www.mcshanesexchange.com. Subway/El: Brown Line to Armitage.

**The Second Child**    This self-described "upscale children's resale boutique" may not look all that upscale—it's basically one long, dark room on the second floor of an Armitage Avenue town house—but take a look at the labels on these kids' clothes (Ralph Lauren, Lilly Pulitzer, and the like), and you'll see that they come from very fashionable closets. There's also a nice—if limited—selection of maternity clothes. 954 W. Armitage Ave. (btw. Bissell St. and Sheffield Ave.). © **773/883-0880.** www.2ndchild.com. Subway/El: Brown Line to Armitage.

## COSTUMES

**Fantasy Costumes**  This sprawling costume shop (covering an entire city block) is devoted to make-believe. The store stocks more than a million items, including 800 styles of masks (priced $1–$200) and all the accessories and makeup needed to complete any costume. There's also a full-service wig salon here. 4065 N. Milwaukee Ave. (west of Cicero Ave.). ☏ **773/777-0222.** www.fantasycostumes.com. Subway/El: Blue Line to Irving Park.

## DISCOUNT CLOTHING

If you never, ever pay full price, then these discount stores are sure to satisfy. The only requirement is that you are ready and willing to dig through racks of clothing in search of that one perfect garment—and that you have pledged not to buy an item just because it's cheap (many a fashion mistake has been made "because it was cheap"). Here are some of the best places to score a deal.

**Filene's Basement**  The Boston department store's discount off-shoot has some prime real estate on the Mag Mile. Take the escalator up, and be prepared to invest some time perusing the racks. The first racks you come upon carry merchandise that has just arrived, and is slightly pricier. As the season progresses, items are moved to the markdown racks, where they can be reduced as much as 90% off retail (it's possible to score items for as little as $6 at that point). "The Vault" has designer items at prices 30% to 60% off retail. And, if you're a bride-to-be, the Running of the Brides event (held at the State St. store in July—check the website for the annual date) dangles out the possibility of a designer gown at hundreds (or thousands) off the retail price. Just don't get trampled. Trampled is not an attractive quality in a bride-to-be. 830 N. Michigan Ave. ☏ **312/482-8918.** A second location is in the Loop at 1 N. State St. ☏ **312-553-1055.** www.filenesbasement.com. Subway/El: Blue and Red lines to Monroe; Orange, Brown, Purple Express, Green, or Pink line to Madison/Wabash.

**Fox's**  This no-frills shop near Armitage Avenue offers designer clothing at a steep discount. The downside: Most clothing labels are cut out, so you might not know exactly which A-list name you're buying, but the last time I was here, I heard a woman telling a friend that she'd seen the same clothes in Saks, a sure sign that Fox's stays

# The T-Shirt Deli: Want Chips with That T?

For a new twist on custom clothing, stop by this cozy Bucktown storefront, where you can order up your own personalized T-shirt creation. Browse through the entertaining books of vintage iron-on patches, and you'll find everything from '80s icons such as Mr. T to '70s-style "Foxy Lady" logos. Choose a design (or create your own message), and your shirt will be printed up while you wait. When it's done, the shirt is packaged in a paper bag with a side of potato chips—just like a real deli. 1739 N. Damen Ave. (btw. Willow St. and St. Paul Ave.). ⓒ 773/276-6266. www.tshirtdeli.com. Subway/El: Blue Line to Damen.

up-to-date with the fashion pulse. 2150 N. Halsted St. (at Dickens St.). ⓒ 773/281-0700. Subway/El: Brown Line to Armitage.

**Goodwill Industries**   Clean, spacious, and well-organized, this is a place for thrifters in the know. Most items will run you about $5. Racks are organized by color. Most of the apparel is relatively new and in good condition (not much in the way of vintage here). Other great steals include housewares and paperback books. 1201 W. Washington St. ⓒ 312/563-1187. www.goodwill.org. Subway/El: Pink Line to Lake.

**H & M**   This ever-trendy and cheap Swedish clothing chain gets a bit packed, so prepare for a frenzy when you enter. If you can brave the crowds, you'll be rewarded with some bargains. H & M is always on trend, at low, low, prices. Quality is as you'd expect—some items are better than others, so make sure to give your garment a trial in the dressing room. There's a nice selection of kids' clothing that's fun, trendy, and won't break the bank. 840 N. Michigan Ave. ⓒ 312/640-0060. Another location in the Loop at 20 N. State St. ⓒ 312/263-4436. www.hm.com. Subway/El: Red Line to Chicago.

**Loehmann's**   The Chicago branch of Loehmann's—the nation's only upscale off-price specialty retailer—caters to a sophisticated white-collar crowd, offering professional clothing, shoes, and accessories at bargain prices. Be sure to check out the Back Room, where designer clothes are sold for 30% to 65% less than at department stores. 151

N. State St. ℂ **312/705-3810.** www.loehmanns.com. Subway/El: Red Line to Lake; Orange, Brown, Purple Express, Green, or Pink line to Randolph/Wabash; Blue or Red line to Washington.

**Mandee**   With an age target of late teens to late twenties, this shop specializes in inexpensive, trendy, and let's admit it, sometimes a bit overly alluring clothing. There's a house brand with prices as cheap as $24 for a pair of pants. Sky-high heels are another specialty here. Do not pay full price. Sales of up to 70% off are common. Pair some of their items with your own, more grown-up (and covered-up) wardrobe, and you can come up with some stellar outfits. 1730 Clybourn Ave. (btw. Concord Place and Sheffield Ave.). ℂ **773/755-7502.** www.mandee.com. Subway/El: Red Line to North/Clybourn.

**Marshall's and TJ Maxx**   The company that owns these discount chains has a huge number of stores in the Chicago area. Up to 60% off department store prices—and 85% of the merchandise is from the current season. Constantly changing merchandise (and different merchandise from store to store) means it's worth popping in now and again to see what's new. Sometimes the stores feel a bit messy, but if you can see past that, you'll enjoy your treasure-hunting experience. Both TJ Maxx and Marshall's chains (with 1,600 stores nationwide) are owned by Boston-based retailer TJX. Marshall's: 600 N. Michigan Ave. & 312/280-7506. www.marshallsonline.com. Subway/El: Red Line to Grand. TJ Maxx: 11 N. State St. ℂ **312/553-0515.** www.tjmaxx.com. Subway/El: Blue, Red lines to Monroe; Orange, Brown, Purple Express, Green, or Pink line to Madison/Wabash.

**Nabi**   Cute, contemporary clothing, from casual to dressy, makes this a go-to spot for bargain hunters. No dressing room, but there are long mirrors, and you can manage to try on some things unobtrusively (wear a cami and leggings to the store for modesty). Eight doors down the street, the same retailer has an entire store devoted to accessories. Dig in! 4531 N. Clark St. ℂ **773/275-5544.** Subway/El: Red Line to Montrose.

**New York & Co.**   This company designs its own trendy line of clothing, which is hit and miss in terms of quality. Still, there are very nice items to be found on a budget, even for work. New York & Co. is especially known for their pants, in a myriad of lengths and rises. 25 N. State St. ℂ **312/629-3100.** www.nyandcompany.com. Subway/El:

Blue, Red lines to Monroe; Orange, Brown, Purple Express, Green, or Pink line to Madison/Wabash.

★ **Nordstrom Rack** This is my favorite place to buy high-quality clothes at steep discounts. Nordstrom Rack, the off-price division of Nordstrom, Inc., first opened in the basement of a downtown Seattle store in 1975 as a clearance department, and since then it's become so popular it's grown into its own division. The Rack carries merchandise from Nordstrom stores and Nordstrom.com at 50% to 60% off original Nordstrom prices—brand-name apparel, shoes, accessories, bath and beauty products, home accents, and so on. Heck, they even offer in-store alterations and tailoring at a competitive cost. 24 N. State St. ℂ **312/377-5500.** www.nordstromrack.com. Subway/El: Blue, Red lines to Monroe; Orange, Brown, Purple Express, Green, or Pink line to Madison/Wabash.

**Unique Thrift** Considered by savvy thrifters to be the one of the best (and best-priced) thrift stores in the city. Open until 9pm for late thrifters, this place has a good assortment of funky clothing, household items, shoes and purses, and furniture. On Mondays, everything is 50% off. You absolutely need to go prepared to sort through racks and racks of stuff (and by stuff, I mean lots of not-so-stellar items), so bring your patience. Also, be forewarned that there are no dressing rooms. Cash only. Bonus: There's a Family Dollar store next to Unique. Double your cheap-shopping pleasure! 3748 N. Elston Ave. ℂ **773/279-0850.** www.uniquethriftstore.com. Subway/El: Blue Line to Addison.

**Village Discount** Clothing moves fast at this gigantic and popular rock-bottom-priced retailer, which is a plus for those who pop in often. It's a bit of a chaotic mess at times, but deals abound for those willing to lose themselves in the never-ending racks of clothing. Don't look for vintage here: It's more about grabbing a great T-shirt for a couple of bucks. (Although you never know when you might find a perfect vintage Ivy League sweatshirt for under a buck.) 2032 N. Milwaukee Ave. ℂ **773/486-7603.** www.villagediscountoutlet.com. Subway/El: Blue Line to Western.

**Zara** Headquarters for stylish going-out clothing at more-than-reasonable prices, this Spanish retailer opened in 2008 in the Old Orchard shopping mall in north suburban Skokie, and is well worth a drive north on the Kennedy (take the Old Orchard exit, head east, and you'll see the outdoor mall of the same name). Westfield Old Orchard Mall, intersection of Old Orchard Road and Skokie Blvd. ℂ **847/329-0808.** www.zara.com. To get here, take the Kennedy Expwy. north to the Edens Expwy., take the Old Orchard exit and head east to the entrance of the mall.

## DEPARTMENT STORES

I fully realize that you are scratching your head right now, wondering how I could possibly include department stores in a free and dirt cheap guidebook. Well, let me tell you: Days of paying full price at department stores are long gone. With coupons and a never-ending stream of sales (most merchandise goes on sale a mere 6 weeks after first appearing in stores), savvy shoppers can score some real bargains at a big department store. It is completely possible to buy clothing at 50% to 75% off retail prices these days, as long as you seek out the sales racks and clip coupons. And while department store credit cards are not to be recommended if you are going to carry a balance (interest rates tend to be sky-high), if you are going to pay the card off monthly, the stores make it worth your while to get a card. Particularly if you are furnishing an apartment for the first time, it's wise to sign up for a card at a major department store, where you can buy towels, bath items, kitchen appliances, and clothing, plus receive a 20% savings that's often offered when you sign up for a card.

**Bloomingdale's**   Though nowhere near as large as the New York original, Chicago's Bloomingdale's appeals to stylish shoppers looking for just a bit of urban edge. The shoe department has a good range (with serious markdowns during semiannual sales). Check out the fifth floor for clothing from the new, trendy designers. 900 N. Michigan Ave. (at Walton St.). ℂ **312/440-4460.** www.bloomingdales.com. Subway/El: Red Line to Chicago.

**Macy's**   When Macy's took over Marshall Field's—Chicago's best-known "hometown" department store—in 2006, there was much local hand-wringing about what the buyout meant for Field's grand State Street headquarters. Although Field's iconic green awnings and shopping bags have been replaced by Macy's more dreary black, the good news is that the store itself remains impressive; a testament to the days when shopping downtown was an eagerly anticipated event rather than a chore. This block-long store is second in size only to Macy's

New York City flagship, and its impressive breadth of merchandise and historically significant interior make it a must-see for serious shoppers. A number of exclusive "miniboutiques" are scattered throughout the overwhelming space, including the 28 Shop, which stocks the latest from hot young designers; beauty stations where you can get a manicure and pick up exclusive products; and a gourmet food department developed by celebrity chef Charlie Trotter. The enormous shoe department is another highlight, with everything from killer high heels (at killer prices) and boots to sneakers and casual sandals.

The **Water Tower** store, 835 N. Michigan Ave. (✆ **312/335-7700**), is a scaled-down but respectable version of the State Street store. Its eight floors are actually much more manageable than the enormous flagship, and its merchandise selection is still vast (although this branch tends to focus on the more expensive brands). 111 N. State St. (at Randolph St.). ✆ **312/781-1000.** www.macys.com. Subway/El: Red Line to Washington.

**Nordstrom**    Nordstrom's spacious, airy design and trendy touches (wheatgrass growing by the escalators, funky music playing on the stereo system) gives it the feel of an upscale boutique rather than an overcrowded department store. The company's famed shoe department is large but not overwhelming; more impressive is the cosmetics department, where you'll find a wide array of smaller labels and an "open sell" environment (meaning you're encouraged to try on makeup without a salesperson hovering over you). In keeping with the store's famed focus on service, a concierge can check your coat, call a cab, or make restaurant reservations for you. If you're looking to score a bargain, save your pennies for the annual Anniversary Sale, which takes place in mid-July and features fall merchandise, hot off the press, at amazingly reduced prices. 520 N. Michigan Ave., inside Westfield North Bridge mall, 55 E. Grand Ave. (at Rush St.). ✆ **312/ 379-4300.** www.nordstrom.com. Subway/El: Red Line to Grand.

## FLEA MARKET

FREE **Maxwell Street**    Get an early start on Sunday mornings (7am–3pm) at one of the country's most famous flea markets. From cheap and tasty Mexican food (zucchini flower tacos and cactus and cheese tacos are not to be missed), consumer electronics (fell off the truck?), to inexpensive produce, household goods (cheap toilet paper, anyone?), knock-off designer sunglasses . . . the list goes on and on. The freshly made virgin piña coladas served in whole pineapples will lift your spirits. 548 W. Roosevelt Rd. (btw. Canal and Clinton sts.). ℭ **312/922-3100.** Subway/El: Red Line to Roosevelt, and walk 4 blocks west.

## FOOD

**Fox & Obel** The city's top gourmet market is a foodie paradise, from the wide selection of specialty cheeses to the mouth-watering display of desserts. If you have a few bucks to spare and are looking for a special treat, you won't be disappointed by taking home a wedge of cheese here. Brown Box Dinners here are actually not a bad deal at $7.99 (for a half-chicken, no less). Skip the overpriced cafe, and instead, pretend you're in a European grocery store while you browse the shelves, which is like taking a minitour through the best specialty foods from around the world (and I dare you to walk through the bakery section without buying a loaf of freshly baked bread). An easy walk to Navy Pier and the lakefront, it's a great place to pick up a picnic lunch or a bottle of wine and some pâté or chocolates to enjoy late-night. 401 E. Illinois St. (at McClurg Ct.). ℭ 312/410-7301. www.foxandobel.com. Subway/El: Red Line to Grand, and then 65 Grand bus.

**Goddess & Grocer** This upscale version of a neighborhood deli stocks everything you need for a mouthwatering lunch or dinner on the go—from specialty sandwiches to chicken and pasta dishes to freshly baked cookies and brownies. Expensive, but the cupcakes are super-yummy, as are the sandwiches. The prepared foods are a few notches above the standard takeout (wild Alaskan salmon, wild mushroom risotto), and the staff can put together meals for any occasion, from a catered business lunch to a romantic evening picnic at Millennium Park. There's also a good selection of wine and prepackaged snacks. The same owners run another, smaller, outpost in Bucktown, 1646 N. Damen Ave, at North Ave. (ℭ **773/342-3200**). 25 E. Delaware St. (at Rush St.). ℭ **312/896-2600.** www.goddessandgrocer. com. Subway/El: Red Line to Chicago.

## HOME DECOR & GIFTS

★ **Art Effect** Classifying this wonderfully eclectic Armitage Avenue shop is no easy task (the owners refer to it as a "modern-day general store"). It's got everything from aromatherapy oils and kitchen mixing bowls designed by cookbook author Nigella Lawson to handcrafted jewelry and gag gifts, not to mention a whole room devoted to hippie-chic women's clothing. The merchandise has a definite female slant, with a vibe that's young and irreverent rather than fussy, but the laid-back, friendly sales staff makes everyone feel welcome. The wide, unpredictable selection makes this one of my favorite browsing spots in town. 934 W. Armitage Ave. (at Bissell St.). © **773/929-3600.** www.arteffectchicago.com. Subway/El: Brown Line to Armitage.

**Orange Skin** It may look like an ultracool loft catering only to trend-ier-than-thou style experts, but don't be intimidated: Orange Skin is one of my favorite places to check out what's new in the world of modern interior design (and the staff is more welcoming than you might expect). From colored clear-plastic dining chairs to bowls made of welded steel wires, browsing here is a good way to gauge what's cool in the world of design. Visit the shop's lower level for smaller tabletop items that make good, one-of-a-kind gifts. 223 W. Erie St. (at Franklin St.). © **312/335-1033.** www.orangeskin.com. Subway/El: Brown Line to Chicago.

★ **P.O.S.H.** Love pieces with a past but can't afford fine antiques? This fun shop sells discontinued china patterns from a more elegant time gone by; recent selections included dishes used for first-class service on American Airlines and a tea service once used in an English country inn. If you're looking for a one-of-a-kind souvenir, they also produce a line of Chicago skyline dinnerware. 613 N. State St. (btw. Ontario and Ohio sts.). © **312/280-1602.** www.poshchicago. com. Subway/El: Red Line to Grand.

**Quake Collectibles** Off the beaten tourist path in the Lincoln Square neighborhood (northwest of downtown), this temple to all things kitschy includes an impressive vintage lunch-box collection and ample stacks of old fan magazines a la *Teen Beat,* with Shaun Cassidy tossing his feathered tresses. 4628 N. Lincoln Ave. (north of Wilson Ave.). © 773/878-4288. Subway/El: Brown Line to Western.

**Quimby's** The ultimate alternative newsstand, Quimby's stocks every kind of obscure periodical, from cutting-edge comics to 'zines "published" in some teenager's basement. Their book selection is also decadently different from that at your local Barnes & Noble; catego-ries include "Conspiracy," "Politics & Revolution," and "Lowbrow Art." 1854 W. North Ave. (just east of Damen Ave.). © **773/342-0910.** www.quimbys.com. Subway/El: Blue Line to Damen.

**Stitch** A favorite gift-shopping spot for savvy local fashion experts, Stitch stocks an almost unclassifiable mix of merchandise including candles, luggage, and bed linens. Unlike at the stereotypical, overly cutesy "gift shoppe," the selection here is fresh and contemporary; whatever you buy here is pretty much guaranteed to be cool. 1723 N. Damen Ave. (at Wabansia St.). ✆ 773/782-1570. www.stitchchicago. com. Subway/El: Blue Line to Damen.

★ **Uncle Fun** Cheap alert! Whenever I'm looking for a quirky Christmas stocking-stuffer or the perfect gag gift, I know Uncle Fun will come through for me (1950s-era toy robots for a sci-fi-geek friend? Check. And how about some 3-D Jesus postcards for a Catholic-school grad?) Bins and cubbyholes are stuffed full of the standard joke toys (rubber-chicken key chains and chattering wind-up teeth), but you'll also find every conceivable modern pop-culture artifact, from Jackson Five buttons to Speed Racer's Mach-Five model car. 1338 W. Belmont Ave. (1 block east of Southport Ave.). ✆ **773/477-8223.** www.unclefunchicago.com. Subway/El: Red or Brown line to Belmont.

## MAGIC SHOPS

**Ash's Magic Shop** Mr. Ash, a real-life magician with a love of his craft, stocks his shop with tricks, jokes, books, and videos that will make you believe in magic, too. 4955 N. Western Ave. (at W. Argyle). ✆ 773/271-4030. www.ashs-magic.com. Subway/El: Brown Line to Western.

## MUSIC

**Beat Parlor** If the idea of hanging out with local DJs appeals, then Beat Parlor is your place. In the city where house music was born, Howard Bailey's Bucktown shop sells lots of it, plus plenty of hip-hop and local DJs' mix tapes, on CD and vinyl. The store's two turntables are always in use by cutters checking out new merchandise. 1653 N. Damen Ave. (btw. North and Wabansia aves.). ✆ **773/395-CUTS** (2887). Subway/El: Blue Line to Damen.

**Dusty Groove America** In 1996, using a rickety old PC, Rick Wojcik and John Schauer founded an online record store at www.dusty groove.com. Since then, the operation has expanded in both cyberspace and the real world. Dusty Groove covers a lot of ground, selling soul, funk, jazz, Brazilian, lounge, Latin, and hip-hop music on new and used vinyl and CDs. For the most part, selections are either rare, imported, or both. 1120 N. Ashland Ave. (1 block south of Division St.). © **773/342-5800.** www.dustygroove.com. Subway/El: Blue Line to Division.

★ **Jazz Record Mart**    This is possibly the best jazz record store in the country. For novices, the "Killers Rack" displays albums that the store's owners consider essential to any jazz collection. Besides jazz, there are bins filled with blues, Latin, and "New Music." The albums are filed alphabetically and by category (vocals, big band, and so on), and there are a couple of turntables to help you spend wisely. Jazz Record Mart also features a stage and seating for 50, where local and national artists coming through town entertain with in-store performances. 27 E. Illinois St. (btw. Wabash Ave. and State St.). © **312/222-1467.** www.jazzrecordmart.com. Subway/El: Red Line to Grand.

**New Sound Gospel**    Chicago is the birthplace of gospel music, and now, thanks to artists such as Kirk Franklin, it's also become big business. All the major labels have gospel music divisions, and this store on the city's far South Side is the best place in town to browse the full range of what's available. Not sure where to start? Ask the store's expert staff for advice—here, you'll find everything from gospel's greatest to groups with names such as Gospel Gangstaz. 10723 S. Halsted St. (at 107th St.). © **773/785-8001.** Subway/El: Red Line to 95th/Dan Ryan, then 108 Halsted bus to 107th St.

**Reckless Records**    The best all-round local record store for music that the cool kids listen to, Reckless Records wins brownie points for its friendly and helpful staff. You'll find new and used CDs and albums in a variety of genres (psychedelic and progressive rock, punk, soul, and jazz) here, along with magazines and a small collection of DVDs. There are also locations in Wicker Park at 1532 N. Milwaukee Ave. (© **773/235-3727**), and the Loop, 26 E. Madison St. (© **312/795-0878**). 3157 N. Broadway (at Belmont Ave.). © **773/404-5080.** www.reckless.com. Subway/El: Red or Brown line to Belmont.

## PAPER & STATIONERY

**All She Wrote**    One of the many owner-operated specialty shops along Armitage Avenue, All She Wrote stocks a fun mix of cards and notepaper, all with a lighthearted, whimsical feel. 825 W. Armitage

Ave. (1 block west of Halsted St.). ℂ **773/529-0100.** www.allshe wrote.com. Subway/El: Red Line to North/Clybourn.

**Fly Paper**   Located on a busy stretch of Southport Street in the Wrigleyville neighborhood, Fly Paper has one of the most offbeat and artsy selections of greeting cards in the city, as well as other novelty and gift items. **Paper Boy,** a 10-minute walk away at 1351 W. Belmont Ave. (ℂ **773/388-8811**), is under the same ownership and features a similarly eclectic collection. 3402 N. Southport Ave. (btw. Belmont Ave. and Addison St.). ℂ **773/296-4359.** Subway/El: Brown Line to Southport.

★ **Paper Source**   The acknowledged leader of stationery stores in Chicago, Paper Source is now expanding throughout the country (with locations from Boston to Beverly Hills). The store's claim to fame is its collection of handmade paper in a variety of colors and textures. You'll also find one-of-a-kind greeting cards and a large collection of rubber stamps for personalizing your own paper at home. The River North shop is the store's headquarters, but there's also a location in the trendy Armitage shopping district at 919 W. Armitage Ave. (ℂ **773/525-7300**). 232 W. Chicago Ave. (at Franklin St.). ℂ **312/337-0798.** www.paper-source.com. Subway/El: Red or Brown line to Chicago.

**The Watermark**   Chicago socialites come here to order their engraved invitations, but this stationery store also carries a good selection of handmade greeting cards for all occasions. 109 E. Oak St. (1 block from Michigan Ave.). ℂ **312/337-5353.** Subway/El: Red Line to Clark/Division.

## SHOES, BAGS & ACCESSORIES

**Alternatives**   This locally owned shoe-store chain offers far more than Doc Marten wannabe designs; you'll find cutting-edge styles for men and women that are more affordable than those you'd find in designer boutiques. 942 Rush St. (at Delaware St.). ℂ **312/266-1545.** www.altshoes.com. Subway/El: Red Line to Chicago.

**1154 Lill Studio**   Purse-a-holics and wannabe designers will find fashion heaven at this custom-handbag shop. Pick a style (which includes everything from evening purses to diaper bags), and then browse the huge selection of fabrics to create your own custom interior and exterior. Your finished creation can be picked up in a few weeks or shipped to your home. Not feeling particularly creative? There's also a selection of premade bags. Personal handbag parties can be arranged for groups of five or more. 904 W. Armitage Ave. (at Fremont St.). © **773/477-LILL** (5455). www.1154lill.com. Subway/El: Brown Line to Armitage.

★ **Lori's Designer Shoes**    Lori's looks like a local version of Payless Shoes (shoeboxes stacked on the floor and women surrounded by piles of heels and boots), but the designer names on most of those shoes prove that this is a step above your typical discount store. A mecca for the shoe-obsessed, Lori's stocks all the latest styles, at prices that average 10% to 30% below department-store rates. 824 W. Armitage Ave. (btw. Sheffield Ave. and Halsted St.). © **773/281-5655.** www.lorisdesignershoes.com. Subway/El: Brown Line to Armitage.

## SPORTS STORES

**Niketown**    When Niketown opened almost 10 years ago, it was truly something new: a store that felt more like a funky sports museum than a place hawking running shoes. These days, however, Niketown is no longer unique to Chicago (it's sprung up in cities from Atlanta to Honolulu), and the store's celebration of athletes can't cover up the fact that the ultimate goal is to sell expensive shoes. But the crowds keep streaming in to snatch up products pitched by Niketown's patron saints Michael Jordan and Kobe Bryant. 669 N. Michigan Ave. (btw. Huron and Erie sts.). © **312/642-6363.** http://niketown.nike.com. Subway/El: Red Line to Grand.

**Sports Authority**    The largest sporting-goods store in the city, Sports Authority offers seven floors of merchandise, from running apparel to camping gear. Sports fans will be in heaven in the first- and fifth-floor team merchandise departments, where Cubs, Bulls, and Sox jerseys abound. Cement handprints of local sports celebs dot the outside of the building; you'll also find a golf practice cage inside if you want to practice your swing. 620 N. LaSalle St. (at Ontario St.). © **312/337-6151.** www.sportsauthority.com. Subway/El: Red Line to Grand.

## SOUVENIRS

★ **ArchiCenter Shop** Stop here for the coolest gifts in town. This bright, sleek shop is part of the Chicago Architecture Foundation, so everything in stock—including photography books, tour guides, stationery, artsy Christmas ornaments, puzzles, and kids' toys—has a definite sense of style. Many items bear the stamp of Frank Lloyd Wright. Go for one of the affordable black-and-white photos of the city skyline—this shop is well worth a visit. 224 S. Michigan Ave. (at Jackson St.). © **312/922-3432,** ext. 241. www.architecture.org. Subway/El: Red Line to Jackson.

**Chicago Tribune Store** Yes, you'll find plenty of newspaper-logo T-shirts and Cubs hats here, but this shop, located on the ground floor of the newspaper offices, also has a great collection of books. You can also order reproductions of past *Tribune* front pages or color prints of photos from the newspaper's archives. 435 N. Michigan Ave. (at Hubbard St.). © **312/222-3080.** Subway/El: Red Line to Grand.

**City of Chicago Store** Located in the Water Works Visitor Center right off Michigan Avenue, this is a convenient stop for Chicago-related souvenirs and gifts, including truly one-of-a-kind pieces of retired municipal equipment (although the parking meters we've seen for sale here might be a little hard to stuff in your suitcase). 163 E. Pearson St. (at Michigan Ave.). © **312/742-8811.** Subway/El: Red Line to Chicago.

## TOYS & CHILDREN'S CLOTHING

**Grow** For a look at the future of baby style, trek out to this trendy boutique in the up-and-coming West Division Street neighborhood. The bright, open space showcases streamlined, ultramodern kids' furniture (such as bubble-shaped high chairs that would look right at home on *The Jetsons*), as well as clothing made of organic fabrics. Sure, many of the environmentally friendly products on display are out of most parents' price range, but families that have had their fill of plastic kiddy gear will have fun browsing here. 1943 W. Division St. (at Damen Ave.). © **773/489-0009.** Subway/El: Blue Line to Division.

**Little Strummer** This compact store is located in the Old Town School of Folk Music, which offers music classes for children, and stocks every kind of mini-instrument imaginable, from accordions and guitars to wind chimes and music boxes. There's also a good selection of music-related games and kids' CDs. 909 W. Armitage Ave. (at Halsted St.). ✆ **773/751-3410.** Subway/El: Brown Line to Armitage.

**Psycho Baby** The opening of this everything-for-baby shop was the definitive sign that Bucktown had gentrified. The prices may sometimes cause a double take ($60 for shoes that your kid will outgrow in 3 months), but the creative selection and happy vibe make it fun for browsing. 1630 N. Damen Ave. (1 block north of North Ave.). ✆ **773/772-2815.** www.psychobabyonline.com. Subway/El: Blue Line to Damen.

## VINTAGE STORES

**Beatnix** This solid vintage store, good for day-to-day and dress-up items, also carries a huge selection of old tuxes. Both men's and women's apparel are available. 3400 N. Halsted St. (at Roscoe St.). ✆ **773/281-6933.** Subway/El: Red Line to Addison.

**Buffalo Exchange** This large store is crammed with racks of antique and new fashions from the 1960s, 1970s, and 1980s. It stocks everything from suits and dresses to neckties, hats, handbags, and jewelry. Buffalo Exchange anticipates some of the hottest new street fashions. Choose from two locations in Chicago: 2875 N. Broadway (btw. Clark and Diversey). ✆ **773/549-1999.** www.buffaloexchange.com. El: Red Line to Belmont or Brown Line to Diversey. 1478 N. Milwaukee Ave. (btw. Evergreen and Honore). ✆ **773/227-9558.** El: Blue Line to Damen.

**The Daisy Shop** A significant step up from your standard vintage store, The Daisy Shop specializes in couture fashions. These designer duds come from the closets of the city's most stylish socialites and carry appropriately hefty price tags. Even so, paying hundreds of dollars for a pristine Chanel suit or Louis Vuitton bag can still be considered a bargain, and well-dressed women from around the world stop by here in search of the perfect one-of-a-kind item. 67 E. Oak St. (btw. Michigan Ave. and Rush St.). ✆ **312/943-8880.** Subway/El: Brown Line to Sedgwick.

## WINE & LIQUOR

★ **Binny's Beverage Depot**   Believe it or not, this football field–size warehouse store evolved from a modest packaged-goods store. Today, the family-owned operation is the largest wine and spirits merchant in the city and offers pleasant, friendly service. You can also find frequent sales of up to 70% off, as well as weekly specials on their website. It also features a superb cheese selection in the on-site Epicurean shop. 1720 N. Marcey St. (near Sheffield and Clybourn aves.). ℂ **800/777-9137** or 312/664-4394. www.binnys.com. Subway/El: Red Line to North/Clybourn; also 213 W. Grand Ave. (at Wells St.). ℂ **312/332-0012.** www.binnys.com. Subway/El: Red Line to Grand.

*Visitors to the Magnificent Mile must remember to look up—way up—for one of its most famous attractions, the Tribune Tower (see p. 124).*

# ITINERARIES FOR THE INDIGENT (OR THRIFTY)

ndigent or not, there's no better way to get to know a city than by checking out the neighborhoods on foot. (And, if indigent is a reasonable assessment of your status, there's no cheaper way to get around than with your own two feet.) Chicago is a fine walking city, with plenty of charming neighborhoods filled with interesting architecture, boutiques, and local eateries. Spend some time strolling and you'll experience Chicago the way the natives do. Every block brings interesting window-shopping and people-watching, two activities guaranteed to keep you entertained at no cost.

The orderly configuration of Chicago's streets and the excellent public transportation system make walking a breeze. When you get tired, you can hop on a bus or the El without having to veer too far off course. In this chapter, you'll get some suggestions for walks that will give you the flavor of Chicago's most frequented neighborhoods. It's hard to get lost in Chicago, but if you are ever directionally challenged, here's one key orientation tip: Lake Michigan is always to the east. And if you look up, that soaring black behemoth now known as the Willis Tower (formerly the Sears Tower) will be to the south for the purposes of these tours.

Listed below are four of my favorite neighborhoods for touring in bipedal fashion, plus a bonus day trip to a really unique destination in the great outdoors. Right, then: Let's get started.

## 1 Getting to Know the Loop

### Itinerary 1: Millennium Park & the Michigan Avenue "Cliff"

| | |
|---|---|
| Start | The Michigan Avenue Bridge, Michigan Avenue at the Chicago River. |
| Finish | Intersection of Wabash Avenue and Congress Parkway. |
| Time | Four hours, including a stop for lunch. |
| Best Times | Weekdays between 9am and 5pm. |
| Worst Times | Weekends, when Michigan Avenue Cliff buildings are closed. |
| Tips | If you add in a walking tour of Millennium Park, you'll be covering a lot of ground here, so wear serious walking footwear. Also bear in mind that in good weather, it's really, really fun to wade in the water at Crown Fountain in Millennium Park, so wear appropriate clothing. |

Here's a walk that focuses on Chicago's famous architecture. South Michigan Avenue is less congested than its northerly branch, the Magnificent Mile. Down here you can amble along and take in a couple of Chicago's famous museums and parks, including Millennium Park, which was completed in 2004 and has become Chicago's second-largest tourist draw after Navy Pier. South Michigan Avenue can be strolled in an hour or two, but if you stop to check out building lobbies and have lunch, it can be a half-day event.

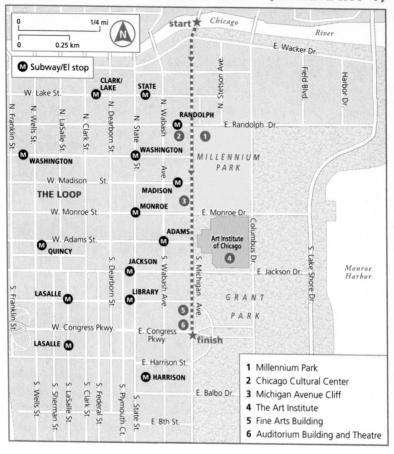

| | |
|---|---|
| 1 | Millennium Park |
| 2 | Chicago Cultural Center |
| 3 | Michigan Avenue Cliff |
| 4 | The Art Institute |
| 5 | Fine Arts Building |
| 6 | Auditorium Building and Theatre |

### 1 Millennium Park

Start on the Michigan Avenue Bridge. Gaze west down the river at the Wrigley Building, Trump International Plaza and Hotel, and the Merchandise Mart. Gaze east down the river to the lake (at the point where river meets lake, you will see the Chicago River locks). Take some amazing photos featuring fabulous you on the bridge with a gorgeous architectural backdrop before your day of touring the Loop. Okay, now we can proceed.

Cross the Chicago River on the Michigan Avenue Bridge and walk south, into the Loop business district. On this easterly fringe of the Loop lie some of Chicago's top cultural institutions and parks. Continue south, past

## Pit Stop

**The Gage** (24 S. Michigan Ave.; ✆ **312/372-4243**) is one good-looking Irish pub—the kind of Irish pub where the chef actually attended culinary school. If you are up for a splurge, ask for a booth in the back, but be aware that entrees can easily set you back $20. Otherwise, grab a seat at the bar and enjoy a libation and a side of frites (energy for the walk ahead).

Lake and Randolph streets. On your left, you will see a clearing: This is **Millennium Park,** on the north end of Grant Park along Michigan Avenue. Admire the dramatic music pavilion designed by Frank Gehry, and check out the large public art displays. Explore Millennium Park at your leisure, and don't miss another photo op at The Bean sculpture (properly known as Cloud Gate). Protocol demands that you lie on the ground under The Bean and have someone take a photo of you reflected up into the sculpture. If this description makes no sense, just wait until you see everyone else doing the exact same thing.

### ② Chicago Cultural Center

At the corner of Michigan and Randolph, directly across Michigan Avenue from Millennium Park, is a huge Beaux Arts–style building, called the **Chicago Cultural Center.** Built in 1897 as the city's public library, the Cultural Center is now your home base for tourist information. Proceed to home base. Go in, pick up all the information you need, and while you're at it, check out the building's stunning interior.

Free tours guide visitors up a sweeping staircase of white Italian marble to admire what is, for my money, the most stunning interior in Chicago. At the top of the staircase is a majestic Tiffany dome, believed to be the world's largest. Even without the free tour, take yourself there. Don't miss it! You'll also discover mosaics of Favrile glass, colored stone, and mother-of-pearl inlaid in white marble.

### ③ Michigan Avenue Cliff

As you stroll south from the Cultural Center, you're seeing the Michigan Avenue Cliff, a particularly impressive great wall of buildings that stretches south to Congress Parkway (location of the Auditorium Building). It's a visual treat for architecture lovers and novices alike.

### ④ The Art Institute

Abutting Millennium Park on the south, facing Adams Avenue, is the **Art Institute.** You can come back here when our tour is done. For now, climb the front steps of the museum and visit the stone lions. At the holidays, the lions sport evergreen wreaths around their necks. This is another don't-miss photo op, so don't miss it. Watch the other people who are sitting on the steps people-watching.

### ⑤ Fine Arts Building

Farther south on the avenue is the **Fine Arts Building,** constructed in 1885 as a showroom for Studebaker carriages, and converted into an arts center in 1917. The building houses two theaters, offices, shops, and studios for musicians, artists, and writers. Frank Lloyd Wright, sculptor Lorado Taft, and L. Frank Baum, author of *The Wonderful Wizard of Oz,* had offices here. Located throughout the building are a number of interesting studios and musical-instrument shops. Take a quick walk through the marble-and-wood lobby, which feels monastic and cloisterlike, or visit the top floor to see the spectacular murals (and to get there, you'll get to ride in an old-fashioned elevator manned by a real, live operator!).

### ⑥ Auditorium Building & Theatre

The last stop on our south Michigan Avenue tour is the **Auditorium Building.** This wonder of architecture was designed and built in 1889 by Louis Sullivan and Dankmar Adler. At the time, it was the heaviest (110,000 tons) modern building on earth, the most fireproof building ever constructed, and the tallest building in Chicago. It was also the first large-scale building to be electrically lighted, and its theater was the first in the country to install air-conditioning. The lobby fronting Michigan Avenue has faux ornamental marble columns, molded ceilings, mosaic floors, and Mexican onyx walls.

If this inspires you, take the elevator to the 10th-floor library reading room and have a look at what was once the city's first top-floor dining room. Soak in the decorative details: They literally don't make them like this anymore—the barrel-vaulted, muraled ceiling and marvelous views of Grand Park and the lake will make architecture fans out of novices.

## Itinerary Index

**Millennium Park**   201 E. Randolph St. (at Michigan Ave.). ✆ 312/742-1168. www.millenniumpark.org. Daily 6am–11pm.

**Chicago Cultural Center**   77 E. Randolph St. (at Michigan Ave.). ✆ 312/744-6630. Mon–Thurs 8am–7pm, Fri 8am–6pm, Sat 9am–6pm, Sun 10am–6pm.

**Art Institute of Chicago**   111 S. Michigan Ave. ✆ 312/443-3600. www.artic.edu. Mon–Wed 10:30am–5pm, Thurs 10:30am–8pm, Sat–Sun 10am–5pm. Summer hours (Memorial Day through Labor Day) Mon–Wed 10:30am–5pm, Thurs–Fri 10:30am–9pm, Sat–Sun 10am–5pm.

**Fine Arts Building**   410 S. Michigan Ave. ✆ 312/913-0537. Mon–Fri 9am–5pm.

**Auditorium Building & Theatre**   50 E. Congress Pkwy. ✆ 800/982-2787. www.auditoriumtheatre.org. Mon–Fri 9am–5pm, open later for performances.

# 2  A Stroll Along the Magnificent Mile

## Itinerary 2: Magnificent Mile

| | |
|---|---|
| **Start** | Michigan Avenue Bridge, Michigan Avenue at the Chicago River. |
| **Finish** | Michigan Avenue and Delaware Street. |
| **Time** | Half a day. |
| **Best Time** | Any day. |
| **Worst Time** | Any summer Saturday when Michigan Avenue is packed with tourists. |
| **Tips** | Load up on cheap bottles of water and snacks, which can save a lot of money during your tours of the city, at the Walgreen's located at the intersection of Michigan and Chicago avenues. |

North Michigan Avenue is known as the Magnificent Mile, from the bridge spanning the Chicago River on the south end to Oak Street on the northern tip. Many of the city's best hotels, shops, and restaurants are to be found on and around elegant Michigan Avenue. But never fear: You won't be dropping any cash here, just taking in the sights as you make your way up this storied avenue. Strolling the entire mile will take you half a day, since you'll want to stop frequently. Of course, if you're determined to avoid the shops, you can do it in less than an hour—but why rush? Linger on the Riverwalk a bit longer.

# MAGNIFICENT MILE (ITINERARY 2)

E. Oak St.
E. Walton Pl.
900 North Michigan Shops
**finish**
E. Delaware Pl.
John Hancock Center
Water Tower Place
Museum of Contemporary Art
E. Chestnut St.
E. Pearson St.
E. Chicago Ave.
**CHICAGO** Ⓜ
E. Superior St.
**RIVER NORTH**
Chicago Place
E. Huron St.
E. Erie St.
E. Ontario St.
**STREETER-VILLE**
E. Ohio St.
**GRAND** Ⓜ
Westfield North Bridge
E. Grand Ave.
E. Illinois St.
Wrigley Building
E. North Water St.
**start** ★
Chicago
Ⓜ Subway/El stop
E. Wacker Dr.

0                    1/4 mi
0          0.25 km

N. Dearborn St.
N. State St.
N. Rush St.
N. DeWitt Pl.
**MAGNIFICENT MILE** N. Michigan Ave.
N. Fairbanks Ct.
N. Wabash Ave.
N. Rush St.
N. St. Clair St.
McClurg Ct.
Columbus Dr.
N. Lake Shore Dr.

94  41
0        3 mi
0        3 km
41
Wrigley Field ■
**C H I C A G O**
Map area
290
THE LOOP
U.S. Cellular Field ■
55
90  41
✈ Midway
94
_Lake Michigan_

1 Chicago Riverwalk
2 Chicago Tribune Tower
3 Chicago Water Tower
4 Fourth Presbyterian Church

## ① Chicago Riverwalk

Start at the **Riverwalk** that goes along the north side of the Chicago River. Walk down the steps on the east side of Michigan Avenue that lead off the Michigan Avenue Bridge. You can walk east for a short distance and see the plaza of the NBC Tower, as well as some of the newest condominium and town-house developments along the river. If you're so inclined,

make a stop at one of the riverfront restaurants. A good choice is Cyrano's Bistrot (p. 66). Get L'Assiette of Four Cheeses for $9.95 and the Pates, Mousses and Rillettes served with grilled country bread and cornichons for $8.95 and share. So French! When you're done strolling the riverwalk, return to the northeast corner of the Michigan Avenue Bridge.

## ② Tribune Tower

Back at the avenue, you can't miss the **Chicago Tribune Tower,** where the venerable newspaper is still put together. The tower is notable for its signature array of stones jutting out from the exterior. The collection was started shortly after the building's completion in 1925 by the newspaper's notoriously despotic publisher, Robert R. McCormick, who gathered them during his world travels. *Tribune* correspondents then began supplying stone souvenirs encountered on assignment. Each one now bears the name of the structure and country whence it came. There are 138 stones in all, including chunks and shards from the Great Wall of China, the Taj Mahal, the White House, the Arc de Triomphe, the Berlin Wall, the Roman Colosseum, London's Houses of Parliament, the Great Pyramid of Cheops in Giza, Egypt, and the original tomb of Abraham Lincoln in Springfield. Inside the *Tribune*'s lobby, there's a brochure telling you where each stone is located. Hey, you just scored a free tour of some of the world's most famous sites. Pat yourself on the back.

## ③ Chicago Water Tower

Continue north along Michigan Avenue. When you reach Chicago Avenue, just ahead of you on the west side of the street is the **Chicago Water Tower** (not to be confused with a mall of the same name, located diagonally across the intersection from the real tower). Michigan Avenue's best-known landmark is dwarfed by high-rises today but still gleams like a fairy-tale castle. Surrounded by lawns and park benches, the tower is illuminated at night, and street musicians often play here (free entertainment; check it out).

Chicagoans are proud of their talisman, one of the few buildings to survive the Great Fire of 1871. (And it serves a real purpose by covering an ugly, 138-ft.-high standpipe used in connection with pumping water from Lake Michigan.) The Gothic-style limestone building now houses an art gallery

## Pit Stop

Step across the street to **Ghirardelli's** (830 N. Michigan Ave., entrance located on DeWitt, just west of Michigan Ave.; ✆ **312/337-9330**) and grab an ice-cream cone ($4.40), or, in chilly weather, a foamy mug of hot chocolate ($3.65). Soak in the old-fashioned ice cream parlor ambiance.

and is a refreshing cultural pit stop. Across the street the pumping station has been transformed into a tourist information center.

④ Fourth Presbyterian Church

On a pleasant weather day, you can take your ice cream cone and walk 1 block north, to the shaded, ivy-covered courtyard of **Fourth Presbyterian Church,** located 1 block north, on the west side of Michigan Avenue at Chestnut Street—a tranquil spot just steps from the hustle and bustle. Eat ice cream, watch the parade of people down Michigan Avenue, and enjoy.

---

### Itinerary Index

**Chicago Riverwalk**   Located at the Michigan Ave. Bridge over the Chicago River, running along the river from the lake, going west.

**Tribune Tower**   445 N. Michigan Ave. ✆ 312/222-4444. Mon-Fri 8am-6pm, Sat-Sun 10am-6pm.

**Chicago Water Tower**   806 N. Michigan Ave. ✆ 312/742-0808. www.ci.chi.il.us/tourism. Daily 10am-6:30pm.

**Fourth Presbyterian Church**   126 E. Chestnut St. ✆ 312/787-4570. Mon-Fri 9am-5pm.

---

## 3 A Walk on the Gold Coast & Old Town

### Itinerary 3: The Gold Coast Mansion Tour

| | |
|---|---|
| **Start** | Michigan Avenue at Oak Street. |
| **Finish** | Wells Street and North Avenue. |
| **Time** | Three hours. |
| **Best Time** | Any day. |
| **Worst Time** | There really isn't one. |
| **Tip** | Make sure you are ready to hoof it in good walking shoes, because we're going to cover some distance. |

Walking north on **Lake Shore Drive** from the intersection of North Michigan Avenue and Oak Street (mecca for ultra-pricey designer fashion in Chicago—take a moment to chuckle to yourself as you remember scoring some major deals thanks to the savvy shopping tips in chapter 7), you will enter a neighborhood known as the Gold Coast. The neighborhood runs along Lake Shore from about Oak Street on the south to North Avenue on the north and includes some of Chicago's most desirable real estate and historic architecture. This is the classic old money neighborhood of Chicago, where many of the city's wealthiest citizens built homes after the 1871 fire. Sadly, starting in the late 1950s, most of the mansions that once lined Lake Shore Drive were slowly torn down and highrises built in their stead, but you can see the remnants of Chicago's storied past in the three mansions still standing near Lake Shore Drive's intersection with Goethe Street. Just strolling the Gold Coast will take you at least an hour and a half, and then I'm going to send you due west along North Avenue into Old Town, so be prepared for quite a hike. You can also combine this walk with a foray into Lincoln Park to make a day's worth of activities. Your choice!

**1** Schiller & Astor Street Mansions

To get a feel for the neighborhood, walk up Lake Shore Drive to **Schiller Street.** Turn left and walk 1 block to **Astor Place.** Turn right onto Astor and enjoy the amble past stately mansions and beautiful brownstones. (Just a block or two farther west, State Pkwy. and Dearborn St. also feature homes fit for magazine covers. Amble to your heart's desire.)

**2** Residence of the Chicago Archbishop

Walking north on either Astor Place or State Parkway, you'll reach the end of the road. This is **North Avenue.** Here, you'll see a redbrick mansion on a large lot. This is the home of Cardinal Francis George, Catholic archbishop of Chicago, and is owned by the Catholic archdiocese of Chicago. Attempt to count the chimneys for yourself (answer: there are 17).

**3** Lincoln Park

You can continue on into **Lincoln Park** (directly across the street to the north of the Archbishop's residence), or head west into Old Town. Alternatively, if you are satiated with this short tour and

## Pit Stop

Don't miss stopping at **Twisted Sister Bakery,** 1543 N. Wells St., where you'll find a homey atmosphere to sit and rest your weary feet, plus surprisingly sophisticated takes on the usual cakes, cookies, eclairs, and cupcakes (about $3 each, $1.75 for Intelligentsia coffee).

# A WALK ON THE GOLD COAST & OLD TOWN (ITINERARY 3)

1 Schiller and Astor Street Mansions
2 Residence of the Catholic Archbishop
3 Lincoln Park
4 Pipers Alley
5 Wells Street Shops

want to hang out and grab a drink, turn back south. Walk south on State Parkway to Division Street. From there going south, you will find a thriving zone of restaurants, bars, and nightclubs, many featuring sidewalk seating—all the better to view the beautiful people that frequent the area.

For those of you continuing on west with our tour, adjacent Old Town is a residential neighborhood best known as the home of the Second City comedy troupe for the past 30-plus years, now found at 1616 N. Wells St. A hippie haven of the 1960s and 1970s, Old Town now includes the newly gentrified Cabrini Green (located on the far southern border of Old Town), America's most notorious housing project, which began falling to the wrecking ball in the late 1990s. Today it's home to retail developments and low-rise mixed-income housing, not something that's particularly worth going out of your way to visit.

The northern part of Old Town, particularly the area north of North Avenue and west of Wells Street, has a lovely residential neighborhood, and on any given day, you will see plenty of strollers and parents with kids in tow. The best street to traverse is Wells Street, which is filled with boutiques and local restaurants. (See below on specific stops.)

④ Pipers Alley

The central intersection of Old Town is the intersection of Wells Street and North Avenue. On the northwest corner is **Pipers Alley,** a shopping complex that is most notable for its large cinema, Starbucks, restaurants, and shops. Directly to the north of Pipers Alley is **Second City.** Stop to walk into Second City's lobby and see the autographed photos of the stars who cut their comedic teeth here.

⑤ Wells Street Shops

Here's where you do some serious window shopping. Walk north up Wells Street. Small retail shops, florists, cafes, bread stores, and more line the street. You can't help but be charmed! When you reach the intersection with Lincoln Avenue, turn back and head south down the opposite side of the street. Cross North Avenue going south. Kids will be magnetically attracted to the colorful fish swimming around the front windows of **Old Town Aquarium,** a shop located on the west side of the street at 1538 N. Wells St. **The Spice House,** 1512 N. Wells St., is famous for its staggering array of (what else?) whole and ground spices. Now, here's a place where you can buy a well-priced souvenir at about $6 a bottle (Indian tellicherry peppercorns, Mexican vanilla extract, freshly ground cinnamon: The list goes on and on).

---

**Itinerary Index**

**Schiller & Astor Street Mansions** Intersection of Schiller and Astor streets. Exterior views only.

**Residence of the Catholic Archbishop** Intersection of North Ave. and State Pkwy. Exterior views only.

**Lincoln Park**    1600 N. Stockton Dr. © 312/742-7726. www.chicagopark
district.com. Daily 6am-10pm.

**Pipers Alley**    1608 N. Wells St. Mon-Fri 9am-5pm, later for theater.

**Wells Street Shops**    Located along Wells St. running north and south
from Eugenie St. south to Schiller St.

# 4  Culture & Style in Andersonville

## Itinerary 4: Andersonville

| | |
|---|---|
| **Start** | North Clark Street and Foster Avenue. |
| **Finish** | North Clark Street and Balmoral Avenue. |
| **Time** | All day. |
| **Best Time** | Start at around 10am, tour a bit, eat lunch, and pick up cookies at the Swedish Bakery. |
| **Worst Time** | After 5pm. The rush hour gets pretty busy around here. |
| **Tips** | Traffic can be pretty heavy along Clark Street at rush hour, and many of the intersections don't have stop lights, just stop signs, so be aware when crossing the street. |

This formerly Scandinavian neighborhood stretches several blocks along North
Clark Street immediately north of Foster Avenue. Since the wave of Scandinavian immigrants ended over 100 years ago, new immigrant groups have moved
in. Today, a burgeoning community of gays and lesbians makes Andersonville
their home. Clark Street going north from Foster is a very walkable small stretch
that includes the **Swedish-American Museum Center** (p. 131), a Scandinavian
deli, a Swedish bakery, and two good Swedish restaurants.

## Pit Stop

Do as the locals do and head to breakfast at **Ann Sather** at 5207 N.
Clark St. (p. 78), where you can order a full breakfast with two sides
($9.95)—and unless you are intent on staying with a diet, you must
choose the gooey fresh-baked cinnamon rolls as one of your sides—
and be ready to share, since they give you two.

## Pit Stop

Stop at **Kopi—A Traveler's Café,** where you can get a mean mango smoothie ($3.75). Pillows and floor-level tables invite lounging, and the global boutique and wall clocks that keep time for countries around the world will have you feeling like the world traveler that you are.

**1** Swedish-American Museum

Even if you're not Swedish, you'll get a kick out of checking out the relics from immigrants who came here from Sweden in the late 1800s. It's touching in fact to see what they brought from home to their new country—worn shoes, intricately painted wooden chests, carefully tatted lace. An art gallery and gift shop occupy the first floor of this charming museum, and exhibits dedicated to the Swedish immigrant experience and a children's immigration museum (complete with a Swedish farm, a ship, and a new farm in America) take up the remaining floors. See p. 131.

**2** Middle Eastern Bakery and Pastry

This grocery, where most products are sold from barrels in bulk, located at 1512 W. Foster Ave., is also known for its deli counter, which features spinach pies, fresh falafel, trays of baklava, pickled vegetables, olives, and soup. If you're looking to stock up on snacks to carry on your travels or something to munch on as you stroll the neighborhood, you'll find plenty of bargains among the bulk goods: dried fruit, nuts, and candies.

**3** Women & Children First Bookstore

Make sure to stop at **Women & Children First** (p. 245), a funky, urban, independent bookstore that is especially noted for its reading series called Women's Voices that features the best female writers today. If you're lucky, you might be able to come back one night during your stay and hear a reading (they are one of the few bookstores that still serve free wine at readings!). More than 30,000 titles pack the shelves here.

**4** The Swedish Bakery

Many locals consider this 80-year-old bakery at 5348 N. Clark St. the best in Chicago. (I know I do.) Handmade Swedish butter cookies are available year-round,

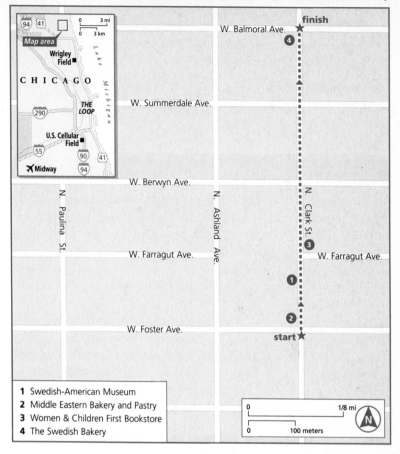

Map labels: finish, W. Balmoral Ave., 4, W. Summerdale Ave., W. Berwyn Ave., N. Paulina St., N. Ashland Ave., N. Clark St., W. Farragut Ave., 3, W. Farragut Ave., 1, 2, W. Foster Ave., start

Inset map: 94, 41, Map area, Wrigley Field, CHICAGO, THE LOOP, 290, Lake Michigan, U.S. Cellular Field, 55, 90, 41, Midway, 94, 0 3 mi, 0 3 km

1 Swedish-American Museum
2 Middle Eastern Bakery and Pastry
3 Women & Children First Bookstore
4 The Swedish Bakery

Scale: 0 — 1/8 mi, 0 — 100 meters, N

and during the holidays you'll find festive heart-shaped spicy ginger cookies (pepparkakor), spice cookies (pfeffernuesse), and marzariner almond tarts. Don't let the crowd of loyal customers dissuade you—take a number, the line moves quickly.

## Itinerary Index

**Swedish American Museum** 5211 N. Clark St. ☎ 773/728-8111. www. samac.org. Tues-Fri 10am-4pm, Sat-Sun 11am-4pm, closed Sun.

**Middle Eastern Bakery and Pastry** 1512 W. Foster Ave. ☎ 773/561-2224. Mon-Sat 9am-8pm, Sun 11am-5pm.

**Women & Children First Bookstore** 5233 N. Clark St. ℭ 773/769-9299. www.womenandchildrenfirst.com. Mon-Tues 11am-7pm, Wed-Fri 11am-9pm, Sat 10am-7pm, Sun 11am-6pm.

**The Swedish Bakery** 5348 N. Clark St. ℭ 773/561-8919. www.swedish bakery.com. Mon-Fri 6:30am-6:30pm, Sat 6:30am-5pm, closed Sun.

# 5 Hiking the Indiana Dunes

My favorite outdoor escape is Indiana Dunes National Lakeshore, 53 miles southeast of Chicago. Taking this trip involves a mandatory car rental (or borrowing a car from a friend, if you're really lucky). Still, given that the fee to enter the Dunes is only $8 per car, this trip is dirt cheap once you get here (bring a cooler with food and you're set). Renting a car for a day is a small price to pay for the kind of experience you're getting.

You may not associate the Midwest with sand dunes, but a trip here will have you rethinking that. The landscape includes 15 miles of dunes and grasses fronting Lake Michigan, reminiscent of Cape Cod, as well as maple and oak forests, marshes, and bogs. To get here, take I-94 E. to Ind. 49 N. (east of Porter). Follow Ind. 49 N. to Route 12. Travel east on Route 12 for 3 miles to the Dorothy Buell Visitor Center.

## Itinerary 5: Hiking the Indiana Dunes

| | |
|---|---|
| **Start** | Wherever you're staying. |
| **Finish** | Indiana Dunes National Lakeshore. |
| **Time** | A full day. |
| **Best Time** | Start out early (by 9am). |
| **Worst Time** | After noon. Traffic getting out of the city can get hairy later in the day. |
| **Tips** | Hit the road early on a weekend day and you'll fly out of the city; start out too late in the day and you'll spend lots of quality time sitting in traffic. Also be aware that you'll need $3 to cross the Illinois Skyway into Indiana. |

### 1 Dorothy Buell Memorial Visitor Center

Stop by the information desk for a free map covering the National Lakeshore. Check out the free 10-minute orientation slide show; there are also interactive video terminals. You'll also find restrooms and a gift shop.

### 2 Calumet Dune Trail

Perfect for novices, this .8-mile paved trail starts behind the Dorothy Buell Memorial Visitor Center and winds through a forest of yellow sassafras and oaks. Signs describe the flora and fauna along the way. If you only have time for one short hike, this is the trail to walk to get a good, representative sample of the natural wonders of the lakeshore, from the gently rolling dunes to a swamp, and finally, the majestic red and white oak trees that create a dense canopy in summer months.

### 3 Chellberg Farm

Those with a historical bent will enjoy touring this restored 1885 brick farmhouse, which belonged to a Swedish immigrant family that lived and worked on this farm for three generations. The Chellberg family sold their farm to the National Park Service in 1927 and their home has been restored to its original late-19th-century appearance (forget electricity and indoor plumbing). There's also a barn filled with farm animals; you can help farmers feed them on Saturdays and Sundays.

### 4 Bailly Homestead

This National Historic Landmark, the former residence of a French Canadian fur trader, dates back to 1822, when it served as a meeting and trading center for Native Americans and Euro-Americans. On Sundays from 1 to 4pm, volunteers dress in period clothing and offer up historical tidbits and insights into

## Pit Stop

It's nothing fancy, but there is a **concession and campground grocery** that's open during the summer months (you can buy wood, ice, groceries, and picnic supplies) and a small fast-food outlet. The crowd tends to include a nice mix of older people, singles, teenagers, and families. 1600 N. Hwy. 25 E., Chesterton, IN. © **219/926-1952.**

life on the homestead (the Homestead is open daily from 11am to 4:30pm during the summer, but weekends only the rest of the year). This is a rare opportunity to catch a glimpse into the lives of early settlers. While you're here, don't miss the unusual family cemetery.

### 5 Mount Baldy

At 125 feet, this is the largest "living" sand dune in the park, meaning that the dune is kept in constant motion by wind and water. Mt. Baldy actually creeps several inches farther from Lake Michigan each year. It got its name thanks to its lack of vegetation, which is the reason why it's mobile—there are no plants anchoring it. The dune is one of the best attractions in the park, popular with everyone from kids to experienced hikers. Climb to the top for a real aerobic workout; you'll be rewarded with a sweeping view of the lake, and on a clear day, you can see all the way to Chicago. On the southern slope, you'll see half-buried trees (as they move, the dunes bury forests, and erosion exposes them again). Once you climb down the "mountain," head for the lake; if it's July or August, the water will be warm enough for a refreshing dip.

### 6 West Beach

Swimming is allowed here from late May to early September, and this top attraction is not only one of the lakeshore's most popular beaches, but also the starting point for a scenic 3-mile boardwalk trail that leads you through dunes, an oak savanna, and jack pine forests on your way to Lake Michigan. It's the perfect trail for sampling the many landscapes found in the National Lakeshore. The beach is my favorite at the lakeshore; it's very popular with swimmers, though you should use caution, as the lake bottom can be uneven and there can be dangerous rip currents (a concern at all of the lakeshore's beaches). This is the only beach where lifeguards are on duty (summer months only) and there's a bathhouse, picnic facilities, vending machines, restrooms, and a $6 parking fee in addition to your $8 admission fee from May to September.

### 7 Kemil Beach

If it's beach-going that you're focused on, check out Kemil Beach, a long stretch of beautiful white sand. While West Beach is my favorite for swimming and sunbathing, this is the best spot on the national lakeshore to watch the sunset. If you get here early enough for one last hike before the sun goes down, don't miss the Dune Ridge Trail, which starts right off the parking lot. This moderate, 1-mile loop requires some climbing, but is

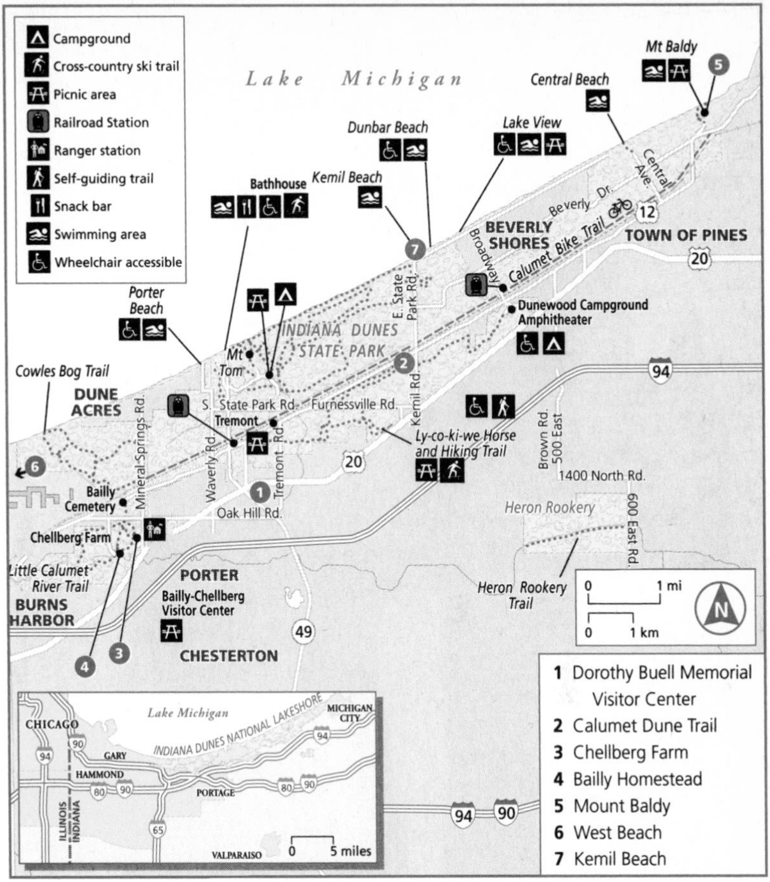

Campground
Cross-country ski trail
Picnic area
Railroad Station
Ranger station
Self-guiding trail
Snack bar
Swimming area
Wheelchair accessible
Lake Michigan
Mt Baldy
Central Beach
Lake View
Dunbar Beach
Kemil Beach
Bathhouse
Porter Beach
Cowles Bog Trail
DUNE ACRES
Mt Tom
INDIANA DUNES STATE PARK
BEVERLY SHORES
TOWN OF PINES
Beverly Dr.
Central Ave.
Broadway
Calumet Bike Trail
Dunewood Campground Amphitheater
E. State Park Rd.
Kemil Rd.
S. State Park Rd.
Furnessville Rd.
Tremont
Tremont Rd.
Mineral Springs Rd.
Waverly Rd.
Oak Hill Rd.
Ly-co-ki-we Horse and Hiking Trail
Brown Rd. 500 East
1400 North Rd.
600 East Rd.
Heron Rookery
Heron Rookery Trail
Bailly Cemetery
Chellberg Farm
Little Calumet River Trail
BURNS HARBOR
PORTER
Bailly-Chellberg Visitor Center
CHESTERTON
0 1 mi
0 1 km
N
CHICAGO
GARY
HAMMOND
PORTAGE
VALPARAISO
MICHIGAN CITY
INDIANA DUNES NATIONAL LAKESHORE
ILLINOIS
INDIANA
0 5 miles
1 Dorothy Buell Memorial Visitor Center
2 Calumet Dune Trail
3 Chellberg Farm
4 Bailly Homestead
5 Mount Baldy
6 West Beach
7 Kemil Beach


nothing a reasonably fit person can't handle, and it will take you through a lovely forested area. Restrooms are available.

## Itinerary Index

**Indiana Dunes National Lakeshore** Porter, IN ✆ 219/395-8914. www.nps.gov. Visitor Center located near the southeast corner of U.S. Highways 49 and 20. Visitor Center hours for summer daily 8:30am-6pm, winter hours 8:30am-4:30pm.

*Here are the fast facts about getting into town, getting around town, and resources for planning your time while you're here.*

# CHICAGO BASICS FROM A TO Z

## 1 Getting into Chicago & Around Town

**Chicago's O'Hare International Airport** (ORD; ✆ 773/686-2200; www.flychicago.com) has long battled Atlanta's Hartsfield for the title of the world's busiest airport. O'Hare is about 20 miles northwest of the Loop. Depending on traffic, the drive to or from downtown can take anywhere from 30 minutes to more than an hour.

O'Hare has information booths in all five terminals; most are on the baggage level. The multilingual employees, who wear red jackets, can assist travelers with everything from arranging ground transportation to getting information about local hotels. The booths, labeled "Airport Information," are open daily from 9am to 8pm.

Most major U.S. and international airlines fly into O'Hare. You'll find the widest range of choices on United Airlines (which is headquartered in Chicago) and American Airlines (which has a hub at O'Hare).

At the opposite end of the city, on the southwest side, is Chicago's other major airport, **Midway International Airport** (MDW; ✆ **773/ 838-0600;** www.flychicago.com). Although it's smaller than O'Hare and handles fewer airlines, Midway is closer to the Loop and attracts more discount airlines, so you may be able to get a cheaper fare flying into here. (Always check fares to both airports if you want to find the best deal.) A cab ride from Midway to the Loop usually takes about 20 minutes. You can find the latest information on both airports at the city's Department of Aviation website: www.flychicago.com.

## GETTING INTO THE CITY

Taxis are plentiful at both O'Hare and Midway, but getting to town is easy by public transportation as well. If you're not carting enormous amounts of luggage and want to save money, I highly recommend taking public transportation, which is convenient from both airports. For $2, you can take the El (vernacular for the elevated train) straight into downtown.

O'Hare is on the Blue Line; a trip to downtown takes about 40 minutes. Trains leave every 6 to 10 minutes during the day, and every half-hour in the evening and overnight.

Getting downtown from Midway is even faster; the ride on the Orange Line takes 20 to 30 minutes. (The Orange Line stops operating each night at about 11:30pm and resumes service by 5am.) Trains leave the station every 6 to 15 minutes. The train station is a fair walk from the terminal—without the benefit of O'Hare's moving sidewalks—so be prepared if you have heavy bags.

A cab ride into the city will cost about $35 from O'Hare (20 miles from downtown), and $25 from Midway (10 miles from downtown). *One warning:* Rush-hour traffic can be horrendous, especially around O'Hare.

Both airports also have outposts for every major car-rental company.

**GO Airport Express** (✆ **888/2-THEVAN** [284-3826]; www.airport express.com) serves most first-class hotels in Chicago with its green-and-white vans; ticket counters are at both airports near baggage claim (outside Customs at the international terminal at O'Hare). For transportation to the airport, reserve a spot through one of the hotels (check with the bell captain). The cost is $27 one-way ($49 round-trip) to or from O'Hare, and $22 one-way ($37 round-trip) to or from Midway. Group rates for two or more people traveling together are less expensive than sharing a cab, and children ages 6 to 12 ride for half-price. The shuttles operate from 4am to 11:30pm.

## GETTING AROUND CHICAGO

The **Chicago Transit Authority,** better known as the **CTA** (© **836-7000** or TTY 836-4949 from any area code in the city and suburbs; **www.transitchicago.com**) operates an extensive system of trains and buses throughout the city of Chicago. The sturdy system carries about 1.5 million passengers a day. Subways and elevated trains (known as the El) are generally safe and reliable, although it's advisable to avoid long rides through unfamiliar neighborhoods late at night.

**Fares** for the bus, subway, and El are $2, with an additional 25¢ for a transfer that allows CTA riders to make two transfers on the bus or El within 2 hours of receipt. Children 6 and under ride free, and those between the ages of 7 and 11 pay $1. Seniors can also receive the reduced fare if they have the appropriate reduced-fare permit (call © **312/836-7000** for details on how to obtain one, although this is probably not a realistic option for a short-term visitor).

The CTA uses credit card–size fare cards that automatically deduct the exact fare each time you take a ride. The reusable cards can be purchased with a preset value already stored, or riders can obtain cards at vending machines located at all CTA train stations and charge them with whatever amount they choose (a minimum of $2 and up to $100). If within 2 hours of your first ride you transfer to a bus or the El,

## Free Ride

During the summer, the city of Chicago operates free trolleys daily between Michigan Avenue and the Museum Campus (site of the Adler Planetarium, the Field Museum of Natural History, and the Shedd Aquarium); the trolleys run only on weekends in the fall and spring. Free trolleys also run year-round between Navy Pier and the Grand/State El station on the Red Line. While the trolleys are supposed to make stops every 30 minutes, waits can be longer during peak tourist season—and the trolleys aren't air-conditioned. If you get tired of waiting, remember that CTA public buses travel the same routes for only $2 per person.

the turnstiles at the El stations and the fare boxes on buses will automatically deduct from your card just the cost of a transfer (25¢). If you make a second transfer within 2 hours, it's free. The same card can be recharged continuously.

Fare cards can be used on buses, but you can't buy a card on the bus. If you get on the bus without a fare card, you'll have to pay $2 cash (either in coins or in dollar bills); the bus drivers cannot make change, so make sure that you've got the right amount before hopping on board.

**By Train**    The CTA operates seven train lines, identified by color: The **Red Line** runs north-south; the **Green Line** runs west-south; the **Blue Line** runs through Wicker Park/Bucktown west-northwest to O'Hare Airport; the **Pink Line** branches off from the Blue Line and serves the southwest side of the city; the **Brown Line** runs in a northern zigzag route; and the **Orange Line** runs southwest, serving Midway airport. The **Purple Line,** which runs on the same Loop elevated tracks as the Orange and Green lines, serves north-suburban Evanston and runs only during rush hour.

I highly recommend taking at least one El ride while you're here—you'll get a whole different perspective on the city (not to mention fascinating views inside downtown office buildings and North Side homes as you zip past their windows). While the Red Line is the most

## Ticket to Ride

Visitors who plan on taking a lot of train or bus trips should consider buying a **Visitor Pass,** which works like a fare card and allows individual users unlimited rides on the El and CTA buses over a 24-hour period. The cards cost $5 and are sold at airports, hotels, museums, Hot Tix outlets, transportation hubs, and Chicago Office of Tourism visitor information centers (you can also buy them in advance online at www.transitchicago.com or by calling ✆ **888/YOUR-CTA** [968-7282]). You can also buy 2-, 3-, and 5-day passes. While the passes save you the trouble of feeding the fare machines yourself, they're economical only if you plan to make at least three distinct trips at least 2 or more hours apart (remember that you get two additional transfers within 2 hr. for an additional 25¢ on a regular fare).

efficient for traveling between the Magnificent Mile and points south, your only views along this underground stretch will be of dingy stations. For sightseers, I recommend taking the aboveground Brown Line, which runs around the downtown Loop and then north through residential neighborhoods. You can ride all the way to the end of the line at Kimball (about a 45-min. ride from downtown), or hop off at Belmont to wander the Lakeview neighborhood. Avoid this scenic ride during rush hour (before 9am and 3:30–6:30pm), when your only view will be of tired commuters.

Study your CTA map carefully before boarding any train. While most trains run every 5 to 20 minutes, decreasing in frequency in the off-peak and overnight hours, some stations close after work hours (as early as 8:30pm) and remain closed on Saturday, Sunday, and holidays. The Orange Line train does not operate from about 11:30pm to 5am, the Brown Line operates only north of Belmont after about 9:30pm, the Blue Line's Cermak branch has ceased operating overnight and on weekends, and the Purple Line does not run overnight.

**By Bus**   The best way to get around neighborhoods along the lakefront—where the trains don't run—is by public bus. Look for the **blue-and-white signs to locate bus stops,** which are spaced about 2 blocks apart. Each bus route is identified by a number and the name of the main street it runs along; the bus that follows Grand Avenue, for example, is the no. 65 Grand.

A few buses that are particularly handy for many visitors are the **no. 146 Marine/Michigan,** an express bus from Belmont Avenue on the North Side that cruises down North Lake Shore Drive (and through Lincoln Park during nonpeak times) to North Michigan Avenue, State Street, and the Grant Park museum campus; the **no. 151 Sheridan,** which passes through Lincoln Park en route to inner Lake Shore Drive and then travels along Michigan Avenue as far south as Adams Street, where it turns west into the Loop (and stops at Union Station); and the **no. 156 LaSalle,** which goes through Lincoln Park and then into the Loop's financial district on LaSalle Street.

**PACE buses** (© **836-7000** from any Chicago area code or 847/364-7223; Mon–Fri 8am–5pm; www.pacebus.com) cover the suburban zones that surround Chicago. They run every 20 to 30 minutes during rush hour, operating until mid-evening Monday through Friday and early evening on weekends. Suburban bus routes are marked with

## Sky Train: Chicago's El

Watch any Hollywood film or TV series set in Chicago, and chances are they'll feature at least one scene set against our screeching elevated train system, more commonly known as the **"El"** (witness *The Fugitive, ER*, and others). The trains symbolize Chicago's gritty, "city-that-works" attitude, but they actually began as cutting-edge technology.

After the Great Fire of 1871, Chicago made a remarkable recovery; within 20 years, the downtown district was swarming with people, streetcars, and horses (but no stoplights). To help relieve congestion, the city took to the sky, building a system of elevated trains 15 feet above all the madness. The first El trains were steam-powered, but by the end of the century, all the lines—run by separate companies— used electricity. In 1895, the three El companies collaborated to build a set of tracks into and around the central business district that all the lines would then share. By 1897, the "Loop" was up and running.

Chicago's El wasn't the nation's first. That honor belongs to New York City, which started running its elevated trains in 1867, 25 years before Chicago. But the New York El has almost disappeared, moving underground and turning into a subway early in the last century. With 289 miles of track, Chicago has the biggest El and the second-largest public transportation system in the country.

nos. 208 and above, and vehicles may be flagged down at intersections where stops aren't marked.

**By Commuter Train** The **Metra** commuter railroad (© **312/322-6777** or TTY 312/322-6774; Mon–Fri 8am–5pm; at other times call the **Transit Information Center** at © **312/836-7000** or TTY 312/836-4949; www.metrarail.com) serves the six-county suburban area around Chicago with 12 train lines. Several terminals are located downtown, including **Union Station** at Adams and Canal streets, **LaSalle Street Station** at LaSalle and Van Buren streets, **North Western Station** at Madison and Canal streets, and **Randolph Street Station** at Randolph Street and Michigan Avenue.

To view the leafy streets of Chicago's northern suburbs, take the **Union Pacific North Line,** which departs from North Western Station, and get off at one of the following scenic towns: Kenilworth, Winnetka, Glencoe, Highland Park, or Lake Forest.

The **Metra Electric** (once known as the Illinois Central–Gulf Railroad, or the IC), running close to Lake Michigan on a track that occupies some of the most valuable real estate in Chicago, will take you to Hyde Park (p. 96). You can catch the Metra Electric in the Loop at the Randolph Street Station and at the Van Buren Street Station at Van Buren Street and Michigan Avenue (both these stations are underground, so they're not immediately obvious to visitors).

Commuter trains have graduated fare schedules based on the distance you ride. On weekends and holidays and during the summer, Metra offers a family discount that allows up to three children under age 12 to ride free when accompanying a paid adult. The commuter railroad also offers a $5 weekend pass for unlimited rides on Saturday and Sunday.

**By Taxi**   Taxis are a convenient but very expensive way to get around the Loop and to get to the dining, shopping, and entertainment options found beyond downtown, such as on the Near North Side, in Old Town and Lincoln Park, and in Bucktown/Wicker Park.

Taxis are easy to hail in the Loop, on the Magnificent Mile and the Gold Coast, in River North, and in Lincoln Park, but if you go far beyond these key areas, you might need to call. Cab companies include **Flash Cab** (✆ 773/561-4444), **Yellow Cab** (✆ 312/TAXI-CAB [829-4222]), and **Checker Cab** (✆ 312/CHECKER [243-2537]).

The meter in Chicago cabs currently starts at $2.25 for the first mile and costs $1.80 for each additional mile, with a $1 surcharge for the first additional rider and 50¢ for each person after that. Due to recent high gas prices, you'll also have to pay an additional $1 fuel surcharge whenever gas prices are above $3/gallon.

**By Car**   One of the great things about visiting Chicago is that you don't need to bring or rent a car to get around: Public transportation and taxis are plentiful, and most of the main tourist attractions are within walking distance of downtown hotels. If you do drive here, Chicago is laid out so logically that it's relatively easy for visitors to get around the city by car. Although rush-hour traffic jams are just as frustrating as they are in other large cities, traffic runs fairly smoothly at most times of the day. Chicagoans have learned to be prepared for unexpected delays; it seems that at least one major highway and several downtown streets are under repair throughout the spring and summer months (some say we have two seasons: winter and construction).

Great diagonal corridors—such as Lincoln Avenue, Clark Street, and Milwaukee Avenue—slice through the grid pattern at key points in the city and shorten many a trip that would otherwise be tedious on the checkerboard surface of the Chicago streets. On scenic **Lake Shore Drive** (also known as Outer Dr.), you can travel the length of the city (and beyond), never far from the great lake that is Chicago's most amazing natural feature. If you're driving here, make sure you take one spin along what we call LSD; the stretch between the Museum Campus and North Avenue is especially stunning.

**Driving Rules**  Unless otherwise posted, a right turn on red is allowed after stopping and signaling. As in any big city with its share of frustrating rush-hour traffic, be prepared for aggressive drivers and the occasional taxi to cut in front of you or make sudden, unexpected turns without signaling. Chicago drivers almost universally speed up at the sight of a yellow light; you'll most likely hear some honking if you don't make that mad dash before the light turns red.

**Parking**  Parking regulations are vigorously enforced throughout the city. Read signs carefully: The streets around Michigan Avenue have parking restrictions during rush hour—and I know from bitter first-hand experience that your car will be towed immediately. Many neighborhoods have adopted resident-only parking that prohibits others from parking on their streets, usually after 6pm each day (even all day in a few areas, such as Old Town). The neighborhood around Wrigley Field is off-limits during Cubs night games, so look for yellow sidewalk signs alerting drivers about the dozen-and-a-half times the Cubs play under lights. You can park in permit zones if you're visiting a friend who can provide you with a pass to stick on your windshield. Beware of tow zones, and, if visiting in winter, make note of curbside warnings regarding snow plowing.

Parking is also expensive. Most restaurants provide valet parking for $10 to $12. Downtown you might also opt for a public garage, but you'll have to pay premium prices. However, several garages connected with malls or other major attractions offer discounted parking with a validated ticket.

If you'll be spending an entire day downtown, the best parking deal in the Loop is the city-run **Millennium Park** garage (© **312/742-7644**), which charges $17 for up to 8 hours (enter on Columbus Dr., 1 block east of Michigan Ave., btw. Monroe and Randolph sts.). A little farther south are two municipal lots underneath **Grant Park,** with one entrance at Michigan Avenue and Van Buren Street and the other at Michigan Avenue and Madison Street (© **312/616-0600**). Parking costs $14 for the first hour and $22 for 2 to 8 hours. Other downtown lots (where prices are comparable or even higher) include **Midcontinental Plaza Garage,** 55 E. Monroe St. (© **312/986-6821**), and **Navy Pier Parking,** 600 E. Grand Ave. (© **312/595-7437**). There's also a large lot next to the **McCormick Place Convention Center,** 2301 S. Lake Shore Dr. (© **312/791-7000**).

**By Bicycle**   The city of Chicago has earned kudos for its efforts to improve conditions for bicycling (designated bike lanes have been installed on stretches of Wells St., Roosevelt Rd., Elston Ave., and Halsted St.), but it can still be a tough prospect trying to compete with cars and their drivers, who aren't always so willing to share the road.

The **Active Transportation Alliance** (© **312/427-3325;** www. activetrans.org), a nonprofit advocacy group, publishes several bicycling maps with tips on recommended on-street routes and parkland routes, as well as a guide to safe cycling in the city.

**Bike Chicago** rents all sorts of bikes, including tandems and four-seater "quadcycles," as well as in-line skates, from three locations: North Avenue Beach, Millennium Park, and Navy Pier (© **888/BIKE-WAY** [245-3929]; www.bikechicago.com). Bike rentals start at $8.75 an hour or $30 a day. Helmets, pads, and locks are provided free of charge. The shops are open daily from 9am to 7pm, weather permitting.

**Towaway Zones**   When the City of Chicago turned its parking meters over to a private company, the rates at parking meters exploded (from $0.25 per hour to $1.00 per hour in many cases). And if you're staying for 3 hours, that quickly adds up to a ridiculous number of quarters. Word is that meters are going to be changed to accept credit cards, but at press time this is not the norm at most meters. Meanwhile, be aware. Don't take a risk: The odds are always against you if you park illegally. You'll shell out a minimum of $25 for the most minor parking violation, plus another $100 or more for towing, plus storage fees. You'll easily be shelling out $250 to $275 total, not to mention the hassle of getting the car back.

## Surfing Around Chicago: The Best City Sites

These Chicago-based sites provide up-to-date listings on everything from restaurants to walking tours.

- **www.choosechicago.com** is your best bet for comprehensive tourism information on hotels, special promotions, and citywide events from the Chicago Convention & Tourism Bureau (and ℂ **877/CHICAGO** [244-2246] also happens to be the phone number for the bureau's tourism information line).

- **www.metromix.com** is the *Chicago Tribune*'s entertainment-oriented site.

- **www.encyclopediaofchicago.com** is a collaboration between the Newberry Library and the Chicago Historical Society that is chock-full of fun facts and useful information about the city's history, architecture, and the lives of some of its famous and infamous personalities.

- **www.chicago.citysearch.com** offers reviews of restaurants, bars, shows, and shops.

- **www.centerstage.net** is good for entertainment news.

- **www.chireader.com** is the site of the *Chicago Reader,* the city's alternative weekly paper.

- For a blogger's view of the city, check out **www.chicagoist.com**.

- **www.chicagobites.com** is a popular food blog that posts weekly reviews of local restaurants.

- **www.craigslist.org**. What can you not find on this site? Craigslist plays host to job postings, apartment listings, personals, and almost anything you can think of. You can refine your search by region, from the city itself, to various neighborhoods.

- **www.yelp.com**. Yelp is an absolute gold mine of real opinions. Search for services such as haircuts or auto repairs, find a doctor or restaurant, and read reviews by fellow city dwellers before you step out the door. When your friends aren't close by to give recommendations, it's the best substitute around.

# 2 Visitor Resources

Before your trip, visit the website of the **Chicago Office of Tourism,** Chicago Cultural Center, 78 E. Washington St., Chicago, IL 60602 (© **877/CHICAGO** [244-2246] or TTY 866/710-0294; www.choose chicago.com), to find out about upcoming events and attractions (they'll also mail you a packet of materials if you want). Click the "Maps & Transportation" link at the top of the home page for links to maps of Chicago neighborhoods. You can even create your own personalized map of sights you'd like to visit. The **Illinois Bureau of Tourism** (© **800/2CONNECT** [226-6632] or TTY 800/406-6418; www.enjoyillinois.com) will also send you information about Chicago and other Illinois destinations.

In addition to the above websites, which give general travel information, see "Surfing Around Chicago: The Best City Sites" for a list of the best Chicago websites.

Once you're here, you may want to visit one of the Office of Tourism's visitor centers to pick up information on special events. The main visitor center, located in the Loop and convenient to many places that you'll likely be visiting, is on the first floor of the **Chicago Cultural Center,** 77 E. Randolph St. (at Michigan Ave.). The center has a phone that you can use to make hotel reservations, and several couches and a cafe where you can study maps and plan your itinerary. The center is open Monday through Friday from 8am to 6pm, Saturday from 9am to 6pm, and Sunday from 10am to 6pm; it's closed on holidays.

The **Chicago Water Works Visitor Center** is in the old pumping station at Michigan and Chicago avenues in the heart of the city's shopping district. The entrance is on the Pearson Street side of the building, across from the Water Tower Place mall. It's open daily from 7:30am to 7pm. This location has the added draw of housing a location of **Hot Tix,** which offers both half-price day-of-performance and full-price tickets to many theater productions around the city, as well as a gift shop. Part of the building has been converted into a theater, including a small cabaret space for tourist-oriented shows and a larger playhouse for the acclaimed Lookingglass Theatre Company.

The city has two daily newspapers, the *Chicago Tribune* and the *Chicago Sun-Times.* Both have cultural listings, including movies, theater, and live music, not to mention reviews of the latest restaurants that are sure to have appeared in the city since this guidebook went to press. The Friday editions of both papers contain special pull-out sections with more detailed, up-to-date information on special events happening over the weekend. The Tribune also publishes *Red Eye,* a weekday tabloid aimed at younger readers with a mix of "lite" news items, entertainment news, and quirky features.

For the short-term visitor, the weekly magazine *Time Out Chicago* lists just about everything going on during the week, from art openings to theater performances. In a class by itself is the *Chicago Reader,* a free weekly that is an invaluable source of entertainment listings, classifieds, and well-written articles on contemporary issues of interest in Chicago. Published every Thursday (except the last week of Dec.), the weekly has a wide distribution downtown and on the North Side; it is available in many retail stores, in building lobbies, and at the paper's offices, 11 E. Illinois St., by about noon on Thursday. Another free weekly, *New City,* also publishes excellent comprehensive listings of entertainment options. Appealing to a slightly younger audience than the *Reader, New City* has an editorial tone tending toward the edgy and irreverent. Published every Wednesday, it's available in the same neighborhoods and locations as the *Reader.*

Of the many free tourist-oriented publications, the most widely read is *Where Chicago.* The handbook-sized weekly contains maps and information on current events. You can find them in most hotels, shops, and restaurants in the major tourist areas.

## 3 Health, Safety & Local Laws & Customs

**Climate**   When I tell people from more temperate climates that I live in Chicago, their first question is how I handle the winters. Actually, winters here are no worse than in other northern cities, but it still isn't exactly prime tourist season. I tell friends the ideal time to visit is summer or fall. Summer offers a nonstop selection of special events and outdoor activities; the only downside is that you'll be dealing with the biggest crowds and periods of hot, muggy weather. Autumn days are generally sunny, and the crowds at major tourist attractions grow thinner—you don't have to worry about snow until late November at the earliest. Spring is extremely unpredictable, with dramatic fluctuations of cold and warm weather, and usually lots of rain. If your top priority is indoor cultural sights, winter's not such a bad time to visit:

## When You've Got to Go . . .

Toilets can be found in hotel lobbies, bars, restaurants, museums, department stores, railway and bus stations, and service stations. Large hotels and fast-food restaurants are often the best bet for clean facilities. Restaurants and bars in resorts or heavily visited areas may reserve their restrooms for patrons. Starbucks can usually be counted upon to take pity on you even if you don't buy anything (particularly if it's a kid who has to go!).

no lines at museums, the cheapest rates at hotels, and the pride that comes with slogging through the slush with the natives.

Chicagoans like to joke that if you don't like the weather, just wait an hour—it will change. (In spring and autumn, I've been known to use my car's heat in the morning and the air-conditioning in the afternoon.) The key is to be prepared for a wide range of weather with clothing that can take you from a sunny morning to a chilly, drizzly evening. As close to your departure as possible, check the local weather forecast at the websites of the *Chicago Tribune* newspaper (www.chicagotribune.com) or the **Weather Channel** (www.weather.com).

Liquor Laws   In Chicago, beer, wine, and other alcoholic beverages are sold at liquor stores and supermarkets. Bars may sell alcohol until 2am, although some nightclubs have special licenses that allow alcohol sales until 4am. It is legal in Illinois to bring your own liquor into a restaurant for your party to consume. If a restaurant does not have a liquor license, you should ask permission to bring in a bottle of wine, out of courtesy. Do not carry open containers of alcohol in your car or any public area that isn't zoned for alcohol consumption. The police can fine you on the spot. And nothing will ruin your trip faster than getting a citation for DUI (driving under the influence), so don't even think about driving while intoxicated. Legal drinking age is 21; proof of age is required.

Phone Facts   The area codes for Chicago are 312 and 773. The 312 code is for the central business district and centrally located neighborhoods (such as the near North Side) and 773 covers all other areas. As is the case with most big metropolitan areas, though, the number of area codes in Chicago is expanding with the population and use of the Internet and other digital services, and by the time this book goes to press, there may well be a new area code for the city. For now, dial 1-before the area code in the city. When in doubt, dial the operator. Local calls are free on private phones, 50¢ in a pay phone. For directory assistance, dial © **411.**

**Safety** Chicago has all the crime problems of any urban center, so use your common sense and stay cautious and alert. At night, you might want to stick to well-lit streets along the Magnificent Mile, River North, Gold Coast, and Lincoln Park, which are all high-traffic areas late into the night. That said, Chicago is still a big city; muggings can—and do—happen anywhere.

Late at night, avoid wandering dark residential streets on the fringes of Hyde Park and Pilsen, which border areas with more troublesome reputations. You can also ask your hotel concierge or an agent at the tourist visitor center about the safety of a particular area.

## Free 411

It's bound to happen: The day you leave this guidebook back at your crash pad for an unencumbered stroll through Bucktown, you'll forget the address of the great happy-hour spot you had earmarked. If you're traveling with a mobile device, call © **GOOG-411** (466-4411), a free voice-activated service where you say where or what you're looking for, and it will (sometimes) connect you with the business you're looking for. If you're calling from a mobile device, GOOG-411 can even send you a text message with more details and a map: Just say "text message" or "map it." Cool, eh?

You can also send a text message to © **GOOGL** (46645) for a lightning-fast response. Within 10 seconds you'll receive a text message with the address and phone number. This nifty trick works in a range of search categories: Look up weather ("weather philadelphia"), language translations ("translate goodbye in spanish"), currency conversions ("10 usd in pounds"), movie times ("harry potter 60605"), and more.

## Where to Surf (the Net) in Chicago

**With Your Own Computer**

More and more hotels, resorts, airports, cafes, and retailers are going Wi-Fi, becoming "hotspots" that offer free high-speed access or charge a small fee for usage.

In the Loop, **Millennium Park, Daley Plaza** (along Washington St. btw. Dearborn and Clark sts.), the **Chicago Cultural Center,** 78 E. Washington St., and the **Harold Washington Library Center,** 400 S. State St., all have wireless access. Elsewhere in downtown Chicago, Starbucks, the sandwich chain Cosí, and McDonald's have numerous locations with Wi-Fi access. Wireless hotspots in Lincoln Park include **Panera Bread,** 616 W. Diversey Pkwy. (© **773/528-4556**), and **Argo Tea,** 958 W. Armitage Ave. (© **773/388-1880**). Free public Wi-Fi is available at all Corner Bakery and Panera Bread locations in the city.

To find more public Wi-Fi hotspots in Chicago, go to **www.jiwire. com**; its Hotspot Finder holds the world's largest directory of public wireless hotspots.

**Without Your Own Computer**

Almost every hotel in Chicago has a business center with Internet access for guests (although you usually have to pay extra to use it). Most youth hostels and public libraries also offer Internet access.

Screenz Computing Center has a location in Lincoln Park at 2717 N. Clark St. (© **773/348-9300; www.screenz.com**) and in Andersonville at 5212 N. Clark St. (© **773/334-8600; www.screenz.com**) They are open 9 am–midnight. Windy City Cyber Cafe (© **773/384-6470; www. windycitycybercafe.com**) is located at 2246 W. North Avenue and is open 6 am–10 pm Mon-Fri and 8 am–10pm Sat-Sun. Rates are $6/hour.

The Harold Washington Library Center, 400 S. State St., and all Chicago public libraries, offer free Wi-Fi Internet access and access to public computers, which at Harold Washington are located on the third floor.

The El is generally quite safe, even at night, although some of the downtown stations can feel eerily deserted late in the evening. Buses are a safe option, too, especially nos. 146 and 151, which pick up along North Michigan Avenue and State Street and connect to the North Side via Lincoln Park.

Blue-and-white police cars are a common sight, and officers also patrol by bicycle downtown and along the lakefront and by horseback at special events and parades. There are police stations in busy nightlife areas, such as the 18th District station at Chicago Avenue and LaSalle Street in River North and the 24th District station (known as Town Hall) at Addison and Halsted streets.

**Smoking Laws**   On January 1, 2008, Chicago put a smoking ban in place for all "public places." Smoking is now prohibited in restaurants and bars. Although there have been arguments against it, so far the law has been enforced in most establishments. Hotels are also offering more nonsmoking rooms, which often leaves those who like to puff out in the cold—sometimes literally.

**Weather**   For weather information, call or surf to the **National Weather Service** (© **831/656-1725;** www.nws.noaa.gov). I also find that WGN-TV (Channel 9) has reliable weather forecasts (www. wgntv.com).

# INDEX